MW00425034

All What Jazz

by the same author

Fiction
Jill
A Girl in Winter

Poetry
The Less Deceived (Marvell Press)
The North Ship
The Whitsun Weddings
High Windows

Non-fiction
Required Writing:
Miscellaneous Pieces 1955–1982

All What Jazz

A Record Diary 1961–1971

PHILIP LARKIN

faber and faber
LONDON · BOSTON

First published in 1970
by Faber and Faber Limited
3 Queen Square London WC1N 3AU
This revised edition first published in 1985
Reprinted in 1986

Photoset by Wilmaset Birkenhead Merseyside
Printed & bound in Great Britain by
Redwood Burn Limited, Trowbridge, Wiltshire

British Library Cataloguing in Publication Data

Larkin, Philip
All what jazz.
1. Jazz music
I. Title II. Daily Telegraph
785.42 ML3506

ISBN 0-571-13475-0
ISBN 0-571-13476-9 Pbk

To
DONALD MITCHELL

Contents

'But if something [i.e. Ornette Coleman] sounds terrible, man, a person should have enough respect for his own mind to say it doesn't sound good. It doesn't to me, and I'm not going to listen to it. No matter how long you listen to it, it doesn't sound any good.'

Miles Davis, *Down Beat*, **13th June 1968**

'Others just give up and reject Ornette Coleman's sounds, saying that it is not jazz any more. But they should have said the same of Miles Davis and others, and for the very same reasons.'

Hugues Panassié, *The Real Jazz*, **1960**

These articles were first printed in the *Daily Telegraph* on the dates given, and are reprinted with the permission of that paper.

What I originally wrote was sometimes cut: I have not restored these cuts. Indeed, I have made a few others, scrapping paragraphs that were significant, if at all, only at the time they were printed. Almost nothing, however, has been altered, except the titles. These were usually supplied by the paper, and I have therefore in most cases invented new ones.

Introduction

1

I have rescued these articles from their press-cuttings book because for all their slightness and superficiality they contain occasional sentences that still amuse me or seem justified. Moreover, as I read them I discern a story which, though ordinary enough, it might be entertaining to bring out into the open.

To tell it means going back some way. Few things have given me more pleasure in life than listening to jazz. I don't claim to be original in this: for the generations that came to adolescence between the wars jazz was that unique private excitement that youth seems to demand. In another age it might have been drink or drugs, religion or poetry. Whatever it happens to be, parents are suspicious of it and it has a bad reputation. I can tell adolescents don't feel like this about jazz today. For one thing, there are so many kinds that to talk about jazz as such would leave them puzzled as well as cold. Then again, it has become respectable: there are scholarly books on it, and adult education courses; it's the kind of interest that might well be mentioned on a university entrance form. And there's so much of it: records, wireless, television, all dispense it regularly. In the thirties it was a fugitive minority interest, a record heard by chance from a foreign station, a chorus between two vocals, one man in an otherwise dull band. No one you knew liked it.

Nevertheless, it had established itself in my life several years before I consciously heard anything that could properly be called real jazz. This happened by way of the dance band, a now-vanished phenomenon of twelve or fourteen players (usually identically uniformed) that was employed by a hotel or restaurant so that its patrons could dance. Their leaders were national celebrities, and had regular time on the radio: 5.15 to 6.00 in the afternoon, for instance, and half-past ten to midnight. They were in almost no sense 'jazz' bands, but about every sixth piece they made a 'hot' number, in which the one or two men in the band who could play jazz would be heard. The classic 'hot' number was 'Tiger Rag': it had that kind of national-anthem status that 'When The Saints Go Marching In' had in the fifties. Harry Roy had a band-within-a-band called The Tiger-Ragamuffins. Nat Gonella's stageshow had a toy tiger lying on the grand piano. Trombonists and tuba-players became adept at producing the traditional tiger growl. I found these hot numbers so exciting that I would listen to hours of dance music in order to catch them when they came, in this way unconsciously learning many now-forgotten lyrics. Those hot numbers! When the bands began to visit the local Hippodrome, I was able actually to see them played, the different sections suddenly rising to play four bars then sitting sharply down again; the shouts of 'Yeah man', the slapped bass, the drum breaks. It was the drummer I concentrated on, sitting as he did on a raised platform behind a battery of cowbells, temple blocks, cymbals, tomtoms and (usually) a chinese gong, his drums picked out in flashing crimson or ultramarine brilliants. Even the resident Hippodrome drummer, a stolid man with horn-rimmed glasses, excited me enough for me to insist that our tickets were for his side of the house, so that I could see what he was doing. I wanted to be a drummer. My parents bought me an elementary drum kit and a set of tuition records by Max Abrams (that will date the anecdote), and I battered away contentedly, spending less time on the rudiments than in improvising an accompaniment to records.

I recount this simply to show that I was, in essence, hooked on jazz even before I heard any, and that what got me was the rhythm. That simple trick of the suspended beat, that had made the slaves shuffle in Congo Square on Saturday nights, was something that never palled. My transition to jazz was slow. The first jazz record I ever owned was Ray Noble's 'Tiger Rag' (it had a drum break). The second, rather surprisingly, was The Washboard Rhythm Kings' 'I'm Gonna Play Down By the Ohio'. The third was Louis Armstrong's 'Ain't Misbehavin''. After that they came thick and fast. Sitting with a friend in his bedroom that overlooked the family tennis-court, I watched leaves drift down through long Sunday afternoons as we took it in turn to wind the portable HMV, and those white and coloured Americans, Bubber Miley, Frank Teschmacher, J. C. Higginbotham, spoke immediately to our understanding. Their rips, slurs and distortions were something we understood perfectly. This was something we had found for ourselves, that wasn't taught at school (what a prerequisite that is of nearly everything worthwhile!), and having found it, we made it bear all the enthusiasm usually directed at more established arts. There was nothing odd about this. It was happening to boys all over Europe and America. It just didn't get into the papers. It was years before I found any music as commanding as Jimmy Noone's 'The Blues Jumped a Rabbit', Armstrong's 'Knockin' a Jug' or 'Squeeze Me', Bessie Smith's 'Backwater Blues', or the Chicago Rhythm Kings' 'I Found a New Baby'.

At Oxford my education grew. I met people who knew more about jazz than I did, and had more records, and who could even parallel my ecstasies with their own. The shops, too, were full of unreturned deletions, some of which have never been reissued to this day (the Sharkey Bonano Vocalions, for instance, or Louis Prima's 'Chasin' Shadows'). I wish I could say that we could recite Black Swan matrix numbers, or knew what was available on Argentine HMV, or played instruments and formed a band, or at least had enough musical knowledge to discuss the records we played intelligently. Only one of our circle could read music: he played the saxophone, but his taste didn't really accord with mine: he was too fond of phrases such as 'not musically interesting' or 'mere rhythmic excitement'. True, our response to Fats Waller's 'Dream Man' or Rosetta Howard's 'If You're a Viper' was a grinning, jigging wordlessness, interspersed with a grunt or two at specially good bits. For us, jazz became part of the private joke of existence, rather than a public expertise: expressions such as 'combined pimp and lover' and 'eating the cheaper cuts of pork' (both from a glossary on 'Yellow Dog Blues') flecked our conversations cryptically; for some reason, Kaminsky's plaintive little introduction to 'Home Cooking' became a common signal, and any of us entering the steam-filled college bath-house would whistle it to see if it was taken up from behind any of the bolted partition doors.

If I say that on leaving Oxford I suffered a gap in my jazz life I am probably reporting a common experience. Most jazz enthusiasts found the war a compulsory hiatus in their devotion. If they were not away in the services, and their collections broken up, the American Federation of Musicians' recording ban of 1942–4 descended on them, together with the general shortage of consumer goods, including records, that hostilities brought increasingly as the war went on. For my part, I was in a series of provincial lodgings where jazz was not welcome, and when I was united with my collection in 1948 and had something to play it on there followed a period when I was content to renew acquaintance with it and to add only what amplified or extended it along existing lines – new records by old favourites, replacements of discs previously abandoned or broken. When the long-playing record was introduced in the middle fifties, I was suspicious of it: it seemed a package deal, forcing you to buy bad tracks along with good at an unwantedly-high price. (The dubbing or remastering of 78s as LPs, too, was regarded as a damaging practice.) This deepened my isolation.

All this is not to say that I was ignorant of the changes taking place on the jazz scene. I knew, for instance, that what I had known as one music had now bifurcated into trad and mod. In Britain one heard a good deal more of the former, thanks to the revivalist boom, but I don't know that I went overboard about it; I liked Lyttelton, and later on the energetic little Barber band that could pack any concert hall between Aberdeen and Bristol. I heard it in Belfast in 1954: a thousand people squashed into the smallish Plaza dance hall, and a thousand more milled outside, the more enterprising getting in through a small square window in the men's lavatory. This was the pre-Ottilie period, when after 'Panama' and 'Chimes Blues' and 'Merrydown Rag' Lonnie Donegan would come forward with his impersonation of Leadbelly. There was no bar: I went and stood on the landing, pursued by the high nasal Glasgow-American version of some incident from transatlantic railway history. All the same, there seemed an element of slightly-unreal archaism about much of the trad of the period, particularly from California, and I could never bring myself to take these grunting and quavering pastiches seriously. On the whole, therefore, I thought it best after the war to suspend judgment, out of an almost-academic shyness about going into a 'new period'. For modern jazz I was even less well briefed. What I heard on the wireless seemed singularly unpromising, but I doubt if I thought it would ever secure enough popular acceptance to warrant my bothering about it.

2

What I am doing, I suppose, is demonstrating that when I was asked to write these articles I was patently unfitted to do so and should have declined. The reason I didn't was that I still thought of myself as a jazz lover, someone unquestionably on the wavelength of Congo Square, and although I knew things had been changing I didn't believe jazz itself could alter out of all recognition any more than the march or the waltz could. It was simply a question of hearing enough of the new stuff: I welcomed the chance to do so, feeling confident that once I got the feel of it all would be made clear. Secondly, I hadn't really any intention of being a jazz *critic*. In literature, I understood, there were several old whores who had grown old in the reviewing game by praising everything, and I planned to be their jazz equivalent. This isn't as venal as it sounds. Since my space was to be so limited, anything but praise would be wasteful; my readers deserved to be told of the best of all worlds, and I was the man to do it. It didn't really matter, therefore, whether I liked things at first or not, as I was going to call them all masterpieces.

But there came a hitch. When the records, in their exciting square packages, began obligingly to arrive from the companies, the eagerness with which I played them turned rapidly to astonishment, to disbelief, to alarm. I felt I was in some nightmare, in which I had confidently gone into an examination hall only to find that I couldn't make head or tail of the questions. It wasn't like listening to a kind of jazz I didn't care for – Art Tatum, shall I say, or Jelly Roll Morton's Red Hot Peppers. It wasn't like listening to jazz at all. Nearly every characteristic of the music had been neatly inverted: for instance, the jazz tone, distinguished from 'straight' practice by an almost-human vibrato, had entirely disappeared, giving way to utter flaccidity. Had the most original feature of jazz been its use of collective improvisation? Banish it: let the first and last choruses be identical exercises in low-temperature unison. Was jazz instrumentation based on the hock-shop trumpets, trombones and clarinets of the returned Civil War regiments? Brace yourself for flutes, harpsichords, electronically-amplified bassoons. Had jazz been essentially a popular art, full of tunes you could whistle? Something fundamentally awful had taken place to ensure that there should be no more tunes. Had the wonderful thing about it been its happy, cake-walky syncopation that set feet tapping and shoulders jerking? Any such feelings were now regularly dispelled by random explosions from the drummer ('dropping bombs'), and the use of non-jazz tempos, 3/4, 5/8, 11/4. Above all, was jazz the music of the American Negro? Then fill it full of conga drums and sambas and all the tawdry trappings of South America, the racket of Middle East bazaars, the cobra-coaxing cacophonies of Calcutta.

But, deeper than this, the sort of emotion the music was trying to evoke seemed to have changed. Whereas the playing of Armstrong,

Bechet, Waller and the Condon groups had been relaxed and expansive, the music of the new men seemed to have developed from some of the least attractive characteristics of the late thirties – the tight-assed little John Kirby band, for instance, or the more riff-laden Goodman units. The substitution of bloodless note-patterns for some cheerful or sentimental popular song as a basis for improvisation (I'm thinking of some of the early Parkers) was a retrograde step, but worse still was the deliberately-contrived eccentricity of the phrasing and harmonies. One of the songs I remember from my dance-music childhood was called 'I'm Nuts About Screwy Music, I'm Mad About Daffy Tempos', and I've often meant to look it up in the British Museum to see whether the rest of the lyric forecast the rise of bop with such uncanny accuracy. This new mode seemed to have originated partly out of boredom with playing ordinary jazz six nights a week (admittedly a pretty gruelling way of earning a living), and partly from a desire to wrest back the initiative in jazz from the white musician, to invent 'something they can't steal because they can't play it'. This motive is a bad basis for any art, and it isn't surprising that I found the results shallow and *voulu*. Worst of all was the pinched, unhappy, febrile, tense nature of the music. The constant pressure to be different and difficult demanded greater and greater technical virtuosity and more and more exaggerated musical non-sequiturs. It wasn't, in a word, the music of happy men. I used to think that anyone hearing a Parker record would guess he was a drug addict, but no one hearing Beiderbecke would think he was an alcoholic, and that this summed up the distinction between the kinds of music.

What I was feeling was, no doubt, a greatly-amplified version of the surprise many European listeners felt when, after the war, records of Parker and his followers began to arrive across the Atlantic. 'America has gone mad!' wrote George Shearing on reaching New York during this period (it didn't take him long to follow suit), and whereas Shearing was (presumably) taking only Parker and Gillespie on the chin, I was taking everything up to 1961 – Monk, Davis, Coltrane, Rollins, The Jazz Messengers, the lot. I was denied even the solace of liking this man and disliking that: I found them all equally off-putting. Parker himself, compulsively fast and showy, couldn't play four bars without resorting to a peculiarly irritating five-note cliché from a pre-war song called 'The Woody Woodpecker Song'. His tone, though much better than that of some of his successors, was thin and sometimes shrill.* The impression of mental hallucination he conveyed could also be derived from the pianist Bud Powell, who cultivated the same kind of manic virtuosity and could sometimes be stopped only by the flashing of a light in his eyes. Gillespie, on the other hand, was a more familiar type, the trumpeter-leader and entertainer, but I didn't relish his addiction to things Latin-American and I found his sense of humour rudimentary. Thelonious Monk seemed a not-very-successful comic, as his funny hats proclaimed: his *faux-naif* elephant-dance piano style, with its gawky intervals and absence of swing, was made doubly tedious by his limited repertoire. With Miles Davis and John Coltrane a new inhumanity emerged. Davis had several manners: the dead muzzled slow stuff, the sour yelping fast stuff, and the sonorous theatrical arranged stuff, and I disliked them all. With John Coltrane metallic and passionless nullity gave way to exercises in gigantic absurdity, great boring excursions on not-especially-attractive themes during which all possible changes were rung, extended investigations of oriental tedium, long-winded and portentous demonstrations of religiosity. It was with Coltrane, too, that jazz started to be *ugly on purpose*: his nasty tone would become more and more exacerbated until he was fairly screeching at you like a pair of demoniacally-possessed bagpipes. After Coltrane, of course, all was chaos, hatred and absurdity, and one was almost relieved that severance with jazz had become so complete and obvious. But this is running ahead of my story.

The awkward thing was that it was altogether too late in the day to publicize this kind of reaction. In the late forties battle had been joined in the correspondence columns between the beret-and-dark-glasses boys and the mouldy figs; by the early sixties, all this had died down. Setting aside a qualification or two I should like to make later, one can say only that to voice such a viewpoint in 1961 would have been journalistically impossible. By then Parker was dead and a historical figure, in young eyes probably indistinguishable from King Oliver and other founding fathers. There was nothing for it but to carry on with my original plan of undiscriminating praise, and I did so for nearly two years. During this time I blocked in the background by

*I fancy, however, that Parker was improving at the time of his death, possibly as a result of meeting Bechet in France (Bechet was always ready to instruct the young).

subscribing to *Down Beat* again (there were none of the FRISCO CHIRP'S VEGAS DEBUT headlines I remembered from my schooldays), and read a lot of books. I learned that jazz had now developed, socially and musically: the post-war Negro was better educated, more politically conscious and culturally aware than his predecessors, and in consequence the Negro jazz musician was more musically sophisticated. He knew his theory, his harmony, his composition: he had probably been to the Juilliard School of Music, and jazz was just what he didn't want to be associated with, in the sense of grinning over half a dozen chords to an audience all night. He had freed his music as a preliminary to freeing himself: jazz was catching up with the rest of music, becoming chromatic instead of diatonic (this was the something fundamentally awful), taking in other national musical characteristics as the American Negro looked beyond the confines of his own bondage. Practically everyone was agreed about all this. It was fearful. In a humanist society, art – and especially modern, or current, art – assumes great importance, and to lose touch with it is parallel to losing one's faith in a religious age. Or, in this particular case, since jazz is the music of the young, it was like losing one's potency. And yet, try as I would, I couldn't find anything to enjoy in the things I was sent, despite their increasing length – five, seven, nine minutes at a time, nothing like the brilliant three-minute cameos of the age of 78s. Something, I felt, had snapped, and I was drifting deeper into the silent shadowland of middle age. Cold death had taken his first citadel.

And yet again, there was something about the books I was now reading that seemed oddly familiar. This *development*, this *progress*, this *new language* that was more *difficult*, more *complex*, that required you to *work hard at appreciating it*, that you *couldn't expect to understand first go*, that needed *technical and professional knowledge* to evaluate it *at all levels*, this *revolutionary explosion* that *spoke for our time* while at the same time being *traditional* in the *fullest*, the *deepest* . . . Of course! This was the language of criticism of modern painting, modern poetry, modern music. *Of course!* How glibly I had talked of modern jazz, without realizing the force of the adjective: this was *modern* jazz, and Parker was a modern jazz player just as Picasso was a modern painter and Pound a modern poet. I hadn't realized that jazz had gone from Lascaux to Jackson Pollock in fifty years, but now I realized it relief came flooding in upon me after nearly two years' despondency. I went back to my books: 'After Parker, you had to be something of a musician to follow the best jazz of the day.'* Of course! After Picasso! After Pound! There could hardly have been a conciser summary of what I don't believe about art.

The reader may here have the sense of having strayed into a private argument. All I am saying is that the term 'modern', when applied to art, has a more than chronological meaning: it denotes a quality of irresponsibility peculiar to this century, known sometimes as modernism, and once I had classified modern jazz under this heading I knew where I was. I am sure there are books in which the genesis of modernism is set out in full. My own theory is that it is related to an imbalance between the two tensions from which art springs: these are the tension between the artist and his material, and between the artist and his audience, and that in the last seventy-five years or so the second of these has slackened or even perished. In consequence the artist has become over-concerned with his material (hence an age of technical experiment), and, in isolation, has busied himself with the two principal themes of modernism, mystification and outrage. Piqued at being neglected, he has painted portraits with both eyes on the same side of the nose, or smothered a model with paint and rolled her over a blank canvas. He has designed a dwelling-house to be built underground. He has written poems resembling the kind of pictures typists make with their machines during the coffee break, or a novel in gibberish, or a play in which the characters sit in dustbins. He has made a six-hour film of someone asleep. He has carved human figures with large holes in them. And parallel to this activity ('every idiom has its idiot', as an American novelist has written) there has grown up a kind of critical journalism designed to put it over. The terms and the arguments vary with circumstances, but basically the message is: don't trust your eyes, or ears, or understanding. They'll tell you this is ridiculous, or ugly, or meaningless. Don't believe them. You've got to work at this: after all, you don't expect to understand anything as important as art straight off, do you? I mean, this is pretty complex stuff: if you want to know how complex, I'm giving a course of ninety-six lectures at the local college, starting next week, and you'd be more than welcome. The whole thing's on the rates, you won't have to pay. After all, think what asses people have made of

*Benny Green: *The Reluctant Art* (London, MacGibbon & Kee, 1962), pp. 182–3.

themselves in the past by not understanding art – you don't want to be like that, do you? And so on, and so forth. Keep the suckers spending.

The tension between artist and audience in jazz slackened when the Negro stopped wanting to entertain the white man, and when the audience as a whole, with the end of the Japanese war and the beginning of television, didn't in any case particularly want to be entertained in that way any longer. The jazz band in the night club declined just as my old interest, the dance band, had declined in the restaurant and hotel: jazz moved, ominously, into the culture belt, the concert halls, university recital rooms and summer schools where the kind of criticism I have outlined has freer play. This was bound to make the re-establishment of any artist-audience nexus more difficult, for universities have long been the accepted stamping-ground for the subsidized acceptance of art rather than the real purchase of it – and so, of course, for this kind of criticism, designed as it is to prevent people using their eyes and ears and understandings to report pleasure and discomfort. In such conditions modernism is bound to flourish.

I don't know whether it is worth pursuing my identification of modern jazz with other branches of modern art any further: if I say I dislike both in what seems to me the same way I have made my point. Having made the connection, however, I soon saw how quickly jazz was passing from mystification ('Why don't you get a piano player? and what's that stuff he's playing?') to outrage. Men such as Ornette Coleman, Albert Ayler and Archie Shepp, dispensing with pitch, harmony, theme, tone, tune and rhythm, were copied by older (Rollins, Coltrane) and young players alike. And some of them gave a keener edge to what they were playing by suggesting that it had some political relation to the aspirations of the Black Power movement. From using music to entertain the white man, the Negro had moved to hating him with it. Anyone who thinks that an Archie ('America's done me a lot of wrong') Shepp record is anything but two fingers extended from a bunched fist at him personally cannot have much appreciation of what he is hearing. Or, as LeRoi Jones puts it, 'Listening to Sonny Murray, you can hear the primal needs of the new music. The heaviest emotional indentation it makes. From ghostly moans of spirit, let out full to the heroic marchspirituals and priestly celebrations of the new blackness.'

By this time I was quite certain that jazz had ceased to be produced. The society that had engendered it had gone, and would not return. Yet surely all that energy and delight could not vanish as completely as it came? Looking round, it didn't take long to discover what was delighting the youth of the sixties as jazz had delighted their fathers; indeed, one could hardly ask the question for the deafening racket of the groups, the slamming, thudding, whanging cult of beat music that derived straight from the Negro clubs on Chicago's South Side, a music so popular that its practitioners formed a new aristocracy that was the envy of all who beheld them, supported by their own radio stations throughout the world's waking hours. Perhaps I was mistaken in thinking that jazz had died; what it had done was split into two, intelligence without beat and beat without intelligence, and it was the latter which had won the kind of youthful allegiance that had led me to hammer an accompaniment to Ray Noble's 'Tiger Rag' when I was 12 or 13. Beat was jazz gone to seed, just as 'modern jazz' was: B. B. King or Ornette Coleman? A difficult choice, and if I were to come down (as I should) on the side of the former, it wouldn't be under the illusion that I was listening to the latterday equivalent of Billie Holiday and Teddy Wilson, Pee Wee Russell and Jess Stacy, or Fats Waller and his Rhythm.

3

My slow approximation through these articles to the position just stated is the story I promised lay in them, and the amusement – at least, for me – is watching truthfulness break in, despite my initial resolve. As I said, it's an ordinary tale, and perhaps hardly worth telling. On the other hand, once I had worked out to my own satisfaction what had happened to post-war jazz, I couldn't help looking round to see who, if anyone, had anticipated me. Jazz writers as a class are committed to a party line that presents jazz as one golden chain stretching from Buddy Bolden to Sun Ra, and their task is facilitated by the practice jazz magazines have of employing several reviewers (the trad man, the mod man, the blues man) to ensure that nobody ever has to write about anything they really detest. This is good for trade, lessens the amount of ill-will flying about the business, and gives the impression that jazz is a happy and homogeneous whole. But was there no one among them who had realized what was going on, apart from myself?

I don't mean to suggest that there are not many knowledgeable critics to whom the party line is a sincere reality, nor to imply that they are given to mendacity. When a jazz writer says, 'You can hear Bessie in Bird', or 'Shepp's playing pure New Orleans street marches', I'm quite prepared to believe he means it, as long as I have permission to mark his mental competence below zero. I also take leave to reflect that most of them are, after all, involved with 'the scene' on a commercial day-to-day basis, and that their protestations might be compared with the strictures of a bishop on immorality: no doubt he means it, but it's also what he draws his money for saying. Would any critic seriously try to convince his hearers that jazz was dead? 'Jazz dead, you say, Mr Stickleback? Then we shan't be wanting next month's record stint, shall we? And don't bother to review "Pharaoh Sanders: Symbol and Synthesis" for the book page. And – let's see – we'd better cancel that New Wave Festival you were going to compère. Hope you make the pop scene, daddyo.' And so they soldier on at their impossible task, as if trying to persuade us that a cold bath is in some metaphysical way the same as a hot bath, instead of its exact opposite ('But don't you see the evolutionary development?').

But of course there was Hugues Panassié, the venerable Frog, who matter-of-factly refused to admit that bop or any of its modernist successors was jazz at all, simply adducing their records as evidence. It was a shock to find myself agreeing with Panassié: back in 1940 I had considered him rather an ass, chiefly because he overvalued Negro players at the expense of white ones ('the natural bad taste of the Negro' was a favourite phrase of the time), in particular the forcible-feeble Ladnier. But in appealing to the ear, rather than regurgitating the convoluted persuasions of the sleeves, he was producing the kind of criticism I liked, and I had to take back much of what I had thought of him in consequence. Then there was Brian Rust, authoritative discographer, who in his introduction to *Jazz Records 1932–42*, claimed that by 1944 'jazz had split, permanently, the followers of the bop cult demanding – and getting – music in an ever-freer form till (at least in the writer's opinion) it ceased even to be recognizable as jazz at all'. He also said that if he played Charlie Parker records to his baby it cried. And it was amusing to find Benny Green, who had made very merry with the bewilderment of old-style fans at the chromatic revolution, devoting the last pages of his book to sarcasms about Ornette Coleman and 'some nebulous lunacy called Free Form': nothing is funnier than an upstaged revolutionary. Now and then, too, a reviewer got the wrong record, as in 1961 when the editor of *Down Beat*, Don DeMicheal, took off on Ornette in heart-warming style ('the resulting chaos is an insult to the listener'), ending 'If Coleman is to be a standard of excellence in jazz, then other standards might as well be done away with.' Only once (August 1967) did I let fly in this way, and then it was like hitting the stumps with a no-ball: the piece wasn't printed.

Such examples* could indeed be multiplied, but might only seem added strokes to a self-portrait of the critic as ossified sensibility. To say I don't like modern jazz because it's modernist art simply raises the question of why I don't like modernist art: I have a suspicion that many readers will welcome my grouping of Parker with Picasso and Pound as one of the nicest things I could say about him. Well, to do so settles at least one question: as long as it was only Parker I didn't like, I might believe that my ears had shut up about the age of 25 and that jazz had left me behind. My dislike of Pound and Picasso, both of whom pre-date me by a considerable margin, can't be explained in this way. The same can be said of Henry Moore and James Joyce (a textbook case of declension from talent to absurdity). No, I dislike such things not because they are new, but because they are irresponsible exploitations of technique in contradiction of human life as we know it. This is my essential criticism of modernism, whether perpetrated by Parker, Pound or Picasso†: it helps us neither to enjoy nor endure. It will divert us as long as we are prepared to be mystified or outraged, but maintains its hold only by being more mystifying and more outrageous: it has no lasting power. Hence the compulsion on every modernist to wade deeper and deeper into violence and obscenity: hence the succession of Parker by Rollins and Coltrane, and of Rollins and Coltrane by Coleman, Ayler and Shepp. In a way, it's a relief: if jazz records are to be one long screech, if painting is to be a blank canvas, if a play is to be two hours of sexual intercourse performed *coram populo*, then

* To which should certainly be added Henry Pleasants, author of *Serious Music – And All That Jazz!* (1969).

† The reader will have guessed by now that I am using these pleasantly alliterative names to represent not only their rightful owners but every practitioner who might be said to have succeeded them.

let's get it over, the sooner the better, in the hope that human values will then be free to reassert themselves.

4

I hope the reviews themselves (and I really can't keep them from the reader much longer) are tolerably free from such polemics. I tried in writing them to be fair and conscientious, and there was many a time when I substituted 'challenging' for 'insolent', 'adventurous' for 'excruciating', and 'colourful' for 'viciously absurd' in a thoroughly professional manner. Although my critical principle has been Eddie Condon's, 'As it enters the ear, does it come in like broken glass or does it come in like honey?', I've generally remained aware that mine was not the only ear in the world. Above all, I hope they suggest I love jazz. I began by saying how much pleasure in life it has given me, and when I imagine how much I should have missed if, instead of being born on 9 August 1922 I had died then, I realize how great my debt is. How dreadful to have lived in the twentieth century, but died before King Oliver led his men into the Gennett studios at Richmond, Indiana, or before Frank Walker auditioned Bessie Smith ('fat and scared to death') or Bubber Miley joined Duke Ellington's Washingtonians! If I have any 'message' for my readers, it's that.

My readers . . . sometimes I wonder whether they really exist. Truly they are remarkably tolerant, manifesting themselves only by the occasional query as to where they can buy records: just once or twice I have been clobbered by a Miles Davis fan, or taken to task by the press agent of a visiting celebrity. Sometimes I imagine them, sullen fleshy inarticulate men, stockbrokers, sellers of goods, living in 30-year-old detached houses among the golf courses of Outer London, husbands of ageing and bitter wives they first seduced to Artie Shaw's 'Begin the Beguine' or The Squadronaires' 'The Nearness of You'; fathers of cold-eyed lascivious daughters on the pill, to whom Ramsay Macdonald is coeval with Rameses II, and cannabis-smoking jeans-and-bearded Stuart-haired sons whose oriental contempt for 'bread' is equalled only by their insatiable demand for it; men in whom a pile of scratched coverless 78s in the attic can awaken memories of vomiting blindly from small Tudor windows to Muggsy Spanier's 'Sister Kate', or winding up a gramophone in a punt to play Armstrong's 'Body and Soul'; men whose first coronary is coming like Christmas; who drift, loaded helplessly with commitments and obligations and necessary observances, into the darkening avenues of age and incapacity, deserted by everything that once made life sweet. These I have tried to remind of the excitement of jazz, and tell where it may still be found.

P. L.

1968

Footnote to the Second Edition

I went on writing these articles for three more years, and the additional pieces are printed here for the sake of completeness. While I enjoyed doing them (listening to new jazz records for an hour with a pint of gin and tonic is the best remedy for a day's work I know), they seem on re-reading to carry a deepening sense of depression. The kind of jazz I liked was dying with its masters: George Lewis, Pee Wee Russell, Johnny Hodges, finally Armstrong himself, the great oak uprooted at last. What claimed to be succeeding it grew more and more astringently chaotic. As James Lincoln Collier has written: 'Music in which we cannot find some principle of order, which seems to lack relationships, will make us anxious. We stop concentrating on it; our minds drift away; we become, as we term it, "bored".'* I certainly did. And what was actually succeeding it – the inescapable whanging world of teenage pop – had dominated the music industry to such an extent that the 'hot record' was becoming as hard to get as when my story started. Review copies were supplied less and less willingly (EMI was always a generous exception); imported foreign labels abounded elusively.

Consequently in July 1971 I wrote suggesting that the late Alasdair Clayre should review pop records every other month in place of me. Alasdair, a charming and remarkable Fellow of All Souls who in addition to pursuing his academic interests composed and sang his own particular kind of pop music, had liked the idea (he had already reviewed for the *Gramophone*), but all that happened was that my pieces for October and November weren't printed. In December I brought my contributions to an end.

I am sure I was right. I had said what I thought about jazz, and

* *The Making of Jazz* (1978), p. 476.

there was no point in repeating myself. Nor were there any signs that I was swaying the mob. When this book first came out in 1970 the reviews were, on the whole, friendly and fair, but they couldn't by any stretch of the imagination be called concurrent. What a pity, they mostly implied, that someone who appreciates one kind of jazz should be so insensitive to all the others. It is true that I can treasure an American comment that 'to understand what the lumpen-jazzmen and their scribes are doing to jazz, this breakthrough book is essential reading', but there was plenty to balance it. Not that I always minded. One of my severest castigators had, three months previously, respectfully noticed a Lennon–Ono album in which, by accident or design, two of the four sides were blank.* I wish I had got that into my introduction.

My readers were more sympathetic. A REME major asked me if I had heard '*Jazz Workshop* on BBC 2 at 00.30 hours on Mondays' ('the most appalling noise'). A gentleman from Stafford painstakingly transcribed the words of 'I'm Nuts About Screwy Music' from his Ballyhooligans version ('I'm daffy about groovy tempos/I'm groovy about daffy changes'). I wondered then, as I do now, how many people really like what came after Armstrong and Ellington. Would the Arts Council give a grant for the analysis of suggestions received by (not played on) *Jazz Record Requests*, and so settle this point?

What I have heard of jazz since then suggests no decisive change for better or worse. The ultimate absurdity of free form surfaces now and again, but there are numerous flirtations with ethnic and rock, and regressions into modes already exhausted. No new dominant figures have emerged, which in a music so dependent on individual invention is bound to be stultifying. When I look at record reviews today, at least half discuss reissues; not always of any antiquity – jazz publishing is a short-run business – but with a heartening number of anthologies or even definitive editions of major traditional figures, which argues that the jazz I was brought up on still commands a paying audience. If I haven't been proved right, I haven't been proved wrong either.

* 'Sides two and four consist entirely of single tones maintained throughout . . . constant listening reveals a curious point: the pitch of the tones alters frequently, but only by microtones. . . This oscillation produces an almost subliminal "beat" which maintains interest.' *Melody Maker*, 15 November 1969.

In any case, my views haven't changed. If Charlie Parker seems a less filthy racket today than he did in 1950 it is only because, as I point out, much filthier rackets succeeded him; pretty much the same, *mutatis mutandis*, could be said about Picasso and Pound. But if I have any regrets about *All What Jazz*, it is that it seemed to type me as a disliker rather than a liker. I still insist I love jazz: the great coloured pioneers and their eager white disciples, and the increasingly remote world that surrounded their music, dance halls, derby hats, band buses, tuxedos, monogrammed music-stands, the shabby recording studios where they assembled, and the hanging honeycomb microphones that saved it all for us.

P. L.

1984

1961

The White World

In their introduction to an excellent paperback, *Jazz on Record* (Arrow Books), Charles Fox, Peter Gammond and Alun Morgan lament the capricious attitude of record companies towards the issue and reissue of jazz recordings. This, they tell us, is miserly and unbalanced, causing a situation in which whole artists, whole epochs are withheld from us. 'It is almost as if a book publisher was able to decide that they would suppress half the classics of English literature.'

This is well said. Even the ordinary listener has plenty to complain of, the tired or raucous 'name' performances, the jumbling of sessions, the duplication, the deletion. For the fan, who knows what is *not* issued, the situation is well-nigh unbearable. The problem is to convince the record companies that the issue of jazz as jazz, and not as a poor relation of rock and roll, is commercial, and the only possible answer seems to be to buy such material when it does appear to the best of one's taste and means.

A special obeisance is due, therefore to Philips for their monumental four-volume 'Thesaurus of Classic Jazz'. This comprises fifty-two sides made between 1926 and 1930 by New York's leading jazz musicians and gives a revealing cross-section of a field poorly represented for a long time now. This is the music of the Jazz Age, but the Jazz Age did not really like jazz. The nearest it got to it was this brand of bright, skilful, melodic, but slightly bloodless music played by the 'hot men' of its favourite orchestras – Whiteman's, Goldkette's, Roger Wolfe Kahn's.

These men – Red Nichols, Miff Mole, Adrian Rollini – drew their inspiration from predominantly white originals, the Original Dixieland Jazz Band, the New Orleans Rhythm Kings and Bix Beiderbecke, rather than from the Negroes. In consequence their jazz had a refined, genteel air that suited palates not ready for Armstrong, Ellington, and the bands of the Savoy Ballroom.

But there is much to be said for Nichols. He used his popularity to record the best men in his circle and give their music an audience: it is thanks to Nichols that we know the musical beginnings of

Goodman, Teagarden, and Pee Wee Russell. And there are plenty of good things on the forty-odd sides given over to his groups: Jimmy Dorsey's mature clarinet style, at once melodious and intense, in comparison with the immature yet potentially much greater Russell; Mole's remarkable control and sobriety of tone; the two-fisted approach of Arthur Schutt, the only white pianist the Negroes admired; and finally, of course, the limpid Nichols cornet, so Bix-like in phrasing that one almost overlooks the absence of Bix's fire and shimmer. Nearly every side is relaxed, nearly every one in irreproachable taste.

Yet it is not only the stiff rhythm sections and the empty syncopations that make this all one can say. The first, non-Nichols, record shows at once that even the white man could go deeper into the jazz territory. Three Trumbauer tracks feature the wonderful triumvirate Bix, Trumbauer and Eddie Lang in their indestructible private world (the 1927 'Three Blind Mice' shows them all at their best), and four 1929 tracks by Eddie Lang's Orchestra, including the familiar 'Hot Heels' and 'Freeze an' Melt', have a drive and dash foreshadowing the famous Venuti-Lang sides of 1931.

Almost anything else currently available is in agreeably violent contrast, nothing more so than the blues. There is an increasing wealth of fine material in this genre now on sale (I hope to deal with some of it in a future article), and the latest is Little Brother Montgomery, who, on 'Little Brother' (Columbia) demonstrates his dry, agile piano technique and high, tremulous vocals.

This 54-year-old idol of Champion Jack Dupree, who was also here not long ago, has an eclectic approach to his music, handling other people's party pieces ('Cow Cow Blues', 'Pinetop's Boogie Woogie') as authoritatively as his own insistent country-style 'New Vicksburg Blues'. Ken Colyer, tasteful and tentative, joins in on three tracks, including 'Buddy Bolden's Blues'. In this, Little Brother rather endearingly sings the familiar phrase as 'open up that wonder'. It makes one think he is talking to the record companies.

11 February 1961

Having a Ball

Perhaps it was the novelty of a swing band concert that sold out the Carnegie Hall on 16 January 1938. Even so, Goodman himself was nervous: he wanted a comedian to come on and tell jokes, just in case. Watching Toscanini's auditorium fill up, Harry James said, 'I feel like a waitress on a date with a college boy.'*

They need not have worried. As we can tell from the re-mastered 'Benny Goodman Carnegie Hall Jazz Concert', reissued in Philips's Giant Jazz Gallery, the audience was sold from the start. And well it might be, for this was the swan-song of one of the key bands in jazz history (shortly after, Krupa, James, Teddy Wilson and Lionel Hampton all turned leader).

There was a trio by Ellingtonians Hodges, Cootie and Carney. Bobby Hackett did Bix's 'I'm Coming Virginia'. And for good measure there was the shape of things to come: Lester Young blowing two choruses in a jam session on 'Honeysuckle Rose'.

At this distance it is easy to point out faults. The two-voice orchestrations, staccato brass and silky reeds had an arid texture that wasn't helped by the killer-diller concept of excitement, and apart from Stacy and Goodman himself the regular band lacked first-class soloists. The Trio and Quartet had too often a helter-skelter approach, putting a premium on sheer virtuosity. But the combination of musicianliness and feeling, the attack of 'Life Goes to a Party' or 'I Got Rhythm', and individual items such as Goodman's six choruses and the ride-out in 'One O'Clock Jump', or Stacy's extraordinary introspective meditation at the close of 'Sing, Sing, Sing', earn this historic Sunday evening its place among immortal jazz occasions.

The jam session was the gimmick of the thirties. Nothing's arranged, we were told. Everyone just plays. Well, perhaps they did. Isolated pockets of them, despite time and the Musicians' Union, still do, such as Buck Clayton, Vic Dickenson, Pee Wee Russell and Bud Freeman ('Newport Jazz Festival All Stars', London). And a bouncing, lively record it is, with a joyous ''Deed I Do' and a longish blues called 'Pee Wee Russell's Unique Sound', that is very good listening, though nowadays Russell rarely emerges from an almost Chinese mood of recession and withdrawal.

John Lewis and the Modern Jazz Quartet have been busy in the studios with Jimmy Giuffre, the Beaux Arts String Quartet, and sundry horn-players, flautists, et al, to produce a group of tracks called 'Third Stream Music' (London). This term was coined by

*Or, according to Bobby Hackett, 'I feel like a whore in church.' (*Down Beat*, 7 March, 1968.)

Gunther Schuller to mean music that partakes of both jazz and classical techniques, and he conducts his own piece, 'Conversation', in which Lewis and Jackson perform swingily among pluckings and whimperings from the Beaux Arts. Two tracks with Giuffre ('Da Capo' and 'Fine') have more cohesion and spirit, reminiscent of 'The Train and the River', and all in all the record has Lewis's virtues of rather miniature sophistication and polish.

11 March 1961

The Persistence of the Blues

No one would contest that the blues are fundamental to jazz. This simple twelve-bar chordal progression – common, subdominant and dominant seventh – underlies the Ellington concerto and the Parker experiment as much as the exuberances of a 1920 jug band or the balladry of an itinerant guitarist. Yet for all its formal simplicity it is rarely monotonous. Somehow in this most characteristic music of the American Negro has been imprisoned an inexhaustible emotional energy. You can go on playing or listening to the blues all night.

In this country we have had to wait a long time for direct access to the real thing. Despite its omnipresence in the instrumental jazz of both races, the usual denotation of 'the blues' is that vast corpus of vocal music, by Negroes for Negroes, in which is recorded nearly every facet of their lives.

Large quantities of this were issued by American record companies on special, and often fugitive, 'race' labels. Thousands of sides were cut during the twenties and thirties, often under deplorable acoustic conditions and with little or no pre-arrangement, but understandably very few of them found their way to Britain. Before 1939 Bessie Smith was the only blues singer represented to any extent on an English label.

Now, happily, the situation is different. In the first place, in the past few years a number of genuine blues artists have actually visited us and gone round the country, usually with the Barber or Lyttelton bands. Big Bill Broonzy, Jimmy Rushing, Sonny Terry and Brownie McGhee, Little Brother Montgomery and Memphis Slim are among those who have demonstrated the real unadulterated blues in our cities, and an exhilarating experience it has been.

Secondly, there are currently available one or two books written with knowledge and enthusiasm that will set the general reader in the path of proper appreciation. *The Country Blues* by Samuel B. Charters (Michael Joseph) gives an absorbing account of this branch of the music and the lives of its chief exponents, men such as Blind Blake, Blind Lemon Jefferson, Leroy Carr and the modern practitioners Muddy Waters and Lightnin' Hopkins.

Paul Oliver's *Blues Fell This Morning* (Cassell), on the other hand, is a study of Negro life and society through the lyrics of 350 blues records. And for a book to transport you instantly to the heart of the Southern States where the blues are still sung as part of Negro daily life, *Been Here and Gone* by Frederic Ramsey (Cassell) is a most moving interpretation of this life in text and photographs.

It is in the third field, records, where improvement has been richest. In contrast to the position ten years ago, it is now possible to obtain at least a sample of a wide range of performers.

Both tyro and connoisseur, for instance, should enjoy the anthology records 'Blues Fell This Morning' (Philips) and 'The Country Blues' (RBF 1, jazz shops only), based on the books mentioned above, and there can be few more impressive records in this field than 'Angola Prisoners' Blues' (Collector). Recorded at a Louisiana State Penitentiary, this last is a prime example of Negroes using the blues as a direct expression of their feelings without the stimulus of audience or payment.

Then Jazz Collector's two EP series 'The Male Blues' and 'The Female Blues' give us Blind Lemon Jefferson, Blind Blake, Ma Rainey and others, and Fontana's 'Treasures of North American Negro Music' includes fine Leroy Carr and Blind Willie Johnson selections. The two American labels, Folkways and Riverside, are now on sale here and note should be taken of 'American Folk Music' (Folkways), containing work by Furry Lewis, Rabbit Brown and the great Sleepy John Estes. Riverside offer a good John Lee Hooker LP welcomely free from electric amplification, and a splendid Ma Rainey, Bessie Smith's tutor and often her equal.

Meantime the bigger British companies are issuing everything from field recordings of root folk music to this year's rhythm and blues. London's 'Southern Folk Heritage Series' give examples of primitive American music of a wild vivacity that must be heard to be believed. The supervisor, Alan Lomax, took his tape-recorder to public baptisms, penitentiaries, and kitchens to catch this musical border-country between Africa and the New World. At the other end of the scale is 'Jimmy Witherspoon at the Renaissance' (Vogue) and Joe Turner's 'Big Joe is Here' (London), robust rocking performances with strong band backings.

Yes, the blues are really with us today, the tradition extending from the pure form of these recordings down to its infinite vulgarization by Elvis and his host of adored imitators.

15 April 1961

Bands Across the Sea

Although it is now an international language, jazz (despite such exponents as Joki Freund, Jerzy Matuskiewicza and Hidehiko 'Sleepy' Matsumoto) remains solidly American. Fans elsewhere know that it is American musicians who matter. They want their latest records, to hear them in the flesh, to play alongside them in clubs and backstage. Such intermingling vitalizes the home product.

But in fact an American musician can no more play with British ones than an American docker can give a hand down at Tilbury. Let him try, and the Ministry of Labour, the Musicians' Union, and the American Federation of Musicians will all hit him at once. Gone are the days when Spike Hughes could assemble his Negro Orchestra in New York, or Benny Carter and Coleman Hawkins, still in their overcoats, stand jamming in London's Nest Club, while the house sax sat weeping helplessly. For many years there was a complete ban. Today, an American band as a stage act is allowed in this country only if balanced by the comparable engagement of a British band in America. (An eye for a tooth, as you might say.) Club dates are out. Mixed recording sessions are out. The profession (in both countries) must be protected.

All this makes 'Chris Barber's American Jazz Band' (Columbia) the more remarkable. Barber, a young trad leader of considerable energy and intelligence, has already done much for British jazz. His own brisk eclectic style has replaced lumbering revivalism as the trad groups' ideal, and he was the first to tour the country with such fine Negro artists as Big Bill Broonzy and Sister Rosetta Tharpe, whom otherwise we might never have heard. Now he presents eight tracks made on his last visit to America with an all-Negro line-up, including Sidney de Paris and Edmond Hall. The numbers are mostly standards such as 'Tishomingo Blues', 'See See Rider', and

'Oh Baby', and they are given easy, confident treatment in which Barber's rather woolly trombone romps along splendidly with the veterans de Paris and Hall, the whole undersprung by some sparkling Wallerish piano by Hank Duncan.

This is a good record in its own right, but its chief significance is that the American Federation of Musicians let it be made. This is another cold war in which a thaw would be welcome.

Meantime releases of every style and period abound. Many relate to Duke Ellington, who at 62 and in his fortieth year as a band leader commands as much respect as ever. There are his own 'Piano in the Background' (Philips) and 'Duke Ellington Presents' (Parlophone), for instance, both largely restylings of familiar numbers. New orchestrations by Gerald Wilson and Bill Mathieu give the first disc the edge (it also has the more Ellington originals), though the other has a delightfully unsickly version of Johnny Hodges' solo 'Daydream'.

Hodges, of course, is a jazz unchangeable, and in 'Blues-a-Plenty' (HMV) his clear, timeless, rather sad alto is as undisturbed as ever. Well supported by Eldridge and Webster, he leads the group with undisputed authority in mixed blues and ballads.

And then there is 'Portrait of Duke Ellington' by Dizzy Gillespie (HMV), eleven of Duke's numbers restyled by Carl Fischer. This is a curiosity of course, but to me sounds more like a rather screwy Ellington record than Duke reinterpreted in an entirely different tradition. Should Diz fall on hard times, however, he could have a fascinating career as Ellington's solo trumpet.

Basie, too, abounds. 'The Count Basie Story' (Colombia) offers 1960 remakes of twenty-three classics of his pre-1950 groups, but here there is no attempt at stylistic redevelopment, original orchestrations and even solos being retained. Fiery ensembles preclude bathos.

'Just the Blues' (Columbia) lets Joe Williams loose with plenty of Basie piano in support of his passionate, somewhat lachrymose singing; this is sincere enough work, though a little mannered for a big band to accompany. If I wanted a blues record, I should buy 'The Blues Roll On', volume seven in London's Southern Folk Heritage Series. I find these unknown Arkansas folk artists tremendously exciting.

All modernists will want 'The Clifford Brown Memorial Album' (Blue Note), two 1953 sessions (one new here) demonstrating the mellow agility of this young trumpeter, who but for a fatal accident in 1956 would certainly have stayed with the leaders. Included are his favourite 'Easy Living' and the showpiece 'Brownie Speaks', with strong support from Gryce, John Lewis, Blakey and Lou Donaldson, who plays beautiful alto on 'You Go To My Head'.

13 May 1961

Bechet and Bird

Not long ago a well-known writer tried to get the word 'great' banned from critical vocabulary, on the grounds that it cannot constitute a meaningful advance on 'good'.

A better reason, in jazz at any rate, would be that it has been too devalued on record sleeves to constitute a meaningful advance on anything. But if we call, for instance, Kaminsky, Carter and Teddy Wilson good (and we can hardly do less), what word are we to use to show recognition of that extra inimitable power that practice cannot give?

I ask because records have recently appeared by two players with nothing in common except that they manifestly stood head and shoulders above their contemporaries: Sidney Bechet and Charlie Parker.

Bechet, the New Orleans veteran who died in Paris on his sixty-second birthday, had led a lonely life as a jobbing clarinet and soprano sax player until he emigrated to France and became a national idol during the fifties. He never influenced anyone of importance except Johnny Hodges, and at times found work so scarce that he set up a tailoring business (is it Mezzrow who had one of his suits?).

Parker, on the other hand, had when he died, aged 34, seen jazz re-fashion itself pretty well in his image and heard his own solos coming back at him from a thousand horns. His technique and invention were prodigious, whereas no one would pretend Bechet had any more of either than he needed. Yet both alike on these records display unquestioned individual authority, unclouded and absolute. This is jazz and this is Bechet (or Parker) playing it.

It may be thought that there is already too much recorded Bechet for any fresh collection to be termed indispensable. 'Jazz Classics No. 1' (Blue Note) is none the less an exception. It joins 'The Sidney Bechet Memorial Album' (Fontana) and 'Shake It and Break It' (deleted HMV) as essential examples of him in his prime, playing with his peers. For one thing, it contains the marvellous 'Blue Horizon', six choruses of slow blues in which Bechet climbs without interruption or hurry from lower to upper register, his clarinet tone at first thick and throbbing, then soaring like Melba in an extraordinary blend of lyricism and power that constituted the unique Bechet voice, commanding attention the instant it sounded.

The same full-throated felicity fills the celebrated 'Summertime' (1939), which according to *Down Beat* made even the accompanists clap, and other tracks show him standing up for himself in groups led (if Bechet could ever be led) by Max Kaminsky, Sidney de Paris and Bunk Johnson. But more delightful than these are duets with his fellow Creole clarinettist, Albert Nicholas, 'Weary Way Blues' and 'Blame It on The Blues'. Supple, light-textured and swinging, these have Bechet's soprano sounding almost like a trumpet beside his less forceful colleague.

From the first staggering cadenza in the Parker-Gillespie 'Night in Tunisia' we are in a different world. 'Diz 'n' Bird in Concert' (Vogue) has one side made up of tapes taken at a Carnegie Hall concert in 1947, and they show Parker in such fast flight that only Gillespie could follow him. Parker's recorded output includes bad takes and rehearsals – his every note will sell – and here the tracks concentrate on the chief soloists, not always presenting complete performances.

Listening to Parker, one has the impression of a man who not only could translate his ideas into notes at superhuman speed, but who was simultaneously aware of half a dozen ways of resolving any given musical situation, and could somehow refer to all of them in passing beyond it. In his extended solos in 'Groovin' High' and 'Confirmation' idea succeeds idea so unhesitatingly and at such high pressure that the hearer acquits him of any premeditated desire to astonish. Clearly, his only problem was how to get it out fast enough.

This is important, because the new modern jazz that Parker and Gillespie founded was in part a reaction against the ossified platitudes of 1940 big-band jazz which they were both forced to play. Driven to desperation by the fag-end of the swing era, they and a few other young Negro musicians produced a music among themselves that was technically, melodically and rhythmically beyond their elders and their audience alike. By doing so, they recaptured for their race the jazz initiative, and, incidentally, split the world of this music into two camps. But on the evidence of these solos alone it would be absurd to call Parker's music a reaction. As well call leaping salmon a reaction.

10 June 1961

Cool, Britannia

Not so long ago, the unlikelihood of the Briton as jazzman would have been perfectly expressed by thinking of him in a bowler hat. Result: complete incongruity, like Mrs Grundy dancing the can-can. Yet today the bowler is worn with jolly unselfconsciousness by some of this country's most popular groups as part of their stand uniform. Nobody laughs. In fact, they cheer. British jazz has arrived, in Britain at any rate.

But British jazz could not capture an audience until the rhythm club (records) had given place to the jazz club (live blowing), and this did not happen until the traditional revival in the late forties. Even then, it remained for Graeme Bell's Australian Jazz Band to show that this was dance music, not dissection material. Suddenly everyone started jiving.

Today, we have a jazz boom. The quickest way to get with the sixties is to catch a jazz concert, Barber, Bilk or Ball. If you are over 30, you may be the oldest person in a crowd of, say, 2,000, but you will still be infected by an enthusiasm as intense as it is innocent. This crowd has never heard 'Golden Leaf Strut', and Frank Teschmacher might be Mayor of West Berlin for all they know, but this is the music they enjoy, beards, bowler hats, banjos and all. The numbers – Ellington, regimental marches, 'Careless Love', folk songs, 'Any Old Iron', 'Mack the Knife' – are recognizable for the first chorus: after that, they become just another trad excursion, simple, invigorating, loud. You might be excused for leaving at the interval.

The boom has drawbacks. For one thing, it means that record companies are readier to issue British traditional than reissue o.p. performers like Luis Russell or the Billy Banks Rhythmakers. For another, it means that non-traditional British musicians feel themselves hard done by.

Of the random samples of British jazz to hand over the past few months, only one has been modern: 'Tubbs' (Fontana), in which Tubby Hayes demonstrates his polished bop tenor-playing, forceful in 'The Late One', tender in 'R.T.H.', and some modish big band arrangements such as the soul-full waltz 'Tubbsville'. Terry Shannon and Bobby Pratt ably support.

And only two have been mainstream: the Fairweather-Brown All Stars' 'Dr. McJazz' (Columbia) and Bruce Turner's Jump Band 'Jumping at the NFT' (77 Records). Both these groups feature tightly orchestrated small-group arrangements, the former riffish originals (the ballad 'Monday' seems nearly a masterpiece to me), the latter less experimental, its leader's Hodges-like alto crossing the Kirby-like approach to the others. Yet all these albums are both skilled and thoughtful, and Turner's in particular shows warmth.

Of the traditionals, 'Chris Barber's Blues Book Vol. One' (Columbia) offers a mixture of Ottilie Patterson solos, ranging from the classics 'Backwater Blues' and 'Blues Before Sunrise' to Ottilie's more recent rhythm-and-blues manner in 'Mama, He Treats Your Daughter Mean'. These white ears find this a monotonous mode, and prefer the softer, almost accidental charm of 'Me and My Chauffeur'. But Mr and Mrs Barber are doing well to popularize the fruits of their American tours.

Mr Acker Bilk, by now almost a folk-hero, stays closer to the tradition in 'The Golden Age of Bilk' (Columbia), offering several familiar vehicles such as 'Buona Sera', 'Should I', and 'Pretty Boy'. There is a robust, four-ale quality about this group's music, stemming from the leader's personality (though not his oddly-sensitive clarinet) and the rough-edged, driving trombone of Jonathan Mortimer. Another bowler set, Dick Charlesworth and his City Gents ('Meet the Gents', Top Rank), show a greater variety of mood, from 'Kitty's Dream' to 'Yes, We Have No Bananas', in all of which the clouded, rather melancholy tone of Bob Masters's trumpet is the primary fascination. Alex Welsh and his Band look to Chicago rather than New Orleans, and on 'It's Right Here for You' (Columbia) display their brisk extrovert charm, with drumbreaks, yelping vocals, and the Russell-type clarinet of Archie Semple. Joseph Reinhardt, Django's brother, provides fine guitar.

And what can be said about The Temperance Seven? If you have one of the 250,000 copies of 'You're Driving Me Crazy' you will know what I mean if I call it Boy Friend jazz. If not, then take a spin at 'Pasadena' (Parlophone) to find out.

15 July 1961

Panassié Stomps

The revised edition of Hugues Panassié's *The Real Jazz* (Yoseloff), reminds me of his earlier *Hot Jazz*, in which as far back as 1934 he attempted to settle the outline of jazz. It has the same meaningless French thoroughness ('John Ewing is perhaps the closest to Trummy Young. Henry Coker has an amazing wealth of ideas, is very versatile, and plays all kinds of styles. Al Hayse is a pure swingman') and the same grotesque translations.

But even more, it reminds me of the fable of the Emperor's New Clothes. As it is well known, about 1940 the young Negroes broke away from the exhausted and limiting swing-era conventions, and set jazz going in a new direction with new rhythms, new harmonies, new intonations. But they did not carry the older players with them (Cab Calloway: 'Quit playing that Chinese music in my band'), nor indeed all the younger ones; hence the jazz world became divided into two camps, traditional and modern. Each has its own fans (the promoters of the recent Earlswood Jazz Festival attribute its success to the fact that they catered for only one group) and its own players. Even the magazines have a traditional reviewer and a modern reviewer.

None the less, Panassié is the first critic to say out loud that he rejects the common critical attitude – 'Well, jazz had to develop. You can't stop progress. All these new men have solid blues backgrounds. You've got to like the best from both kinds' – and says uncompromisingly that modern jazz is a freak, an aberration: 'Despite all that has been said by the "intellectualists" on the subject, be-bop music is NOT jazz. This is no mere opinion. This is fact.' Parker was a good alto in his Jay McShann days, but 'when he developed what was called bop, he ceased to be a real jazz musician'.

Many people will find this book simply silly. Others will breathe a sigh of pleasure at hearing their shyest thoughts uttered.

'Music, to create harmony, must investigate discord,' says Plutarch's epigraph to the new edition of *The Encyclopaedia of Jazz* (Arthur Barker), and Leonard Feather has done a great deal of investigating to expand his original 360 pages to 527. The biographical entries, which are the book's *raison d'être*, have increased to 2,000, adding players as different as John Coltrane and John Lee Hooker. The book's sole gleam of humour, under 'Bolden, Charles

"Buddy"' ('the sound of his horn, according to those who heard him play, was comparable to that of John Peel'), has been allowed to remain. Otherwise, it concentrates on life and work, adding occasional evaluations and comments.

As before, it has blocks of fascinating photographs, historical and musicological essays, and many amusing though rather pointless items such as birthdays, lists of 'kings of jazz', reports on the blindfold test (records, not whisky), and so on. One may not always agree with Mr Feather – why does he keep calling Charlie Shavers one of the nine best trumpeters of all time? – but his book can be read as well as referred to with pleasure as well as profit. A must.

12 August 1961

Make Me a Palate

Back from a holiday where the only music came from waiters' beach radios, my scoured palate revels in the accumulation of recent records. While an exciting multilayered sandwich works slowly down the spindle of my record-player, I realize afresh the truth of Baudelaire's words: 'Man can live a week without bread, but not a day without the righteous jazz.'

Prestige (how quickly these American labels have become an essential part of the British jazz scene!) has issued two delightful guitar records by Al Casey and Tiny Grimes. In 'Buck Jumpin'', Casey, who was born in 1915 and was for many years part of Fats Waller's Rhythm, returns to unamplified guitar for a set of standards, notably 'Body and Soul'. His warm and supple single-string style eschews gimmickry, and it is a pleasure to hear another Wallerite, Rudy Powell, supporting on midstream alto. 'Casey's Blues' is, as you might imagine, the best track. Tiny Grimes, although only two years younger, has moved in more forward-looking company, including Tatum, Young and Parker, and his more abrupt electric guitar work bears traces of this. Solos are shared more evenly with Ray Bryant and Jerome Richardson (tenor and flute).

There is some danger that the tenor sax may become the club bore of jazz, droning on in front of a docile rhythm section for track after track, and nearly every month produces such a session. Though it may be a little late to mention 'The Soul of Ben Webster' (HMV), it should be noted as an exception, for not only does Webster yield occasionally to the plangent trumpet of Art Farmer and Jimmy Jones's piano, but Harold Ashby's tenor is there to provide comparison. 'Chelsea Bridge' and 'When I Fall in Love' are masterpieces of shapely phrasing.

'Stan Getz At Large' (HMV, two volumes) and 'Coltrane Jazz' (London) make a violent contrast in this field. Getz, fluctuating effortlessly before a Danish rhythm section, dispenses the dry vintage of neo-Young perhaps a little too passionlessly, while John Coltrane, that relentless experimenter, intersperses the vinegary drizzle of his tone with chords (yes, two notes at once) that hardly seem worth the effort. Getz is the pleasanter listening – almost too pleasant – but Coltrane is thinking harder, and is still far ahead of his followers; witness 'Harmonique'.

The Modern Jazz Quartet has sometimes been condemned for an inbred academicism emanating from its leader, John Lewis, in whose hushed and respected aura vibra-harpist Milt Jackson is to be seen struggling like a fly in amber. To me their music, though narrow, has a natural swing under its shimmering restraint, and it has never seemed better than on 'The Modern Jazz Quartet European Concert' (London, two volumes). Most tracks are familiar items – 'Django', 'Bags' Groove' – but are freshly-rendered, and I love the ghostly barrelhouse of 'Pyramid'. Perhaps an audience helped.

Humphrey Lyttelton also has an audience in 'Humph Returns to the Conway' (Columbia), in which his new six-piece line-up traverses its wide repertoire from rhythm and blues ('Ti-Ri-Lee') through Ellington to some very modernish cutting on tenor. Lyttelton's Armstrong numbers are a shade effortful, and I dislike the habit of playing 'Bugle Call Rag' as 'Ole Miss', but gusto and good humour make this record more enjoyable than many of greater pretension.

Blue Note's Thelonious Monk anthology, 'Genius of Modern Music, Vol. One', shows the foundations of Monk's now familiar piano approach by tracks from the forties – unexpected, at times outlandish, supremely confident, with occasional contrived hamfistedness and an over-use of descending runs. The passage of time has done nothing to dull 'Epistrophy', 'In Walked Bud', 'Round About Midnight', and the rest of his celebrated originals. Now go straight on to 'The Golden Age of Ragtime' (Riverside), a series of transcribed piano rolls demonstrating this quaint formal ancestor of jazz, with its rich counter-melodies and pervasive pre-1914 melancholy.

And lastly, once more thanks for the inexhaustible vitality of the blues. 'Champion Jack's Natural and Soulful Blues' (London) has Jack Dupree's unabashed yelling as he splashes up and down the keyboard in 'Bad Life' and 'Bad Luck Bound to Change', strong, simple and moving. Equally invigorating is 'Jimmy Rushing and the Smith Girls' (Philips). Mr Five-By-Five's tone is unshakably jubilant, and backing by Hawkins and Clayton make fast and slow tracks alike successful. Finally, Brownie McGhee and Sonny Terry combine again in 'Down Home Blues' (Prestige): this music is as natural as breathing, and one wants it to go on as long.

9 September 1961

Survival of the Hottest

I suppose that, apart from Bix (who died in 1931 'of everything', as novelist Frank Norris said), the most original white jazz player has been his friend, clarinettist Pee Wee Russell. If he has never enjoyed Beiderbecke's renown, it may be because at 56 he is still unromantically alive. No one familiar with the characteristic excitement of his solos, their lurid snuffling, asthmatic voicelessness, notes leant on till they split, and sudden passionate intensities, could deny the uniqueness of his contribution to jazz.

Pee Wee began life as just another of the hard, rather piercing white clarinets of the Nichols-Lanin scene in the twenties, but his individuality soon manifested itself. After Teschmacher's death in 1932 he became the leading 'Chicago' clarinet, and was featured on numerous Condon sides from 'Home Cooking' (1933) to the flood of wartime Commodores.

Success encouraged him to indulge his melodramatic sense of timing, to widen his range of tone, and to employ grotesque tricks of overblowing to convey an almost inarticulate emotionalism. In the not over-subtle world of the American nightclub, a reputation for funny noises at times obscured his harmonic ingenuity and instinctive lyricism.

The appearance of 'Swingin' With Pee Wee' (Prestige) confirms that Russell is not only still a major jazz artist, but that he is managing to separate himself from the decline of the Condon vogue wherein he made his name. Since his illness in 1951, he has recorded with a variety of companions, from players perhaps twenty years his junior, like Jimmy Giuffre and Ruby Braff (who obligingly hushes the accompaniment when Russell has a pianissimo fit) to middle-aged mainstreamers like Vic Dickenson and Buck Clayton. In the present disc he and Clayton front a rhythm section of Tommy Flanagan, Wendell Marshall and Osie Johnson.

In my recollection this is the first time Pee Wee has recorded with a single trumpet since the classic (and deleted) 1932 sides with Henry Allen, and if the excitement is not quite so great there is still an abundance of solos and uninhibited two-horn ensembles. In all-Negro company Russell is inclined to keep his tone pure, and only on the blues 'Englewood' and 'Midnight Blue' does he grow at all catarrhal.

For the rest he is clear and challenging, a master of the unexpectedly right, producing in 'Anything For You', 'Lulu's Back In Town' and 'Wrap Your Troubles in Dreams' long solos as good as anything I have heard in the last ten years. And yet Clayton is almost as good, at once daring and composed, and the rhythm section springy and well-recorded though a shade well-bred. This is not only good Russell, but splendid jazz into the bargain.

Art Farmer's economical trumpet is displayed to advantage on 'Farmer's Market' (Esquire) with Hank Mobley and Kenny Drew; an out-of-tempo meditation 'Reminiscin'' shows Farmer combining the natural beauty of his instrument with a modern intonation.

There have been a good many Cannonball Adderley records recently: 'African Waltz' on the LP of the same title (Riverside) is a lumbering affair, and the rest of the tracks show off Cannonball's big band playing mostly Ernie Wilkins arrangements. For a less interrupted view of its leader's Carter-Parker alto 'Cannonball Takes Charge' (Riverside) presents him against various rhythm sections, taking charge indeed. His full, decided treatment of 'Poor Butterfly', 'I Remember You', 'Hang My Tears Out To Dry', and other standards makes a satisfying positive album that should please most tastes.

Among the first Pye Jazz label discs is an LP by Britain's leading trad group Kenny Ball, a hard-driving sparkling little band with a higher level of musicianliness than most. At times they sound mechanical, and passages lifted from classic records are certainly derivative, but if there is anyone who still wants a copy of 'Samantha' here it is, along with pleasant versions of 'Tin Roof Blues', 'Blue Turning Grey', and a marathon 'High Society' that took some twenty years off my reactions.

Nor should 'Bunny' (Camden) be overlooked, even though Berigan's trumpet at this distance of time is less interesting than his band with its dry, thirtyish, swinging sound. Joe Bushkin makes sporadic, delightful appearances. Lastly, the month's blues is without doubt 'Lightnin'' (Prestige). This is Lightnin' Hopkins at his most relaxed, his voice and guitar blending so perfectly the words hardly signify. Samuel B. Charters called him 'the last singer in the grand style' and this justifies the claim splendidly. Leonard Gaskin's bass stalks alongside.

14 October 1961

Looking Back at Louis

I know some public libraries buy records, but do they buy jazz records? If not, Parlophone's 'Louis Armstrong: His Greatest Years' would be an ideal start. The first two discs comprise the first thirty-two sides Armstrong made under his own name in Chicago between November 1925 and May 1927, and it is clear that when the full set of four is complete we shall have the nearest thing to a scholar's standard edition that the jazz record world is likely to produce. Tracks are in chronological order, annotated by that Porson of early jazz, Brian Rust.

At this time Armstrong's power and reputation were growing almost monthly. He had finished a two-year stint with King Oliver in Chicago, and a year with Fletcher Henderson in New York. Now he was back in Chicago, playing with two bands every night (one of which billed him as 'World's Greatest Trumpet Player'), with this Okeh contract to fulfil as well.

Louis was not yet a leader, and these groups, the Hot Five and the Hot Seven, existed only in the studio, but their records are classics, not only for what they are, but as evidence of Armstrong's enormous talent bursting out of its chrysalis. On the first sides his loud, clear cornet drives along exuberantly, but by 1927 the original hilarious 'family' atmosphere with its spoken jive and missed cues has given place to a much surer understanding dominated by Armstrong's greater maturity. He reaches more confidently for high notes; his cadenzas are more individual; he draws on greater depths of feeling. 'Georgia Grind' and 'Cornet Chop Suey' are good but they cannot compare with 'Alligator Crawl' or 'Melancholy Blues'.

With the latter, the great virtuoso of 1928–29 is waiting in the wings, and the remaining discs of this magnificent project will show him assuming the stage.

Another degree of thaw in the exchange freeze-up between Britain and the United States was registered last month when tenorist Zoot Sims arrived to play British club dates (as opposed to theatres) with the blessing of both unions. Tubby Hayes has gone to America to do likewise. Other appearances scheduled for November are Dizzy Gillespie and John Coltrane in a Jazz At The Philharmonic package, and the Dave Brubeck Quartet, who come just in time to see their new EP 'Take Five' (Fontana) enter the Top Twenty. This modest tricky-rhythmed piece seems an odd candidate for mass acclaim.

For the stay-at-home there is plenty of consolation among the new issues. The Alex Welsh-Archie Semple 'Night People' (Columbia) is a delightful series of duets with piano and bass, modelled on Wild Bill Davison and Pee Wee Russell without being swamped by them. Wild Bill's emotionalism becomes slightly smarmy in Welsh's hands, but for the most part these are crisp, relaxed, tuneful tracks, particularly 'Solitariness', 'Night People' and Semple's solo 'The Lady Sings the Blues'.

While on home ground, let me apologize for calling the Temperance Seven 'Boy Friend jazz' some months back. Their new LP 'The Temperance Seven 1961' (Parlophone) exhibits a repertoire far too extraordinary to be summarized so briefly. Until now, revivalists have concentrated on the good parts of twenties jazz; here is a group concentrating on the, shall we say, more characteristic parts. 'Hard-Hearted Hannah', 'Vo-Do-Do-De-O Blues' and the rest constitute a kind of surrealist archaism well supported by the band's bizarre walking-out dress, and the flickering Bix-like trumpet of Cephas Howard only confuses us more. Paul McDowell's 'Falling In Love Again', sung first in English, then German, is my track of the month. It is the jazz equivalent of 'The Blue Angel' and 'Doctor Caligari' combined.

There have been several Cannonball Adderley discs lately, but even if you have some of them do not neglect 'The Cannonball Adderley Quintet in San Francisco' (Riverside), which pre-dates most of them (1959) and is an exhilarating live performance from the Jazz Workshop. Pianist Bobby Timmons's 'This Here' ('part shout and part moan'), 'Spontaneous Combustion' and 'Hi-Fly' show the Adderley brothers creating their familiar illusion that somewhere on the far side of modernism is hot jazz again.

11 November 1961

Horn in a Dilemma

That inexhaustible stimulus to the imagination *A Pictorial History of Jazz* (1955) devotes seven pages to Bix Beiderbecke. They trace the seven years of his life that changed him from a loose-lipped jug-eared Iowa boy in shirt-sleeves to the solemn, tuxedoed, moustached member of the Whiteman Orchestra who shares a page with a photostat of his own death certificate: in New York, of lobar pneumonia, on 6 August 1931.

I am reminded of these pictures by two recent issues, 'Bix Beiderbecke and the Wolverines' (Riverside) and 'The Bix Beiderbecke Legend' (RCA), which cover the beginning and end of his career respectively. As everyone knows, Bix at 21 was the star of the Wolverines, a Mid-West roadhouse group that won a great campus reputation in 1924, cut a dozen or so records and finished up in New York. It was here that Bix left them; clearly he was meant for bigger things. Unfortunately, bigger things meant a trumpet chair in one of the highly paying commercial bands of the time. Nine of the RCA tracks, therefore, are made with Whiteman, and three more with Jean Goldkette (including a new attribution from 1924). In two cases different takes are given of the same numbers, as if to show that every note Bix waxed is still precious.

Well, of course, it is. Yet after playing both records through (especially as the 'Legend' finishes with one of Bix's late, clouded, heart-breakingly sad half-choruses on 'I'll Be A Friend') one is left miserable at the utter waste of the most original talent jazz ever produced.

For there is no doubt of Bix's originality: the astonishingly flighted solo on the Wolverines's 'Royal Garden Blues' shows him able even at 21 to produce triumphs owing nothing to Armstrong. And there is no doubt it was wasted: to hear him explode like Judgment Day out of the Whiteman Orchestra (as on 'No Sweet Man') only to retire at the end of sixteen bars into his genteel surroundings like a clock-cuckoo is an exhibition of artistic impotence painful to witness. Bix should have been dominating his own group, not decorating the Whiteman cake.

What went wrong? There is, of course, the well-worn story of his alcoholism and unstable personality. But his dilemmas went deeper than that. First, in 1927, there was no living to be earned in jazz, whereas Bix knew that as Whiteman's featured trumpet he could command the best salary in the business. Secondly, in an odd way Bix liked Whiteman and his 'symphonic jazz'. His interest in classical music increased yearly and the world of Grofé and Gershwin was as near to it as his lack of musical education enabled him to get. 'Bix was growing away from us,' Mezz Mezzrow said. 'Finally he drifted clean out of our sphere. Losing his head over "serious" music made him go way tangent . . .' Perhaps Bix would have been better off with either more gifts or less. But the playing on these records can still put to flight such thoughts of inadequacy.

Bix today would undoubtedly have been a modern, like the Negro trumpeter Kinny Dorham, who was born in the year the Wolverines made their records. His LP 'Whistle Stop' (Blue Note) fascinates by its leader's smooth, unhesitant horn and the musicianly approach of the other four. Dorham, who has composed and taught as well as played with most star modern groups, is here heard with Hank Mobley and Philly Joe Jones in seven of his originals. The title number carries long gripping solos by all concerned but Dorham's one-minute 'Epitaph' nearly steals the show. Guitarist Jim Hall has also taught (School of Jazz, Lenox, Mass.), and the delightful 'Good Friday Blues' by the Modest Jazz Trio (Vogue) features him with Red Mitchell and Red Kelly. The blues has the latter-day 'Americana' flavour of Mose Allison and Guiffre, but the other numbers – notably 'I Was Doin' Alright' – might slip by as cocktail-music except for the superb economy of piano and guitar.

Philips have reissued fourteen splendid Billie Holiday tracks ('This Is My Last Affair'), all dating from the thirties, when she was in best voice and company. This was before Lady Day began to 'use her voice like an instrument' – a fatuous notion for any singer relying so obviously on actual lyrics – and 'A Fine Romance', 'Carelessly' and 'You Let Me Down' demonstrate her insinuating yet forceful appeal. Of altoist Johnny Hodges in 'Gerry Mulligan Meets Johnny Hodges' (HMV) it can be said only that he uses his instrument like a voice, floating irresistibly through everything he touches. These six numbers, all credited to either or both players, are like delicious bubbles blown extempore in the studio; jazz-lovers of all shades are urged to catch them before they vanish.

9 December 1961

1962

Rose-Red-Light City

Every age has its romantic city and ours is New Orleans. Canal Street, Basin Street, Rampart, Burgundy, Gravier, nearly every thoroughfare stays in our memory by reason of some unforgettable music: even its veterans, who must have known them for what they were, an appallingly vicious squalor corralled into a red light district by Alderman Sidney Story in 1897, can say nothing in its dispraise.

'Yes, New Orleans was always a musical town – a happy town,' mused Clarence Williams. In its way, it was a kind of Cockaigne: parades, picnics, funerals, all had their brass bands, and every citizen, shoeblack, cigarmaker, bricklayer, was half a musician. Their music has become synonymous with a particularly buoyant kind of jazz that seems to grow from a spontaneous enjoyment of living.

That the spell is still potent is proved on the one hand by the continued popularity of the city's old-timers, and on the other by their young British followers. Riverside, for instance, has begun a series called 'New Orleans: the Living Legends', of which the latest example is Kid Thomas and his Algiers Stompers. This is crude, uncertainly-pitched stuff, and Thomas (born 1896) has a trumpet tone at once thin and rough, but Louis Nelson's trombone and the exuberant drumming of Sammy Penn give it a compelling attraction, whether in blues numbers or the plangent 'Girl of My Dreams'.

Similar material is found on two LPs bearing the Storyville label (the alderman has the strangest of immortalities): 'New Orleans Styles', including sides by Oscar Celestin with Alphonse Picou on clarinet, Kid Ory's Creole Jazz Band, and Wilbur De Paris's New Orleans Jazz; and a curious assortment in the form of a guided tour of present-day New Orleans music with spoken links by George Lewis, featuring Celestin again, Johnny St Cyr's Hot Five, Bill Matthews, and Lewis's own group with Kid Howard. I preferred the first of these, but both will interest the antiquarian.

That British traditional jazz turned from the Armstrong-Oliver pattern to that offered by George Lewis and modern New Orleans bands was largely the work of Ken Colyer, who visited the Crescent

City as a seaman and brought back an inspiration that is the foundation of Barber and Bilk today. On 'This Is the Blues' (Columbia) is heard a beautiful selection of his unhurried traditional numbers, 'When the Sun Goes Down', 'Tishomingo Blues', and 'See See Rider'. Like Bilk, Colyer combines a robust public personality with the tenderest of instrumental tones.

Two other notable British groups are Terry Lightfoot's New Orleans Jazzmen ('World of Trad' on Columbia) and Dick Charlesworth and his City Gents ('Yes Indeed It's the Gents' on HMV), each providing good driving performances of standard numbers. Bob Masters's soft-spoken trumpet gives the latter disc the edge.

Parlophone has now finished its four-volume edition of the early work of the First Citizen of New Orleans, Louis Armstrong, taking 'The Greatest Years' up to December, 1928, and 'Tight Like This'. This is the Complete Shakespeare of jazz, and buyers should act accordingly. But it is to be hoped that Parlophone will follow the example of French Odeon and extend the series to seven discs.

Another alumnus from Algiers (now a suburb of New Orleans) is Henry Allen, who was with Oliver in 1927. The restless, unpredictable Allen trumpet on 'Red Allen Plays King Oliver' (HMV) has little kinship with his masters, but 'Yellow Dog Blues' and 'How Long Blues' show him at his patchy best. Lastly, a Storyville EP of three Crescent City stalwarts, Jelly Roll Morton, Barney Bigard and Zutty Singleton, produce as the Jelly Roll Morton Trio some fine spirited 1929 pieces that everyone should have.

The Blackhawk in San Francisco is a long way from the Tenderloin District, and the music Miles Davis played there on a certain Friday and Saturday nights ('Miles Davis in Person', Fontana, two discs) has little relation to the Bolden tradition. Davis has a moody and perverse persona, and his trumpet affects me in the same way; on 'Walkin'' or 'Neo', for instance, he runs phrases to death with a calculated perversity, and spends whole blocks of bars trying to emaciate his tone to a still further degree of unpleasantness. There is, however, a gusty informality in the atmosphere, the well-sprung rhythm section of Wynton Kelly, Paul Chambers and Jimmy Cobb encourage Davis and Hank Mobley to long bouts of free expression very far from the egg-walking hushedness of some of Davis's studio pieces.

For blues lovers, there is no choice this month: they simply must spend their money on Alexis Korner's 'Kings of the Blues' (RCA), three EP volumes of thrilling music by Gus Cannon's Jug Stompers,

Big Maceo, Sleepy John Estes and others. All are delightful, but if a choice must be made, the four spring-like 1928 tracks of the Stompers have most individuality.

13 January 1962

Without the Duke

In his time – and that time is getting on for forty years – Duke Ellington has had some great soloists. Yet I can think of hardly one who did not become indefinably less once he moved outside the full orchestra. Compare, for instance, Bigard with Ellington to Bigard with Armstrong. It is easy to see why. In an Ellington composition, solos are the result of collaboration between leader and player. The player improvises, but he improvises Ellington's way. And when his solo appears it is at a premeditated moment in the rich confection of an Ellington arrangement: he is on his own, but with what a safety-net under him!

Johnny 'Rabbit' Hodges, inscrutable 56-year-old alto player with Ellington since 1928 (bar a five-year break in the fifties), comes nearest to being the exception to this rule – not, perhaps, a complete exception, for he is contractually unable to record outside the Ellington orbit, but for the past twenty years he has led small Ellington groups and featured his own material. New tracks by Rabbit occur every six months or so, and the latest is 'Not So Dukish' (HMV Verve), on which he has all-star support from Eldridge, Nance, Webster, Hamilton, and other Ellingtonians. There is a story that a French conductor once asked Hodges how he got the veritable artistry of his tone, to which Hodges replied, 'I just lucked it out, bubber, I just lucked it out.' So bland, so clear, so voluptuously voiced with *portamento* and *glissandi* and yet so essentially hot, Hodges' alto tone sounds the reverse of accidental. But it is not unduly studied. In 'M.H.R.', for instance, when we do not hear him till chorus six, his supple naturalness makes all previous soloists sound lumbering.

Yet listening to 'Blues With a Feeling' (1928) from 'Jungle Jamboree' (Parlophone), we realize from the stabbing plaintiveness of his soprano solo that latterday still-rather-Dukish Ellington units with their neat riffy tunes and unruffled ensembles have lost much of the original Ellington emotion. This LP is one more selection of early Ellington, vintage 1927–30, which everyone should, and no doubt will, have.

It is a shock to realize that Rex Stewart, who leads the Condon group in 'Tiger Rag and All That Jazz' (Vogue) was with Ellington for eleven years, whereas Bubber Miley, who stamped Ellington's growl trumpet on the public mind for ever, was with him less than three. Condon's line-up cannot now compare with the old 1940 days of Kaminsky and Russell, and Stewart, good-humoured and adaptable though he is, sounds too squealing and intense for the Condon mode. He has a good solo on 'Lazy River', though, and the playing is generally spirited, lone survivor Bud Freeman excelling on 'Livery Stable Blues' with the rough, baying tenor of his old days.

Django Reinhardt, perhaps the only European jazz natural, also had a spell with Ellington on his unsuccessful tour of the States in 1946. In *Django Reinhardt*, by Charles Delaunay (Cassell), we learn how, time and again, Duke had to spin out shows before the unpunctual Django appeared to do his feature. Django was a gypsy, and dispensed a particularly exciting form of guitar jazz, nimble and richly-chorded. 'Django and Stephane' (HMV) provides fourteen hitherto unpublished tracks made with his old side-kick violinist Stephane Grappelly in 1949.

I must be the last person in England to hear Dave Brubeck's LP of new tempo-rarities, 'Time Further Out' (Fontana), in which the Quartet waltz and otherwise gyrate through nine time-signatures ranging from 3/4 to 9/8. Brubeck's sleeve-note points out that jazz is very unenterprising in this direction, when field-hollers and Maori dances manage 5/4 and 6/4, and his new titles, especially 'Blue Shadows In The Street', are pleasantly fascinating. But they reminded me of John Hammond's comment on Benny Carter's 'Waltzing the Blues': 'In monkeying with the structure of the blues, Benny has robbed them of all warmth and feeling.' This was in 1936, but I have never forgotten it.

10 February 1962

After the Moderns

Despite the different facets of jazz today – the veterans, the blues, trad, mainstream, hard bop, soul, free form – the two primary questions about it are, first, is modern jazz driving out traditional;

and, second, if it is, can modern jazz keep the hold on public taste that traditional jazz had?

The answer to the first is yes. Jazz is always what the young American Negro is playing, and today he is a modernist. Armstrong and George Lewis, Ellington and Basie, Pee Wee Russell and Buck Clayton all maintain a traditional approach, but they are all over 50 now and are not being replaced.

The answer to the second is less clear. To some extent modern jazz, like other modern arts, is a performer's art – it began, by all accounts, as a private language: 'Something they can't steal because they can't play it.' Its revolutionaries, however, are already elder statesmen, and are beginning to be reissued. Excellent cross-sections of the earlier work of Gillespie and Monk are provided by 'The Greatest of Dizzy Gillespie' (RCA) and 'Thelonious Monk Volume Two' (Blue Note), and there is a third, 'The Essential Charlie Parker' (HMV), that has not yet reached me: everyone wanting to lay a foundation of classic modern performances in his collection should have them.

Listening to Gillespie, one realizes how impossible it was to imagine what the next great jazz trumpet stylist would sound like, yet how unmistakable he was when he came. His solos on the 1946 small band Victors – 'Night In Tunisia', 'Anthropology' and the others – are still tremendous; free, rocketing phrases, each punched out powerful and precise. Beside him, the rest of the group seems hardly to have emerged from the John Kirby era. For me, however, he is an up-tempo genius; his pure, slightly inhuman tone has little emotional depth on the slower 'Dizzier and Dizzier' (1949), and I have always felt that his eccentric personality – his very 'dizziness' – impairs his power to move.

Thelonious Monk ('the guy who started it all') has been more a seminal influence as composer and arranger than by his piano performances, which are technically somewhat unsure and – perhaps intentionally – ham-fisted.

His chording is always rich and strange, however, and on recordings from the fifties with Milt Jackson, Kinny Dorham and the exquisite alto of Lou Donaldson – the 6/4 'Carolina Moon', 'Straight No Chaser' and 'Skippy', for instance – he mixes his harmonic innovations with a forthright stride style reminiscent of Waller or The Lion.

Gigi Gryce, alto and composer of Jazz Lab Quintet fame, has

produced an exciting all-blues LP, 'Saying Somethin'!' (Esquire), with a new young trumpeter, Richard Williams. These tracks follow the usual routine of ensemble figures, solos, fours and out that shows the two horns to advantage, Williams in particular excelling on the souly 'Jones' Bones'. The eight-bar opener, 'Back Breaker', has some lovely Gryce alto, and a more old-fashioned sound that justifies the leader's avowed intention of 'integrating . . . straight jazz and commercial jazz'. More power to his elbow, and the sooner we hear more of Williams the better.

Tenorist Gene Ammons (son of the mighty Albert) has veered right through the spectrum from cool to rhythm-and-blues and part-way back: the title-piece of 'Blue Gene' (Esquire) has him forcefully blowing the blues before a popping of conga drums, with Idrees Sulieman and Pepper Adams in support. Three long blues tracks, however, seem to exhaust everyone's ideas, and the minor-keyed 'Hip Tip' has a freer, less strained air, Billie Holiday's accompanist Mel Waldron contributing especially well.

Cannonball Adderley can usually be relied on, and the tracks with brother Nat and pianist Junior Mance on 'Cannonball Enroute' (Mercury) are none the worse for being about four years old. Adderley has the rare virtue of sounding neither screwball nor neurotic, yet always pushing towards excitement: I favour him for this reason.

The present state of jazz largely depends on such performers as these: its future may be shaped by tenorist John Coltrane, who with Milt Jackson on 'Bags and Trane' (London) offers a unique mingling of his bleak tone with Jackson's luscious vibraharp. As a novelty it has much to commend it. As a taste of things to come it is a thought glacial.

10 March 1962

Ranging Through the Decades

Laymen may suppose that once a jazz record is issued it remains available indefinitely everywhere. Far from it. The LPs of Luis Russell and The Rhythmakers on Argentine HMV are unobtainable in Oxford Street: the thirty-seven Basie LPs issued in the past eleven years are by now mostly deleted. There is a constant struggle in the jazz record world between new performances and old, exacerbated by the fact that jazz offers little scope for reinterpretation or editing of its classics – it is not 'Weary Blues' we want but Armstrong's 1927 'Weary Blues'. And all too often jazz loses its places in the catalogue because it cannot compete with something called 'Eine Kleine Twist-Musik'.

All the more credit is, therefore, due to Parlophone for following up their four-disc 'Louis Armstrong: His Greatest Years' with 'Jazz Sounds of the Twenties'. These three discs are period anthologies made by 'Big Bands' (Oliver, Moten, Creath), 'Dixieland Bands' (ODJB, Johnny Bayersdorffer, Original New Orleans Rhythm Kings), and 'Small Groups and Piano Solos' (Clarence Williams, The Chicago Footwarmers, Waller, James P. Johnson). As the names show, this is an attempt to resurrect an era by performances as worthwhile as they are rare by bands many of which no reasonable listener could today expect to hear. Pre-electric recording and dated instrumental technique make the historical sense necessary to enjoy some tracks, and the gaiety and colour is sometimes tiny and distant, like a miniature. But the third disc in particular, with its knock-about ad-libs and engaging piano solos, is gay and colourful.

Sidney Bechet was used to wresting the lead from trumpeters with his soprano sax, but he met his match in flamboyant cornettist Wild Bill Davison. 'Sidney Bechet Giant of Jazz, Vol. 1' (Blue Note) gives all six sides of their first pitched battle of 1945, an encounter so thrilling that it was repeated in 1949 and 1950.

The result is a magnificent draw. The clash of styles – Bechet's throbbing *cantabile* and Davison's hoarse and thrusting over-emphasis – sets each one off: Bechet at his imperturbable best and Wild Bill rising to the occasion to produce some of his most uninhibited solos, as in 'Shine' and 'Way Down Yonder'. These are far beyond his usual reputation as an Armstrong-derivative. Art Hodes's rolling piano completes the décor.

Going back to 1939, there are twelve of the original Solo Art tracks on 'Giants of Boogie Woogie' (Riverside), in which that mighty triumvirate Albert Ammons, Meade Lux Lewis and Pete Johnson rumble their way through characteristic pieces, notably Ammons' 'Bass Goin' Crazy' and Johnson's 'Climbin' and Screamin''. A more piquant piano reissue is provided by 'Jazz at the Savoy: the 20's' (Decca), which presents the legendary Spanish-American Cantab. Fred Elizalde, who went from the Footlights

Revue to the Savoy in the middle twenties, where he used an American group with Nichols-Lanin affiliations without the Musicians' Union seeming to mind. The band numbers are unremarkable, but there is peculiar who's-for-tennis charm in Elizalde's solos. A buy for Old Nostalgians.

Bunk Johnson was almost a reissue in himself, but 'Bunk Johnson's Band 1944' (Storyville) reminds us how these New Orleans American Music recordings are already embedded in a different kind of history – that of British traditional jazz. Johnson, too, sounds surprisingly sophisticated by comparison with some of the old-timers we have had to endure lately, and this record can be recommended to anyone still not knowing what Bolden-era trumpet was like.

However, the present day cannot be completely ignored; there is a critical movement to make clarinettist Pee Wee Russell an honorary modern, and forget that tiresome twenty years' Dixieland. I feel it is at work in 'Jazz Reunion' (Candid), where Russell joins Coleman Hawkins for the first time since 1929 in company with Bob Brookmeyer, Emmett Berry, and pianist-arranger Nat Pierce. There is no doubt that Pee Wee has said all he has to say on the Condon repertoire, but in even a semi-modern context his idiosyncrasies lose their full flavour, and the freedom of LP leads him to ramble as vaguely and vapidly as Tony Scott. Much compensation can be found in 'Tin Tin Deo' and the blues '28th and 8th', and Hawkins is good throughout. In the public 'Jazz At The Modern' (Parlophone) Russell tightens up alongside Shorty Baker and Tyree Glenn, and delivers a characteristic aquarelle 'September In The Rain', Baker's 'Do Nothing Till You Hear From Me' taking the honours, nonetheless, with a finished professionalism.

There is vogue in the States at present for electric organs, and the shudderers should try 'Midnight Special' (Blue Note), one of the eighteen albums made for this label by Jimmy Smith on which he is heard with tenorist Stanley Turrentine. The nasal, blended tones of the instrument have undeniable fascination, and Smith uses them rather as Count Basie (from whom he clearly derives) uses his orchestra; that is, excitingly. Those who have heard the Count on his recent fifth tour, however, may find it an anti-climax.

16 April 1962

Armstrong to Parker

More and more are Charlie Parker and Louis Armstrong mentioned in the same breath as equals. The age in which Armstrong's trumpet technique was adapted to every jazz melody instrument has been succeeded by one in which, to quote Lester Young, 'everyone's playing Bird'. Yet, ironically enough, it is Armstrong who is still with us, flourishing that endless succession of clean handkerchiefs, while Parker has been dead these seven years.

Both men were innovators, though of very different kinds. Armstrong was an acceptor, a central talent into which flowed the many tributaries of jazz; his innovation was a throbbing, personal tone which demanded to be heard alone instead of as part of an ensemble. It has been said that Armstrong was lucky rather than great, that many an obscure trumpeter who never left the South played as well as he did, that he owes his reputation to good publicity and assiduous self-discipline. This is unfair; it would be truer to say that he was the apotheosis of a host of minor talents, of a tradition that lifted him up like a wave, and which he in turn purified.

Parker was a complete contrast. Born in Kansas City in 1920, he came to maturity just when the initial impulse of the twenties and early thirties had spent itself, and the jazz scene was dominated by the large, white, commercial swing bands. The effect of playing their music six nights a week can be imagined. Where Armstrong had accepted, Parker rejected. 'I kept thinking', he said afterwards, 'there's bound to be something else.'

This 'something else', that can be heard again on 'The Essential Charlie Parker' (HMV Verve) and 'Bird Is Free' (Esquire), was, in a word, complication. Parker found jazz chugging along in 4/4 time in the tonic and dominant, and splintered it into a thousand rhythmic and harmonic pieces. Showers of sixteenths, accented on half- and quarter-beats, exhibited a new harmonic fecundity and an originality of phrasing that had scarcely been hinted at before. Parker did not 'follow' anyone, as Armstrong followed Oliver. He just appeared.

His appearance, and that of his music, stung Armstrong into one of his rare bursts of criticism of fellow-musicians. In 1948, he termed it 'that modern malice', complaining that 'you got no melody to remember and no beat to dance to', and recently a reference to 'that ju-jitsu music' prefaced a reiteration of his latterday creed: 'A straight lead is better than any jazz solo you know of.' His concerts show what he means: on favourite slow numbers, 'Georgia' or 'Blueberry Hill', the deliberate unadorned simplicity of his playing and singing still grips huge audiences like a vice. But, of course, Parker gripped audiences too: on 'Bird Is Free' or 'Charlie Parker in Sweden' (Storyville), both taped in the early fifties, standards such as 'Cool Blues', 'Star Eyes' and 'Lester Leaps In' are treated with fresh and vivid audacity. All the same, his music, or what his successors have made of it, remains a minority taste. A local symptom of this is the BBC's decision to ban modern jazz from its weekly 'Jazz Club' on the grounds of public uninterest, a regrettable step in view of Britain's many fine modern musicians such as Tubby Hayes.

The new CBS label (for American Columbia) gets off to a splendid start with a four-disc 'The Fletcher Henderson Story: a Study in Frustration', presenting sixty-four sides made between 1923 and 1938 by successive groups assembled by this unlucky pianist-leader.

No bands had more stars than his: to speak of trumpeters only, Armstrong, Joe Smith, Ladnier, Stewart, Allen and Eldridge. Yet solid commercial success always eluded him. Later in life he had the bitterness of seeing his arrangements send the Goodman band rocketing to fame.

Magnificent depth collections like this one restore one's faith in record companies. It should be bought as a history of the middle-of-the-road jazz orchestra up to the swing era; as a conspectus of Don Redman and Henderson as arrangers; as a study of the early Coleman Hawkins; as a magnificent bouquet of solos by some of the finest Negro musicians. Volume 4 (1932–8), containing the prophetic 'Queer Notions' and two splendid King Porters, is perhaps the best to begin with; listeners should work backwards as means and historical sense dictate.

14 May 1962

Up From the South

For lovers of the traditional blues, today's record lists are unprecedently exciting. Yet the mode itself seems in danger of extinction. Young Negro jazzmen are looking to Africa, to Latin America, to the East, anywhere but to the Mississippi where their forebears were treated like a kind of farm animal. The very popularity of the ignorant, hopeless, vital blues among white people is enough to render them suspect to the young urban emancipated. The country cousin who arrives from the South with an acoustic guitar and a 'race' repertoire is soon laughed into more modish behaviour.

Veterans of the inter-war period however, have followed their reputations to Europe and are enjoying an Indian summer of renown. One of the best of them was the late Bill Broonzy, who after the war tactfully softened his rough style and thereby gained, like Josh White, much white acclaim. Enough of his native plangency remained, nonetheless, in his 'hollers' and 'rooster crows', played off against the deep urgency of his guitar, to make 'Big Bill Broonzy: Last Session' (HMV Verve, three volumes) a memorial to the Southern blues. This 'last session', made in 1957, offers new versions of many of Broonzy's best-known numbers and gives no hint that Broonzy was even then suffering from lung cancer.

Other famous names currently providing new material are the legendary Speckled Red, now around 70, who displays his rare boogie style on 'The Dirty Dozens' (Storyville); Roosevelt Sykes ('The Honeydripper', Columbia), a boisterous, somewhat coarse-toned singer and pianist; and Champion Jack Dupree, who, on an LP bearing his name (Storyville), offers more practised singing over less skilful piano. Dupree is an adept at the kind of keyboard reminiscence originated by Jelly Roll Morton in the Library of Congress ('I think of ol' Big Bill Broonzy, ol' Tampa Red, ol' Memphis Slim', etc.), and makes the most of his rudimentary technique to produce a delightful record.

For the current blues we have 'The Blues' (Columbia), with all the slogging percussion, echo chambers and amplified mouth-harps of rhythm-and-blues. This is essentially coarsened and simplified to stir mass emotion. John Lee Hooker, Memphis Slim and Jimmy Witherspoon are featured, but I preferred Jimmy Reed and Elmore James.

The appeal of classic female singers of the twenties was also public, directed at the coloured-circuit music halls, and 'Jazz Sounds of the Twenties, vol. 4: Blues Singers' (Parlophone) offers fine tracks by Victoria Spivey, Sara Martin, Margaret Johnson and Bertha 'Chippie' Hill, whose famous 'Pratt City Blues' and 'Pleadin' for the Blues' are magnificently supported by 1926 Armstrong. The broad, rolling attack of these singers is powerfully and variously supported by Bechet, Oliver, Ory, Lang and others, making a splendid conclusion to a courageous series.

It took a white man, though, to make a philosophy of the blues, and readers of Mezz Mezzrow's autobiography *Really the Blues* will know how he found in them the key to a relaxed vitality white America lacks. To prove his point, he set up a record company, King Jazz, and produced a sequence of warm, unforced, mellow numbers with some of the coloured players he most admired. Storyville is now reissuing every take of every number cut, and LPs such as 'Out of the Gallion' and 'Really the Blues' are as fresh and vivid as when they were made nearly twenty years ago. Bechet dignified every session he attended, and Lips Page and Sammy Price settle deeply in their respective grooves.

Very different offerings continue to arrive from the 'new thing', tenorist John Coltrane, whose drizzling, snake-charmer tone now seems happiest in narrow, strongly-coloured harmonic patterns as on 'Olé Coltrane' (London) and 'Africa/Brass' (HMV), where he can 'play long' before two basses and a drummer, plucking and popping in some rare time-signature. Coltrane's records are, paradoxically, nearly always both interesting and boring, and I certainly find myself listening to them in preference to many a less adventurous set. 'Dahomey Dance' and 'Aisha', on the former disc, have moments of real beauty and excitement. But what a long way from the Mississippi!

16 June 1962

'You're a Genius!'

Abruptly, two light-toned instruments begin to scribble a series of shrill, rapid yelps in unison against a regular bass and irregular drums. Then one, the alto sax, takes over, leaping and twisting in unpredictable intervals, blending short streams of notes, from nowhere to nowhere, with others whose conventional and even sentimental flavour, like quotes from 'The World Is Waiting For The Sunrise', have in this setting all the surreal incongruity of a hatstand in the sky. Sonorous bayings tail up into whimpers two octaves higher; during the frequent pauses, the bass seems always to be busily ascending or descending the scale, while the drummer indulges in short accelerated patterings.

This is Ornette Coleman and his Quartet, whose latest LP, 'Ornette!' (London), constitutes a report on their present position in outer space. Coleman, a self-taught 32-year-old Negro, who has now trimmed the long hair and beard of his youth, has been in the public ear since John Lewis got him into the Lenox School of Jazz in 1959. He plays a white plastic alto ('it responds more completely') in a manner that dispenses with nearly all the formalities except possibly that of tempo. He has been acclaimed by Charlie Mingus, Leonard Bernstein ('You're a genius!') and Gunther Schuller, who sees in him the first real advance in jazz since Charlie Parker. Others think him a pretentious novelty who is rapidly becoming a bore.

His 500-odd bars on 'R.P.D.D.', however, ranging from lusty honking to meditative diminuendo and exhibiting unfailing resourcefulness at all stages, must be the most remarkable solo released this year so far. Almost equally astounding work comes from bass player Scott La-Faro on 'W.R.U.', where he strums his instrument like a cello or even a guitar, and there is an extended African-type drum solo from Ed Blackwell on 'T. & T.' (the sleeve withholds the meaning of these initials). Only the musical morse contributed by Don Cherry on pocket-trumpet seems unimpressive.

In an art where novelty is too often at a premium Coleman has been both lauded and laughed at. Those who praise him do so not so much for his musical subtlety and technical innovations as for the sheer exuberance and freedom of his playing. This is undeniable, but there is a good deal of silliness mixed with it that shows in standards such as 'Embraceable You' ('This Is Our Music', also London), and which prevents one taking him quite seriously.

Major British companies seem to be vying with each other as to which can issue the most fascinating antiquarian material. In the lead at present is Philips, whose series 'Classic Jazz Masters' has begun with a rich block of LPs and EPs, all worth investigation. Chief among them is 'Bessie's Blues', sixteen sides made by Bessie Smith in 1923–4 with Clarence Williams, Fletcher Henderson and others. This is an indispensable addition to 'The Bessie Smith Story' (four volumes, also Philips), offering titles such as 'Cemetery Blues', 'Mama's Got the Blues', and 'T'aint Nobody's Business' in remarkable re-created form. A long sleeve-note by Paul Oliver draws a detailed comparison between Bessie and Ma Rainey.

Then there is 'Doc Cook Featuring Freddy Keppard, 1923–1928', giving a cross-section of coloured big-band jazz in Chicago in the twenties; six of the thirteen sides include the semi-legendary New Orleansian Keppard, past his peak perhaps but still capable of a ringing cornet lead. Other LPs present Blind Boy Fuller and Clarence Williams, and there are EPs of Papa Celestin, Clara Smith, Luis Russell and Charlie Creath. Finally, Philips have taken on the sterling job of distributing the American Riverside label, whose LP 'Johnny Dodds' comprises more sides from Chicago's twenties, less well reproduced but mostly more exciting.

The 'classic' jazz period, however, was, according to the French critic, André Hodeir, not the twenties but 1935–45. Any listener inclined to dismiss this view should first hear 'Spirituals to Swing, Vol. 1' (Fontana), sixteen tracks from the famous Carnegie Hall concerts sponsored in 1938–9 by John Hammond. Absolutely no historic sense is needed to enjoy a bill of Goodman, Hampton, Christian, Basie and his first, best band, Lips Page, James P. Johnson, and two choice tracks by Ladnier, Bechet and pick-up support. Recording balance is sometimes erratic but this is a fine anthology of performances from an age when the jazz tradition was undivided, and veteran, swing king and youngster, white and coloured, could meet on common ground with common enjoyment.

And from these it is a natural transition to two minor assortments of performances by the late Lester Young, whose bone-hard tenor became slacker and more wistful as the forties proceeded. 'Blue Lester' (Eros) is the better, offering good tracks with Butterfield and the Basie rhythm in 1944, but 'Pres' (Esquire), tape-recorded at a dance in 1952, has also some good ballad pieces to offset some rather dreadful flagwaving. They both re-emphasize how much jazz was lost by his death in 1959.

14 July 1962

Jazz as a Way of Life

An interesting side-effect of jazz is that it has become *la vie de bohème* in the popular imagination. Whereas Somerset Maugham's Philip Carey shocked his reverend uncle by setting up in Paris as a painter, Mr John Wain's Jeremy Coleman, in his new novel *Strike The Father Dead* (Macmillan), shocks his professorial father by setting up in Paris as a jazz pianist. The shift is significant. To desert business or government for the traditional arts nowadays is merely to exchange one kind of establishment for another.

Nor are the arts themselves as exciting as they were. For sheer impact Parker or Armstrong – or even Barber and Bilk – can beat them every time. And, today, it is the jazzman who appears to the young as the true artist, disdaining worldly success, even comfort, who is condemned as a peddler of emotional viciousness.

How far is this true? Mr Wain is sufficiently knowledgeable to block-in his sixties version of the artist's life convincingly (it was a good stroke to make his Negro genius, Percy, a *valve* trombonist), but his novel is not a documentary and does not pretend to be.

A much more factual account is offered by the American jazz writer Nat Hentoff in *The Jazz Life* (Peter Davies), 'an attempt to explore several of the social, economic and psychological elements that make up the context of modern jazz'. Mr Hentoff, in fact, begins where Mr Wain leaves off: given the impulse to play jazz, that is, how can it be put into practice in America today? The jazz musician's status is low because his livelihood is so closely bound up with the nightclub world: police precautions demand that he hold a 'cabaret card', which can be withdrawn on the smallest pretext and which thus puts him entirely in their hands. Nor is this world over-scrupulous in the matter of contracts, payment and working conditions: often, for instance, a club is controlled by racketeers and his union 'is seldom militant for its jazz constituents'. Recording brings nothing but a fixed fee for the date, no matter how well the record sells afterwards. If the musician is a Negro, his lot is much worse. It might be imagined that in the jazz world the reputation of its most celebrated artists – the men who make money for the promoters – would render the colour problem less acute; but this is not so.

Mr Hentoff does not by-pass the continual indignities endured by the Negro entertainer, who may well be refused admission at a club front door over which his name blazes in lights, but he does not run them into the ground. Rather, he brings out the subtler aspects of the colour problem, such as the resentment felt by Negro musicians at the idea that jazz is 'natural' to them, and that they therefore deserve no great applause for playing it. This is all a valuable corrective to jam-session romanticism (the union disapproves of jam sessions, by the way), but Mr Hentoff's book has many lighter pages, such as a hilarious account of an Armstrong recording date, and his illuminating character sketches of Basie, Coleman, Mingus, Monk, Miles Davis and John Lewis.

With the reissue of veteran guitarist Eddie Condon's *We Called It Music* in Corgi Books we are back in Bohemia, in the world of the wonderful new art that carried its devotees through the Depression in a haze of Prohibition gin, all-night sessions, and Bix. Written in facetious understatement, this is in many ways the most amusing jazz book, and since Condon has known nearly everybody from King Oliver onwards (he got his union card in 1922) it can be read as a succession of outrageous anecdotes. Underneath the surface, however, runs his perpetual campaign for 'respectability, and a chance to be heard' for his music. Today he runs a Manhattan nightspot, and has shared the Constitution Hall, Washington, with the National Symphony Orchestra, and may well feel he has achieved much of his life's ambition. Yet by the end of the book one cannot help feeling that Condon's world of whisky and wisecracks, once real and important, has become private and rather irrelevant. This edition has two additional chapters and a discography by Dave Carey.

The notion put forward by Henry Pleasants in *Death Of A Music?* (Gollancz) that the European classical tradition is finished and will be replaced by American jazz and popular music should interest all deck-chair musicologists, though whether they will agree with him is another matter. The effete condition of classical music after 300 years has been reached by jazz itself in under half a century, however, which certainly indicates superiority of a kind.

11 August 1962

Big Noise from Yesterday

The decline of the big band since 1945 is as difficult to explain as it is impossible to deny. The familiar glittering twelve- or fifteen-piece 'dance orchestra', with male and female vocalists and repertoire of sweet and hot numbers has become an anachronism, a kind of musical mastodon.

Admittedly, a surprising number of name bands are still in the business – Charlie Barnet, Benny Goodman, Harry James, Hines, Kenton, Herman – but in all honesty very few still count for much; the crowd-pullers are nearly all small groups, as if only six- or seven-piece outfits nowadays can express the subtlety and vitality of jazz. The situation is all the odder because it is a complete reversal of the traditional position where the public demands big 'commercial' bands and the musicians, though complying, long for the after-hours jam session. Gillespie, Mulligan and Quincy Jones have all had big groups, and lost them through lack of public support; men like Schuller and Gil Evans need the scope of a full orchestra to deploy their talents, but there are no orchestras to be had.

The reason for this seems to be that whereas the old orchestras used to be mixtures of star men and good section guys, today the good section guys are picking up a solid living from studio work and the stars are on their own in small groups. And both groups are probably happier than they would be under the same baton on the road.

These reflections are prompted by one of the most refreshing of recent reissues, 'Stomp Off, Let's Go', by the Bob Crosby Orchestra (Decca: Ace of Hearts). The distinctive sound of this New Orleans-pedigreed group, with its rough-edged trombones, free-ranging clarinet, and hefty two-beat drumming with a top-dressing of crash cymbals, is still as potent today as in 1937–42, when these tunes were recorded. Arrangements of standards such as 'Panama', 'Wolverine Blues' and the title number by bassist Bob Haggart, tended to make every piece a first cousin to his famous synthetic street-march 'South Rampart Street Parade', but they are none the less robustly exciting for that. Here is that collective feeling that only big-band work over a long period can generate.

Although the Crosby band's individuality was its brassy Dixieland appeal (it marched almost accidentally at the head of the whole Dixieland revival), its significance rests on its battery of first-class soloists – tenorist Eddie Miller on 'Little Rock Getaway', Fazola on 'Spain', Jess Stacy on 'Vultee Special', and the numerous occasions when Warren Smith's sergeant-major's trombone, or the trumpet of Yank Lawson, Sterling Bose, Butterfield or Spanier, would break through for eight bars or so before being swept away in the raging ensemble. A band like this may be an historical impossibility today, but the power of its music is undiminished.

Duke Ellington has frequently been accused of declining, but in retrospect his career seems to be one golden age after another. 'The Indispensable Duke Ellington' (RCA Victor, two volumes) offers twenty tracks from 'Morning Glory' (1940) to 'Swamp Fire' (1946), plus 'The Perfume Suite' (1945), a period falling very definitely into two halves on either side of the AFM recording ban of 1942–4. This is a handsome collection and forms a strong link in the indispensable Ellington chain. It is good news that Ellington plans to tour this country next April.

My mention of 'Clarence Williams Jug and Washboard Bands, 1927–1935' (Philips) last month must be amplified in view of the pleasure this disc has given me since. The music of these little groups is curiously fresh and delightful, not so old-fashioned as to require conscious appreciation yet still within earshot of the spirit of the amateur Southern spasm bands. Ed Allen's unpretentious cornet, the clarinet of Cecil Scott or Buster Bailey, a studio piano and kitchen rhythm section make 'He Wouldn't Stop Doing It', 'Beer Garden Blues' and 'You're Bound to Look Like a Monkey' little triumphs of relaxed swing that epitomize Negro high spirits without calling in the often-tedious mugging of Waller or Armstrong. This is not only a good record, it is a completely original one.

8 September 1962

Billie's Golden Years

No jazz artist has the public more firmly by the ear at present than the late Billie Holiday. As a young girl she was recognized by critic John Hammond as a jazz natural almost before she opened her mouth and through his influence was recording at the age of 20 with the finest New York players of her time – Goodman, Berigan, Teddy Wilson and (after the Basie band had struck town) Buck Clayton, Lester Young and that incomparable rhythm section. By 1940 she was a star in her own right, and although she regularly visited the recording studios through the remainder of her unhappy life until her death in 1959, it is generally accepted that the spring and summer of her talent were over by the early years of the war.

This at any rate is the period covered by Philips's monumental 'Billie Holiday: the Golden Years', a three-volume issue of forty-eight tracks made between 1933 and 1941. They constitute a wonderful memorial to her unique talent and to the informal jazz of the thirties. This talent was unique because it showed a singer of popular ballads fitting naturally into a jazz performance: it was also paradoxical, for in addition to exhibiting an intense jazz feeling that shaped the tune to its own ends (Billie Holiday was never popular with the music publishers), it held a strong emotional commitment to the lyrics, so that the Broadway ballads she sang were transfigured without losing their original appeal. There is no better example of this than the 1936 'These Foolish Things', in which her taut, vibrant voice expresses all the human feeling of the words while modifying both rhythm and melody in accord with altoist Johnny Hodges' superb accompaniment. Regrettably, she was not able to hold the balance between these conflicting elements. There came to be something a little willed about her distortions of the melody, while the success of 'Strange Fruit' and the more torchy side of her repertoire led her to specialize to an almost masochistic degree in songs of rejection and yearning.

Little of this is evident in this collection: here is the buoyant Billie of 'This Year's Kisses', 'Did I Remember?' and 'A Fine Romance'. Here, too, is a bouquet of solos from some of the best players of an era that had achieved sophistication and taste without losing drive and simplicity, best exemplified perhaps not by the bland, allusive tenor of Lester Young but Teddy Wilson's crisp, single-fingered piano that was in itself an innovation.

We are a long way from those years with the robust composer-bassist Charlie Mingus, whose Jazz Workshop unit is, as its title suggests, one of the spearheads of forward-looking jazz. A pugnacious personality who has been known to contemplate punching hostile reviewers, Mingus drives his group with frenzied virtuosity, humming and yelping encouragement rather like the late Fats Waller. In 'Jazz Portraits' (United Artists) four attractive tracks from a 1959 concert show his talents as composer and performer along with his regular altoist, John Handy, and tenorist, Booker Ervin, in 'Alice's Wonderland' and 'No Private Income Blues'.

On 'Oh Yeah' (London) Mingus switches to piano for a wildly eccentric session, singing the blues on 'Devil Woman', parodying Fats Waller on 'Eat That Chicken', and in 'Passions Of a Man' leads an orgy of wailing and muttering that sounds like a radio tuned to three stations at once. Multi-instrumentalist Roland Kirk pits his odd saxophones against Ervin's tenor and Jimmy Knepper's trombone. Mingus is also featured on 'Newport Rebels' (Candid), a group that set up in a tent outside the 1960 Newport Festival in protest against its increasing commercialization, and turns in good work with Roy Eldridge and Jo Jones on 'Wrap Your Troubles In Dreams' and 'Mysterious Blues'. The most piquant piece, however, is singer

Abbey Lincoln's ''Tain't Nobody's Business', with Benny Bailey and Eric Dolphy breathing alternate fire in a biting chase chorus.

On 'Miles Davis at Carnegie Hall' (CBS) the sombre and magnificent Davis fronts both his Quartet and Gil Evans's orchestra, pouring out a succession of smoky and sonorous solos that range from the almost mediæval stateliness of his concert manner on 'Spring Is Here' and 'Lament' to more informal tear-ups on 'No Blues' and 'Oleo'. According to the sleeve, Davis actually smiled twice at the audience during the evening and there is indeed a warmth about the entire proceedings that makes this a most enjoyable LP. Hank Mobley and Wynton Kelly support.

Two fine recent blues issues are 'Robert Johnson 1936–1937' (Philips), which offers sixteen of the twenty-nine tracks made by this obscure Mississippi singer in his short life, and 'Last Night Blues' (Fontana), on which Lightnin' Hopkins and Sonny Terry record together for the first time. Johnson, a rough and rather hag-ridden stylist, was clearly a model for younger back-country singers, such as Muddy Waters, forming a sharp contrast to the more reflective humour and sadness of Hopkins, whose guitar-work is increasingly rich and strange.

17 October 1962

Jam Yesterday

All through the thirties the Commodore Music Shop existed precariously on New York's 52nd Street, the only specialist jazz record shop in the world. 'New Orleans was the cradle', said its proprietor, Milt Gabler, 'but we were the iron lung.' In 1938 he began organizing his own sessions, and the results, put out under red-and-gold labels that said what everyone played, became the jewels of many a wartime collection. It is an event of first importance that EMI has at last started to issue the Commodore catalogue here under the label Stateside.

Although Gabler was responsible for several classic performances by great Negro artists such as Jelly Roll Morton and Billie Holiday, his name and label is traditionally associated with the jam-session music of Eddie Condon and that group of second-generation white players who drifted in and out of his orbit. It was to Condon that Gabler turned for a pick-up group, and 'Jam Sessions At Commodore' (Stateside) offers two of the first sides they made, 'Carnegie Jump' and 'Carnegie Drag', named after Goodman's famous Carnegie Hall concert that had taken place a few hours before on 16 January. The quality of the hard, laconic music of Condon, Freeman, Russell, Brunis and the rest is well known, and can be seen to have enduring virtues apart from those of the original Negro tradition from which it derived. None the less, Negro players were always at home on the Condon stand (Bechet, for instance, James P. Johnson and Hot Lips Page), and in 'Basin Street Blues' and 'Oh, Katharina!' Benny Morton and Sid Catlett combine lustily with Kaminsky, Russell and Joe Bushkin. On the reverse are all four sides of 'A Good Man is Hard to Find', a curious 1940 experiment clearly meant to capture the shifting, polyphonic atmosphere of a jam session, and featuring nearly every Condonite of note. Though there are some good solos, the general effect is flaccid, and the end is dire.

The nightclub boom of the war brought fame and success to Condon's music, and by 1944, when 'Chicago Jazz – Muggsy Spanier's Ragtimers' (Stateside) was made, it was degenerating into a somewhat mechanical routine aptly named Nicksieland, after Nick's where Condon played nightly (his own club did not open until 1945). Although Spanier and Russell battle it out on all twelve tracks, producing magnificent versions of 'Sweet Lorraine', 'Snag It' and 'Rosetta', a piece such as 'September in the Rain', where Muggsy repeats his favourite cliché so often I stopped counting, has a trudging quality. It is to be hoped that future Stateside Condon issues concentrate on the halcyon years 1938–40.

Equally memorable releases on this label, also from the Commodore list, are 'Billie Holiday', including her first 'Strange Fruit' which Gabler recorded when no one else would, and her pulsing tight-voiced blues 'Fine and Mellow', and 'Lester Young and the Kansas City Five', two sessions from 1938 and 1944 with Young playing clarinet and tenor respectively.

The autumn has brought numerous good releases on most other labels which must be noticed however briefly: in 'On Tour' (HMV Verve), Zoot Sims and the Gerry Mulligan Concert Jazz Band produce punchy, uncomplicated music, sometimes reminiscent of the Henderson tradition, the Milan 'Go Home' being especially exciting.

'Dizzy Gillespie In Concert' (HMV Verve) demonstrates once again the master's unflagging extrovert mode on 'Night In Tunisia' and a fine 'The Mooche' that carries a long blues chorus. Lovers of the younger, harder boppers will rejoice in the Oliver Nelson-Eric Dolphy 'Straight Ahead' (Esquire), with pianist Richard Wyands, and perhaps even in 'Coltrane Live At The Village Vanguard' (HMV), which in 'Chasin' The Trane' offers the longest (and to my mind the most perversely ugly and boring) of his solos to date. Another Johnny Hodges disc, 'Blue Hodge' (HMV Verve), is a welcome anodyne, with Rabbit alternatively swinging and melting before Wild Bill Davis's electric organ. The return of tenorist Sonny Rollins on 'The Bridge' (RCA) after some three years' general retooling shows him to have dropped many of the rough-necked, 'angry' mannerisms of his fifties approach. Now his tone is lean, keen and uncompromising, yet often unexpectedly tender, as in the ballads 'Where Are You' and 'God Bless The Child'.

10 November 1962

Don't Go 'Way Nobody

A certain defensiveness is discernible among promoters of modern jazz in face of the unwelcome but unavoidable fact that their music is not as popular as Artie Shaw used to be. 'Swings just the way conventional jazz swings,' says the sleeve of 'Jazz Workshop: George Russell and his Smalltet' (RCA), while the liner of 'Tough Tenors: Johnny Griffin and Eddie "Lockjaw" Davis' (Jazzland) has a sentence starting: 'If you are afflicted with fears that jazz is about to wander up some intellectual alley . . .' – thereby conceding that such fears are normal in the scene today. There is no simple answer to this suggestion. The term 'jazz' covers so wide a spectrum nowadays that it connotes almost nothing: then again, 'conventional' jazz, if by this is meant well-worn traditional modes, probably does not swing either.

The situation can probably be best understood with reference to my colleague Peter Stadlen's sage remark that 'swing' depends on just *not* giving the listener what he is expecting in terms of rhythm and pitch. If veteran New Orleans themes now fail to swing because they give us precisely what we are expecting, then it may be that the post-Parker generation fails because we no longer know what to expect. The world we live in, as Mr Benny Green says, is a diatonic world, and until we have chromatic hymns and national anthems and lullabies is likely to remain so; hence the extension of the harmonic and rhythmic range of jazz that has taken place since 1940 has inevitably removed it some distance from our instinctive musical sympathies.

At any rate, there is nothing conventional about George Russell's restless miniatures, whose subtle mixtures of scoring and improvisation are put over with impeccable musicianship by Art Farmer, Hal McKusick and Bill Evans. The harmonies, as befits pieces by the author of *The Lydian Concept of Tonal Organisation*, are daring without being *outré*, and the orchestration, with trumpet, alto and guitar ceaselessly dividing into solo and accompanying voices, is splendidly adroit. While there is plenty of drive in 'Round Johnny Rondo' and 'Ezzthetic', the most memorable track is 'Fellow Delegates', where George Russell and Osie Johnson spell each other on redwood and chromatic drums, producing a fascinating pattern of sound like water dripping irregularly into a huge metal tank. My reservation about this kind of music is its tendency to return to where it began in the last chorus. The suggestion is that it has got nowhere.

A quick (and cheap) conspectus of the contemporary sock-and-soul Negro stylists is offered by the two-disc package 'Riverside Giants of Jazz' ('Two for the Price of One'), an anthology of seventeen tracks by the Adderleys, Monk, Johnny Griffin, Junior Mance, Wes Montgomery, Charlie Rouse and many others. Highlights for me were 'Peri's Scope', by Bill Evans and the Don Rendell- Graham Bond Duet on 'Manumission', not to mention one of the tracks from 'Tough Tenors', mentioned above which offers the sinuous-sinewy styles of Griffin and Davis romping like young otters at play.

'The Soulful Piano of Junior Mance' (Jazzland) gives nine examples of this young artist's polite earthiness (he makes even 'Sweet and Lovely' sound like gospel). More fine piano, too, from Jess Stacy and Ralph Sutton (Ace of Hearts), contrasts the Waller-derived stride of Sutton with Stacy's brittle, dragging understatement of eight standards.

British rhythm-and-blues may sound as anomalous as British sherry, but the large following of Alexis Korner's Blues Incorporated will welcome 'R. & B. from the Marquee' (Ace of Clubs), which showcases hearty derivatives such as 'Hoochie Coochie' and 'I Got My Mojo Working'. The singing is not always on pitch, but Cyril Davies's harmonica and Korner's electric guitar blow up a fine storm if you like this flamboyant Negro mode.

Two reissues to be bought almost automatically are 'Sidney Bechet:

Giant of Jazz Vol. 2' (Blue Note) and 'Midnite in Harlem: Chick Webb and his Band' (Ace of Hearts). This Wild Bill-Bechet set may be a little rougher than the first, but what magnificent vitality these men show on 'Mandy' and 'Cake-Walkin' Babies'. The Webb disc exhibits one of Harlem's great bands that should have got some of the plaudits that went to Goodman.

15 December 1962

1963

The Prospect Behind Us

One of the oddest features of the American jazz scene is the way the past refuses to be over. The visitor to New York may emerge from The Five Spot or The Village Vanguard, confident that he knows where jazz is after its long pilgrimage from New Orleans. But in fact the whole of its history continues to happen simultaneously. In that huge continent at practically any moment a Glenn Miller band is recalling the war, a Tommy Dorsey band the thirties, Arthur Schutt and Ben Pollack (not to mention Louis Armstrong and Duke Ellington) are still in business, there is Bartok jazz and Brazilian jazz, while a visiting group such as Kenny Ball's, bringing our own brisk little wrong-end-of-the-telescope version of New Orleans, may quite possibly run into Kid Ory, who gave Armstrong his first band job back in 1918 and is still huffing and puffing successfully. It would not surprise me to learn that there was a Paul Whiteman Orchestra somewhere in the Middle West still doing the '1812 Overture' with bells, cannons and all.

In Britain the prospect of 1963 largely reinforces this sense of stasis. Trad, everyone agrees, is dead, but it shows no more signs of lying down than modern does of sitting up. The year's first visitor is Ellington himself who opens to-night at Finsbury Park, and, if he is not quite a novelty, interest is heightened by the return to his band of 54-year-old Cootie Williams, for whom he has written a new 'Concerto'.

Gerry Mulligan is also rumoured to be contemplating a visit, bringing a Concert Jazz Band featuring Brookmeyer, Clark Terry, Mel Lewis, Bill Crow and Jene Quill, and so is Stan Kenton, who currently has Bill Holman and Lennie Niehaus in his team of arrangers. Sonny Rollins will be passing through this month en route for the Continent; no doubt efforts will be made to convince him of the desirability of a spell in London.

Of the names entering this year in the ascendant Oliver Nelson's comes first to mind. This virile hard bopper with a Master's degree in music has had a number of successful albums recently, but his latest, 'Nocturne' (Fontana), with the late Lem Winchester on vibes, has been rather coolly received on both sides of the Atlantic. Personally I found it delightful. His plain, passionless tone, entirely free of vibrato or glissando, gives full soaring quantity to 'In a Sentimental Mood' and 'Time After Time', before Duvivier's plucked and bowed bass and Richard Wyand's piano.

'Johnny Hodges With Billy Strayhorn and the Orchestra' (Verve) is a delicious assortment of characteristic tapestries wherein the rich and violent Ellington sound is shot through with Hodges' lucent alto in 'Jeep's Blues', 'Lucky So-And-So', and 'Juice A-Plenty'. This is his best collection since 'The Big Sound' in 1959.

Clarinettist Edmond Hall has always been something of an anomaly, in that the natural rasp of his tone and confessed respect for Benny Goodman have taken him a long way, stylistically, from his birthplace, New Orleans. 'Swing Session' (Stateside) presents ten tracks dating from 1944 when he was fronting a quartet featuring Teddy Wilson, and they reinforce the contention that some of the best jazz results from sympathetic players informally using pop material such as 'Shanty Town', 'Sleepytime Gal', or 'Where Or When'. Hall's familiar clarinet has plenty of scope for its sour message, and Wilson, probably the best supporting pianist in jazz, turns in a handful of curt variations worthy of his Goodman days.

No month is complete without a blues record, and 'The Folk Lore Of John Lee Hooker' (Stateside) offers the best selection I have heard of this distinguished singer and guitarist. Hooker has a curiously archaic manner: after singing a line, his guitar breaks into a series of rapid, aimless little runs proliferating through a whole back-country of melancholy, before he sings the line again with no harmonic progression. It gives the listener the impression of hearing a tradition as ancient as it is fascinating, and should not be missed.

12 January 1963

Playin' My Saxophone

Once the late developer of the jazz instrumental family, the tenor saxophone is now its dominant solo voice. No longer handicapped in an age of amplification by its lack of tonal brilliance, it can supply the more allusive and intimate jazz modes of today in a way denied to the trumpet. Indeed, whereas originally the tenor saxophone adopted the 'trumpet style', the lesson is now being learnt in reverse.

The number of practitioners able to produce an inimitable tenor mode is correspondingly great. Chief among them is Stan Getz, who with Charlie Byrd on acoustic guitar has in 'Jazz Samba' (Verve) produced one of the most purely enjoyable records for a long time. Supple and unflurried, Getz has taken to these rhythms unhesitatingly; one track, 'Desafinado', already enjoys a degree of Top-Twenty popularity. While this is, of course, music from the bossa nova fringe, the swing of 'Samba Dees Days' and the melancholy of 'Samba Triste' would be the same in any language, and the whole disc can be confidently recommended to any level of brow.

Getz, of course, looks back to Lester Young; ten years older, Buddy Tate still prefers the riper tradition of Hawkins. Tate, a Kansas City man who played alongside Herschel Evans with Troy Floyd and ultimately replaced him in Basie's 1939 band, has a passionate attacking tone that quite steals 'Buck and Buddy' (Fontana) from Buck Clayton and Sir Charles Thompson. A less traditional set is found on 'Let's Jam' (Fontana), where Tate joins that fine trumpeter Joe Thomas and Claude Hopkins on some of the latter's originals, 'Safari' and 'Late Evening', mixed with a fruity Tate version of 'I Apologise' and the ever-sparkling 'I Would Do Anything For You'. In the shifting reed scene today, Tate's power and distinction have become something of a touchstone.

Sonny Rollins follows his own tradition: 'Sonny Boy' (Esquire) dates from 1956, and offers five pieces from his pre-withdrawal era, of which the title piece, lean and burstingly unsentimental, is the best, not only for Rollins but for Max Roach's casually tough brushwork. Others, including the sixty-bar a minute 'B. Quick', sound like scrapings of the Rollins barrel. His return to the scene explains the track 'Sonny's Return' on 'Here and Now' by the Art Farmer-Benny Golson Jazztet (Mercury). Golson's tenor, despite modern overlayings, still carries a Byas-like warmth, and with Farmer's flugelhorn deals velvetly with a programme including Ray Bryant's stirring 'Tonk' and his own 'Whisper Not'.

Two more LP's, 'Coltrane Plays The Blues' (London) and 'Coltrane Time' (United Artists), show this player's individual amalgam of bagpipe and squeaker unabated in popularity. Both are of uncertain date: the latter, with composer-pianist Cecil Taylor dropping provocative handfuls of notes behind Coltrane and trumpeter Kinny Dorham, has a greater unity of feeling – the slow 'Shiftin' Down' is especially good – while the former offers six blues tracks for Coltrane's soprano and tenor with McCoy Tyner and Elvin Jones, his long earnest solos giving the listener ample opportunity to judge how natural a blues player he is.

Ears cocked for reissues should catch the twelve Henderson sides made in 1926–7 and 1931 on 'Smack' (Ace of Hearts). The four earlier pieces include the ceremonially splendid blues 'Hot Mustard', in which Ladnier's trumpet rings through some delightful scorings (clarinets against tuba, for instance). None of these tracks was included in the four-volume CBS set issued last year. The sheer blasting noise of 'George Brunis: King of the Tailgate Trombone' (Stateside) is like a naked electric light bulb, but these dozen Commodore sides from the forties have some well-knit numbers and some typically rousing work from Wild Bill Davison, Max Kaminsky, Pee Wee Russell and, of course, Brunis himself, who sings just a little too often. Finally, Philips's re-issue of 'Kid Thomas and his Algiers Stompers' (Riverside) demonstrates once more that if the long-playing record has done nothing else it has enabled the full driving build-up of the New Orleans ensemble to be preserved. This is a warm, happy performance, not least remarkable for the exhilarating clarinet of Albert Burbank, who should not be missed.

9 February 1963

Ambassador Jazz

It is fitting that the two-disc 'Benny Goodman in Moscow' (RCA Victor) should have arrived while I was reading Dr Neil Leonard's *Jazz and the White Americans: the Acceptance of a New Art Form* (University of Chicago Press). For Dr Leonard's book is concerned to trace the gradual subsidence of the hostility from almost every section of 'white America' that jazz met with in the first twenty years of the century. This hostility to the 'snort and jangle' of the new music was not simply aesthetic. Jazz was denounced for its low social and moral origins, its baleful influence on behaviour, and even its suspect political tendencies. Dr Leonard claims that this attack declined slowly from about 1925, and virtually ceased during the war years, at which point his book ends. It contains much valuable documentary evidence, although his 'art form' approach limits full treatment of the question, which surely requires reference to the economics of entertainment and the social position of the Negro to be complete.

Goodman's records, on the other hand, the fruit of his State Department-sponsored trip to Russia last summer, constitute an eloquent example of the United States Government's current realization that jazz is probably the most-loved thing ever to come out of America. From being American folk music it has become world folk music. The artists – Gillespie, Armstrong, Brubeck – who have toured abroad since 1956 as part of the 'cultural ambassador' programme have been ecstatically received, but they have really only been building on a vast enthusiasm that had been fostered by the American Forces Network and such subsequent programmes as Willis Conover's 'Music USA'.

To some extent, the political angle is denied: 'Jazz is no longer strictly American,' a programme director maintained. 'You can't say Verdi is just Italian.' Yet, equally, the notion that jazz is 'musical democracy', the free expression of individuality, is far from absent. If jazz is not presented as such, there is evidence that this, to some extent, is how it is received.

The choice of Goodman by the Kremlin (all such tours are by invitation only) was no doubt due to his Russian-Jewish parentage and his classical affiliations, and he was known to be keen on the idea. Jazz opinion in America felt, justifiably, that he was poorly fitted to represent contemporary trends, and would have preferred to send Armstrong, Ellington, or Gillespie: this, however, was not to be. A fine group of players accompanied him, including Teddy Wilson, Zoot Sims, Joe Newman, Phil Woods, Victor Feldman and Mel Lewis, but reports suggest that he did not get the best out of them. Audiences were enthusiastic, but the latest Russian request for American culture, as reported a week or so ago, says nothing about more jazz. No doubt the State Department was prepared for such swings of feeling.

Listening to the records, one is bound to admit that Goodman plays a judicious mixture of his old book – 'One O'Clock Jump', 'Stealin' Apples' – together with his own brand of chamber music and some more recent pieces such as Tadd Dameron's 'Swift As the Wind' and some good solo items, notably Newman's 'Midgets'. Sims and Woods do a fine duo number on 'Titter Pipes' that produces heavy, almost frightening applause. Yet one can sense the lack of conviction that an agreed musical policy would have given. Or perhaps official art is always a little unreal.

Searching for vitality among recent releases of bossa nova and flute solos is an unrewarding task, but there is plenty on Dizzy Gillespie's 'Carnegie Hall Concert' (Verve). The odd instrumentation – four trombones, four french horns, three drummers, as well as five trumpets and a solitary reedman – seems to upset the balance, but there is a boisterous 'Manteca' that works up to a dazzling climax, and new versions of 'Kush' and 'A Night in Tunisia'. Leo Wright solos lyrically on 'This Is The Way', and there is an appallingly long gabble-babble between Dizzy and Joe Carroll in 'Ool Ya Koo', which may amuse. In all, these are stirring performances.

Stirring, too, is Charlie Mingus's excursion in Mexican motifs in 'Tijuana Moods' (RCA Victor), though it dates from 1957. Like many Mingus offerings, it is next to indescribable; perhaps blues flamenco as treated by an amalgam of Parker, Gillespie and Ellington would be a fair summary, but the leader's insistent virtuoso bass playing, and his hoarse vocal encouragings are all his own. An obscure trumpeter, Clarence Shaw, provides a contrast in fragility, notably in 'Flamingo', but everyone, including the listener, is swept away in the astonishing 'Ysabel's Table Dance'.

Traditionalists needing something to hold on to will delight in 'Bechet' (Riverside), twelve previously unissued tapes, from Rudi Blesh's 'This Is Jazz' series in 1947. In various company – Davison, Spanier, Archey, Sullivan et al – the incomparable master of the soprano sax turns in some splendid versions of his repertoire, some of which (for instance, 'Love For Sale') are, despite muzzy recording, as good as any he ever did. Finally, the Harlem itinerant preacher and guitar-player Blind Gary Davis should be heard in sacred and secular moods on 'Harlem Street Singer' (Fontana) and 'Pure Religion and Bad Company' (77 Records). His harsh, whooping approach, reminiscent at times of Blind Willie Johnson, proves once again how numerous and never-ending are the many tributaries of jazz.

20 March 1963

The Holy Growl

There are no legends about James 'Bubber' Miley. He was a coloured trumpet player who died in 1932 at the age of 29, by which time he had a band sometimes called 'Bubber Miley and his Mileage Makers'. A much earlier photograph shows him aged 19, posed behind blues singer Mamie Smith with his trumpet to his lips, slim and unremarkable. But between these ages he spent three years in a small orchestra taken over by an unknown pianist named Ellington, and it was this that made him an unforgettable part of jazz.

What he did, in brief, was to turn the little group Ellington inherited from Elmer Snowden in 1925 from a 'sweet' to a 'hot' band, and to present Ellington with a ready-made speciality, the jungle style. Miley was a growl trumpeter, and a great user of mutes to give his tone emotional colour. There was nothing new in this: it was at least as old as King Oliver. But Miley's was different: his tone had a snarling, gobbling savagery that stabbed through the coltish orchestrations with primitive authenticity. Ellington was quick to turn it to account and was soon the acknowledged purveyor of 'jungle' music to the patrons of the Kentucky and Cotton clubs in New York – it was a tradition he was never to abandon.

Several rare tracks showing Miley at his best can be found on the first side of 'The Duke In Harlem' (Ace of Hearts), notably 'Immigration Blues', 'Red Hot Band', and 'The Creeper'. His fierce impatience, along with trombonist Joe Nanton's broader mimicry, the dry, rattling rhythm section and Ellington's snatches of bar-room ragtime remind the listener once again what a pinnacle of individuality jazz reached with this team. On the reverse (1929–30), Cootie Williams carries on Miley's work, Hodges and Bigard have arrived, and another great age has begun. But there was no substitute for Miley.

It is good to have the first of the four discs of 'Swing Street' (Columbia), which presents typical small groups that played in and around 52nd Street in the thirties. There was perhaps no need for the entire 'Home Cooking' session, but Condon fans will welcome an alternative take of 'Madame Dynamite'. Wingy Manone's 'Isle of Capri' is a classic of debunking, and the Spirits of Rhythm, with their great guitarist Teddy Bunn, exhibit their evolutionary place between the Mills Brothers and Skiffle. The rest of this set will take the focal point of New York jazz up to 1945.

17 April 1963

Pianists Not For Shooting

I have a weakness for the entertainers of jazz (as opposed to more sombre characters who suggest by their demeanour that I am lucky to hear them), and so for Fats Waller. Admittedly his humour could be excruciating and his piano-playing a baroque triviality. All the same, dozens of his airy, inconsequential records still command, twenty years after his death, a following that stretches from Collectors' Corner to Housewives' Choice.

The two-volume 'Fats on the Air' (RCA) is made up of two sessions for radio: one alone or with Rudy Powell in 1935, the other with his small band in 1939. They consist of familiar stand-bys, separate or grouped into medleys, from his repertoire.

The 1935 numbers – 'Baby Brown', 'Don't Let It Bother You', 'Alligator Crawl' and others – are often run off negligently, ending after the vocal with a 'Mercy me' and a modulation into something else. The 1939 band, with Bugs Hamilton and Sedric, gives a fuller, rougher treatment, achieving in at least one instance ('The Moon Is Low') a pretty powerful success.

These are routine Waller performances, both phrasing and facetiousness trembling on the edge of one big cliché. What saves them is the clean, ringing professionalism of the playing, the energy and good humour, and the moments of irresistible charm,as in the lyric of 'How Can You Face Me', that somehow manage to be vibrant jazz as well.

No one could accuse Thelonious Monk of clean professionalism: indeed, Waller's own title 'Numb Fumblin'' would suit him better than its composer, yet in his latest offering, 'Monk's Dream' (CBS), made by the Quartet with Charlie Rouse, there are constant oddities of harmony and rhythm that suggest an approach as flippant as Waller's own. Indeed, on more than one track – 'Bright Mississippi', for instance – there are distinct echoes of Waller's kind of piano. Monk is full of surprises. Parts of 'Body and Soul' sound like Teddy Wilson, coarsened and magnified, downward runs and all. Two choruses of 'Bolivar Blues' hint that Monk could be to Pee Wee Russell what Hines was to Armstrong. The title-number and 'Sweet and Lovely' are successful and integrated performances – how faithfully Rouse reflects his leader's many moods! – and justify Monk's return to the studio after a longish interval. I am less happy about 'Thelonious Himself' (Riverside), solos made in 1957 and previously issued on London. These seven out-of-tempo meditations show Monk casually striking out his personal interpretations of 'April In Paris', 'Round Midnight' and others, his hesitant chords like suitcases just too full to shut properly. On the eighth side, John Coltrane contributes a solo of characteristic dreariness.

Riverside has put out another collection of piano tracks from Jelly Roll Morton's 1938 Library of Congress recordings entitled 'Rags and Blues'. These include 'Winin' Boy' (two versions), 'See See Rider', 'Mamie's Blues' and a number of others from this epic and ghostly session. Morton is not usually thought of as a blues pianist, yet the gay and scabrous 'If You Was Whisky' shows him swinging as lightly as anyone, calling the lyrics indefatigably in a tired baritone above his tapping shoe. This is a record of enormous and historic charm.

Today styles contrast greatly, as do Phineas Newborn ('A World of Piano' on Contemporary) and Ahmad Jamal ('All of You' on Pye). Newborn's remarkable technique has made his reputation, but on some tracks, notably 'Cabau', he resembles a cheerless Art Tatum, and there is room for greater emotional warmth in his playing. 'Juicy Lucy' is nicely light-hearted, and though the minor key 3/4 piece 'For Carl' lasts seven minutes, its feeling mounts steadily. Jamal, on the other hand, with his sudden deafening crescendoes and stalking Garner-like ballads, has been branded as more of an entertainer. But this is where we came in.

Anyone who missed the American Folk Blues Festival that toured the Continent last autumn and made a single appearance in Manchester should hear 'American Folk Blues Festival' (Polydor), made after hours in Hamburg. The package deal that brought together John Lee Hooker, Brownie McGhee, Sonny Terry, Shaky Jake, Memphis Slim and T-Bone Walker here offers twelve vividly-recorded tracks (Deutsche Grammophon) on which each artist sings and the others take turns on guitar and piano. This leads to a rather samey R. & B. atmosphere, lacking the solitary anguish that is the hallmark of the blues, but McGhee, Memphis Slim and Hooker all make their personal impression. And the month's nicest surprise is a batch of rhythm-and-blues singles from Pye, including Howlin' Wolf, Sonny Boy Williamson, Bo Diddley and our own Cyril Davies. Here the genuine mode can be sipped cheaply.

15 May 1963

The End of Jazz

In New York City Criminal Court recently, Charlie Mingus was referred to as 'a great jazz musician'. Mingus, who had or had not punched his trombonist, Jimmy Knepper, was quick to resent this. 'Don't call me a jazz musician,' he retorted. 'To me the word jazz means discrimination, secondclass citizenship, the whole back-of-the-bus bit.'

This revealing anecdote suggests that what is happening in the Southern States of America today is not without significance for the present and future state of jazz. The American Negro is trying to take a step forward that can be compared only with the ending of slavery in the nineteenth century. And despite the dogs, the hosepipes and the burnings, advances have already been made towards giving the Negro his civil rights under the Constitution that would have been inconceivable when Louis Armstrong was a young man. These advances will doubtless continue. They will end only when the Negro is as well housed, educated and medically cared-for as the white man.

There are two possible consequences in this for jazz. One is that if in the course of desegregation the enclosed, strongly-characterized pattern of Negro life is broken up, its traditional cultures such as jazz will be diluted. The Negro did not have the blues because he was naturally melancholy. He had them because he was cheated and bullied and starved. End this, and the blues may end too.

Secondly, the contemporary Negro jazz musician is caught up by two impulses: the desire to disclaim the old entertainment, down-home, give-the-folks-a-great-big-smile side of his profession that seems today to have humiliating associations with slavery's Congo Square; and the desire for the status of musical literacy, for sophistication, for the techniques and instrumentation of straight music. I should say Mingus's remark was prompted by the first of these, and much of his music by the second. The Negro is in a paradoxical position: he is looking for the jazz that isn't jazz. Either he will find it, or – and I say this in all seriousness – jazz will become an extinct form of music as the ballad is an extinct form of literature, because the society that produced it has gone.

The jazz that isn't jazz is no bad description of Sonny Rollins's 'Our Man in Jazz' (RCA), a live recording at The Village Vanguard that shows Rollins very much on an Ornette Coleman kick, supported indeed by Ornette's Don Cherry and Billy Higgins. In the breakneck 'Oleo', which lasts all one side, Rollins barks and blares his way thrustingly through one-third of the track, spurred on by occasional explosions from the drums and intermittent whimpers, faint as vapour-trails, from Cherry, and if the record had maintained this pace it would be splendid. The poised, less hectic 'Doxy' works to a rocking conclusion and has some delectable solo drumming from Higgins. There is a fiery sardonic excitement on this record: there is also aimlessness and puerility. If you can stand free form, it is worth investigating.

That there is no going back seems to be the message of 'Swing Street, Vol. 2' (Columbia), which is streaked by that peculiarly thirtyish comic corn exemplified by 'The Music Goes Round and Around' (Frank Froeba) and Louis Prima's meet-the-gang vocals ('Let's Have a Jubilee'). On the credit side is Frank Newton's 'You Showed Me the Way' and a variety of piano pieces by Waller, Tatum, Wilson, and that too-little-known artist Clarence Profit, whose 'Don't Leave Me' (previously unissued) is nicely lyrical. These discs are a fascinating enterprise, but I must admit that this one wiped some of the rose off my spectacles as far as its period is concerned.

Duke Ellington is tireless at finding new combinations and presentations of his talents, and 'The Duke Meets Coleman Hawkins' (HMV) is another of these studio encounters which may or may not come off. (By all accounts, an Ellington-Mingus-Roach set was a resounding success.) Here Hawkins sits in with Nance, Brown, Hodges and Carney in a number of pieces reminiscent of the riffy 'Ellington unit' music of twenty-five years ago, and is somewhat gobblingly polysyllabic for his company, though his five choruses on 'Mood Indigo' and an eloquent simplicity in 'Self Portrait' redeem his reputation.

15 June 1963

Venuti and Lang

I made the acquaintance of Joe Venuti and Eddie Lang involuntarily, through finding them on the back of an old black-label Parlophone Armstrong, and I am afraid they suffered in comparison. The opportunity to reassess their music offered by the latest two-disc addition to American Columbia's splendid Thesaurus of Classic Jazz is therefore specially welcome.

'Stringing the Blues' (CBS) offers thirty-two pieces made between 1926 and 1933, the year of Lang's premature death; the emphasis is on the chamber music of the Blue Four and Five, and the gay, musicianly phenomenon that was Venuti-Lang is thus available for extended study. Both children of Italian immigrants (Lang's real name was Massaro) and brought up in the classical tradition in Philadelphia, they developed an astonishing rapport not equalled till the days of Grappelly and Reinhardt. This expressed itself, however, more in a light-hearted series of musical practical jokes than by heightened excitement, for their particular brand of white jazz retained elements of facetiousness and horseplay.

Venuti especially was given to extravagance (he used cheap fiddles so that he could smash them over people's heads) and revelled in the cadenza coda, bridge-break tradition of the twenties. The keynote of his records was the unexpected; players such as Jimmy Dorsey would switch from cornet to clarinet to alto; Adrian Rollini would play goofus and hot fountain pen, a complete stranger would be pressed to play the kazoo, and anything left lying around the studio (an electric buzzer, for instance) would inevitably feature in the ensembles.

Lang was a different proposition. Despite his complete responsiveness to Venuti's fleet violin, he had a leaning towards Negro company, and his duets with Lonnie Johnson ('Two Tone Stomp', 'Guitar Blues') and the legendary Blind Willie Dunn's Gin Bottle Four sides with King Oliver suggest that he would have been happier in a rougher, richer tradition. Venuti made the blues sound like a novelty foxtrot; Lang made them sound like the blues. Was it his support that lent Tommy Dorsey's trumpet such harsh authority on 'You Can't Cheat a Cheater'? To explore these sides is to rediscover a jazz world of confident irresponsibility quite alien to these days of tape surgery.

'Ballads' by John Coltrane (HMV) and 'Hollywood Stampede' by Coleman Hawkins (Capitol) show these very different tenormen coping with the slow and sentimental. Of the two, Coltrane is the more remarkable: his tenor still sounds like an alto with sinus trouble; but, eschewing for once marathon experimentalisms, he traces the outlines of such standards as 'Easy To Remember', 'Over and Over Again' and 'All Or Nothing At All' with commendable economy. The result holds a bleak beauty. Whether, as the sleeve claims, it marks a permanent advance towards self-discipline only time will tell.

The Hawkins disc has a historic aura: made in 1945 with Howard McGhee, it constitutes a splendid sunset of the master's romanticism, giving versions of 'Stardust', 'Talk of the Town' and 'Someone to Watch Over Me' in which he dodges smoothly through the changes with never a flatted fifth to show what time it is. Bop clichés abound in the up-tempo unisons of 'Rifftide' and 'Stampede', however, and Howard McGhee's trumpet announces a different age. Hawkins' subsequent modernism was described by a critic as 'a milestone walking along the road', and the jazz press on both sides of the Atlantic has recently been celebrating a similar advance by Pee Wee Russell.

What has happened is that Pee Wee has been taken in hand by brassman-didact Marshall Brown and is heading a quartet that uses Brown's arrangements to flirt with the free form, the twelve-tone scale and other unfamiliarities. Russell fans will be anxiously watching the British lists for 'New Groove', the combo's first album. It is reassuring to learn that Russell has two ashtrays in his kitchen, one marked 'Birdland' but the other marked 'Eddie Condon's'.

Decca has obligingly made available ('These Cats Are High!') some early Ink Spots recordings of the pre-'Whispering Grass' days, when their book included Leroy Carr's 'When the Sun Goes Down', and a batch of forties ballads by Billie Holiday ('The "Lady" Sings' Volume One). The third volume of 'Swing Street' (Columbia) offers John Kirby, Joe Marsala, Red Norvo, and Slim and Slam's 'Flat Foot Floogie', which recalls Munich year with disagreeable sharpness.

On the modern side is the Jazz Messengers' 'A Night in Tunisia' (RCA), with Jackie McLean's alto and Blakey's Grand Guignol drumming: 'The Artistry of Freddie Hubbard' shows Hubbard's bold and brilliant trumpet with Curtis Fuller and Tommy Flanagan; and Tad Dameron's 'The Magic Touch' (Riverside) presents ten orchestral originals by the chief romantic of bop, ably supported by Clark Terry, Bill Evans and others in a bid for the beautiful.

10 July 1963

Three-Tenor Fight

Few things wring a groan from my lips more readily than the prospect of another solo tenor team in cliché-ridden conflict. What, then, makes 'Soul Battle' (Esquire) such a pleasant exception? Partly, no doubt, the piquant contrast formed by the talents of sophisticated Oliver Nelson, veteran Jimmy Forrest, and rhythm-and-blues stylist King Curtis. Partly too, the cracking rhythm section of Gene Casey, George Duvivier and Roy Haynes that propels each soloist irresistibly onward without recourse to fancy time signatures or Latin-American kitchenware.

But what chiefly distinguishes the session is the way each man subordinates individual mannerisms to the common task of keeping things swinging. Whether it is Nelson on 'Blues for M.F.' or 'Anacruses', Forrest on 'Perdido', or Curtis on 'Blues At The Five-Spot', every solo bursts with immediate vitality. Battle honours go to the young composer-arranger Oliver Nelson, who only a couple of weeks previously (Autumn 1960) had been cutting the third-streamy 'Nocturne' (Fontana, last December). Not only are his solos most musically adventurous, but his harmonic innovation and Coltrane-like tone are unequivocally harnessed to excitement: witness his long spell on 'In Passing', an ingeniously-chorded twelve-bar piece he tosses around with abandon. Yet he does not put Forrest and Curtis in the shade. Their tough, bellowing intonations make an excellent counterbalance (seekers after more Forrest, by the way, should try 'Sit Down And Relax With Jimmy Forrest' on Esquire), and the ear rejoices at their different eloquence. The record's most satisfying part is the chase choruses on 'Perdido', where in four-bar spells the three men underline their common devotion to improvised jazz.

Better than expected, too, is 'Lady Love' (United Artists), live numbers from a 1954 Billie Holiday concert in Germany. Billie has been crammed into our ears since her death, and in any case her work in the fifties could be painfully bad, but here her latterday voice, at once charred and scorching, is heard against Carl Drinkard's piano in a set of standards. In 'Blue Moon' and 'Them There Eyes' she retains something of her old attack and agility; there are fewer excursions into maudlin melodrama, while in the jammed 'Billie's Blues' and 'Lover Come Back' with Norvo and De Franco she proves that despite everything she was still capable of holding her own in a free-for-all with first-class musicians. A heartening record.

Lightnin' Hopkins labours under a rhythm-and-blues accompaniment on two tracks of his 'Lightnin' Strikes' (Stateside), but otherwise his sombre voice and monitory guitar throb unchallenged. The best of the elder Texans, Hopkins, excels in slow directly-personal statements of distress and melancholy such as 'Want To Come Home' and 'Walkin' Round In Circles'. Another valuable blues disc is 'Billie and Dede Pierce' (Riverside), a 'living legends' session of a husband-and-wife team long resident in New Orleans. She plays piano and sings with durable monotony; he blows unpretentious, moving cornet. Coming on the first track of this set, 'St. Louis Blues', after twenty-five minutes of the Jazz Misanthropes' 'Tracheotomy', I nearly wept at its humble ravishing sincerity.

There have been some fine reissues lately. 'McKinney's Cotton Pickers' (RCA Victor) has sixteen sides made between 1929–31 by this great Negro band that included Don Redman, Fats Waller and Joe Smith. 'Washboard Rhythm' (Ace of Hearts) offers five Chicago groups from the twenties (how about an LP of that very different but invigorating band, the Washboard Rhythm Kings?), while Volume Four of 'Swing Street' (Columbia) closes the series with Pete Johnson, Lips Page, Count Basie and a rare pair of Bechet-Noble Sissle sides. 'Ten-Thirty Tuesday Night' (Ace of Clubs) is a batch of Lew Stone recordings with Nat Gonella and Al Bowlly, offering British over-forties a private line back to their youth.

Nearer the present is 'The Greatest of Stan Getz' (Columbia), nine tracks from 1950–1 of which the set with Al Haig and Jimmy Raney is unquestionably the most exciting. The essential source material in 'The Charlie Parker Memorial Volumes' and 'The Dizzy Gillespie Story' is now available on Realm. Disappointment of the month is 'George Wein and the Newport All-Stars' (HMV), in which Braff, Russell, Freeman and nine nice tunes fail to get together. Will Pee Wee's confiding modern snufflings ever reach a coherent artistic statement? Sadness of the month is the death of Bob Scobey. 'The Bob Scobey Story' (Good Time Jazz, two volumes) is a monument to his eager, musical trumpet. The height of his material success, according to *Down Beat*, was making a cigarette commercial in 1959.

10 August 1963

Looking at Parker

The four-word history of jazz is 'Louis Armstrong: Charlie Parker' – Armstrong who integrated and enhanced a great racial tradition, Parker the prism through which it broke up into an infinity of subtler musical components. Armstrong, who built his achievements on a prudent and athletic professionalism, is still with us. Parker died at 34 with the body of a man of 60, the hero of one more legend of the self-destructive artist.

Bird: the legend of Charlie Parker by Robert George Reisner (MacGibbon & Kee), exemplifies rather than explores this legend. Significantly enough, it is composed of eighty-odd personal recollections of Parker arranged in a meaningless alphabetical order of contributors – significantly, because to order, sift and evaluate would run counter to the kind of devotion Bird inspired. The chaos of his life is felt to transcend the limitations of social responsibility just as his music transcends the limitations of hand and brain. Nevertheless, one can piece together the character of this young Negro with the devoted mother (Mrs Addie Parker's nine pages are moving and enlightening) and the fantastic physical and artistic stamina. His early attempts to play jazz were ridiculed: perhaps as a consequence he developed a staggering technical accomplishment that left his contemporaries standing. His long periods of drug addiction made him too unreliable to sustain the engagements his fame would have earned him, and at the end of his life he was near destitution again. 'Man, I'm handing you the keys of the kingdom,' he said to Sonny Stitt a week before his death.

Everybody liked Bird, though there is little in this book to show why: he seems to have acted out a Skimpolian son-mother relation with the world, whereby he traded on the generosity of his admirers. 'He was never hesitant about letting people, who love him, give,' says Benny Harris. 'I asked him about this, and philosopher that he was, he said: "What good is love if you can't take?"' But for all this the legend badly needs clarifying. The Bird of Dave Schildkraut ('his behaviour throughout the tour was exemplary') or Mrs Doris Parker ('he had many suits, went to work always neatly dressed, and on time') is not the Bird who fell asleep on the stand, cheated admiring acquaintances, and at the finish had 'no veins left to inject'. Al Cotton claims that Parker admitted that his attempted suicide in 1954 (he died the following year) was a ruse to escape Union discipline. Some say he was crushingly rude to young musicians, others that he was kind and helpful. All this needs sorting out.

Mr Reisner's hagiography prompts a more reflective look at the first four discs of 'The Charlie Parker Memorial Album', now reissued on the remarkable new label, Realm. These recordings of 1944–8 have a likeness to Armstrong's Hot Five sides: they exhibit a musician of unprecedented fluency and stature among colleagues not his equal. Parker's easy, flexible alto with its complete command of a new harmonic language makes the young Miles Davis sound stiff and mechanical, and on many tracts the rhythm section stumps along unregenerately. The numerous takes of each number make it clear that Bird, despite his frequent clichés (that asinine Woody-Woodpecker phrase, for instance), had an inexhaustible invention.

None the less, the mode of jazz represented by these historic sessions was in many respects unsatisfying. Its ancestry was plainly the neat throttled riffing of swing-era groups such as John Kirby, Goodman's chamber groups, and the Ellington units, and it had its own sterile conventions, such as the unison first chorus repeated at the end, as if to demonstrate that nothing had really happened. Nor is the emphasis placed on playing very fast and very high an artistic asset. To listen to the breakneck dreariness of 'Constellation' or Miles Davis's frenzied stuttering on the 1947 'Bird Gets the Worm' prompts an echo of Dr Johnson's retort 'Difficult, Madam? Would it were impossible!'

It is Parker's solos that carry these records and have caused an alteration in the course of jazz. Granted that his technique and musical instinct for innovation were unrivalled, what was he *like*? His talent was indivisible; one cannot say that he would have been better if he had played more simply or with fewer rhythmic eccentricities; these are features of the wild, bubbling freedom that characterizes him, and that some say earned him his nickname. But freedom from what? As one listens to Parker spiralling away 'out of this world', as the phrase goes, one can only answer 'humanity', and that is a fatal thing for an artist, or an art, to be separated from.

11 September 1963

Thundering Herds

The three-disc 'Woody Herman: The Thundering Herds' (CBS) is a fitting memorial to the last of the line of great white bands that dominated the scene from 1935 to about 1950. Although Herman's career as a bandleader began in 1936, when he reorganized some survivors of the Isham Jones Juniors as 'the band that plays the blues', and is even today still fulfilling engagements, this set concentrates on the key period between 1945 and 1947. This was the time of 'Apple Honey', 'Caldonia', 'Wild Root' and other pieces that sent the band and its soloists to the top of the polls. Five out of six sides are devoted to the music of the 'First Herd', to the work of Bill Harris, Flip Phillips, Chubby Jackson, Dave Tough, and arrangers Ralph Burns and Neil Hefti; the last side features the 'Second Herd', which was formed in autumn, 1947, and contained Shorty Rogers, Zoot Sims, Stan Getz, Serge Chaloff and Al Cohn.

The 1945 Herman band succeeded by reason of its youthful vitality and fresh musical approach: Woody was always ready to experiment, his line-up at times even including such leaders of the New Wave as Dizzy Gillespie and Bud Johnson. Igor Stravinsky liked the band, and they returned the compliment ('the guys were always listening to his early things'). At the same time, the 'First Herd' music had sufficient drive to carry it past the turning to Kenton and the dangers of over-formalization.

The music enshrined in this historic set has something of a hybrid quality, as if the band's musical policy was only patchily consistent. Herman's own reed work inclined rather to the Ellingtonians, Bigard and Hodges, than to the Goodman-Shaw Chicagoan tradition. The orchestrations veered from straight 'heads' ('Blowing Up a Storm') to the fanciest of scores (John LaPorta's 'Non-Alcoholic'), taking in some Billy Cotton comedy on the way ('Put That Ring On My Finger'). Some of the best tracks are by the 1946 Woodchoppers, lit by Red Norvo's vibes. This is a fine memorial to the principal cradle of post-war white soloists.

Another historic orchestra, but one which had no existence outside the studio, was the 1933 Spike Hughes' Negro Orchestra. Spike, who in those days picked a mean bass, signed up all the great Hendersonians in New York* to play his originals and arrangements, and in 'Spike Hughes and his All-American Orchestra' (Decca Ace of Clubs – why the segregationist title?) Allen, Hawkins, Berry, Carter, Wells and the rest snatch some magnificent moments from Hughes' somewhat Europeanized concepts.

Far and away the most exciting of recent blues releases is 'The Legend of Sleepy John Estes' (Esquire). The rediscovery of this almost-mythical singer (at least one reference book says he died in March 1953) adds a major voice to the current blues scene. Lovers of the two sides, 'Drop Down Mama' and 'Married Woman Blues', put

*It was in fact Benny Carter's Orchestra.

out here by Brunswick just after the war, will rejoice to hear that Estes' slurred, whimpering delivery is unchanged, and that his old sidekick Hammie Nixon is in attendance on harmonica. Estes is now blind, and reputedly living in something like poverty, but when these tracks were made last year he was clearly at the top of his magnificent form.

Two fine Leadbelly discs compete for attention, 'Good Morning Blues' (RCA) and 'Huddie Leadbetter's Best' (Capitol). Leadbelly was a gripping blues singer, despite his habit of throwing in five and a half extra bars to every twelve, and there is a tremendously moving moment on 'T.B. Blues' when he breaks out after a recitative into the Shakespearean 'Too late, too late, too late, too late, too late'. The second disc has two examples of his rare piano, and a further group of standards such as 'Rock Island Line' and 'Sweet Mary Blues'.

'Lightning Hopkins Sings the Blues' (Realm) offers a session by this earthy Texas singer made in Houston about 1950, including 'Fast Life Woman' and 'Broken Hearted Blues'.

The earnest, humourless reed work of John Coltrane makes him the Youth Club bore of jazz as far as I am concerned, but 'Duke Ellington and John Coltrane' (HMV) and 'Miles Davis and John Coltrane Play Richard Rodgers' (Fontana) are two interesting examples of the interplay of personalities, the latter, as might be expected, proving more homogeneous. Miles does a solo 'Blue Room' that suggests he will soon be challenging Pat Halcox. Cannonball Adderley is on record as claiming that jazz is emerging from experimentalism into simple happy improvisation. Certainly he does his best for this on 'Jazz Workshop Revisited' (Riverside), working up a fine boisterous storm before a live Frisco audience in a way not to be missed. Finally, the coruscating piano of Oscar Peterson is heard to advantage on 'Affinity' (Verve), including a breakneck 'You Are My Heart's Delight' that ends up as a kind of frenzied reminiscence of Mendelssohn's 'Wedding March'. First rate church music of its kind.

9 October 1963

Snail Race Voluntary

'I usually don't buy jazz records,' Miles Davis told an interviewer recently. 'They make me tired and depressed.' At least half his new LP 'Seven Steps to Heaven' (CBS) has me feeling the same way. For three tracks (made in San Francisco with Victor Feldman) his lifeless muted tone, at once hollow and unresonant, creeps along only just in tempo, the ends of notes hanging down like Dali watches, and since two of the tunes are 'Basin Street Blues' and 'Baby Won't You Please Come Home', an atmosphere approaching burlesque is created, as if Miles were in for a how-unlike-Wild-Bill-Davison-can-you-get competition. This effect is heightened by the fact that some of his lower notes sound like Wild Bill's Bronx cheers after a course at the Juilliard School of Music.

For me the interest of these musical snail races resides in Feldman's piano, where cheerfulness, not to mention feeling, keeps breaking in, notably on 'Basin Street', where he picks up the tempo with manifest relief, and in his long meditative solo on 'I Fall in Love Too Easily'. The other three tracks, recorded in New York with Herbie Hancock in place of Feldman and an interesting new drummer, Anthony Williams, are up-tempo pieces that show Miles fully in control of his own harsh, rather unfriendly mode. His tone, clouding and clearing, scrambles stabbingly into the stratosphere without the fluffs we have somehow come to expect, and on Feldman's 'Joshua' in particular he phrases with almost conversational ease. Tenorist George Coleman offers some modest Coltrane-ish support. I have the impression that in this country at least (*Down Beat* gave this five stars) Miles has lost some of his critical following of late. If so, I should say that it is because like most of his Negro contemporaries his increasing preoccupation with musical theory is in direct ratio to his liability to make an ass of himself.

This could never be said of the unflappable Mac of jazz, Duke Ellington. 'If a guy plays something and nobody digs it', he writes in the sumptuous *Esquire's World of Jazz* (Arthur Barker), 'then he hasn't communicated with his audience.' (The interest of this truism lies in where the implied condemnation falls.) No such charge will be levelled at 'Money Jungle' (United Artists), his trio record with Charlie Mingus and Max Roach, where, in spite of strange company, Duke clings closely to his traditional Blackbird jungle and programme-pieces. In the title number, a minor blues, he thrashes around spiritedly as if defending his reputation against the younger men; the more connected 'Very Special', also a blues, can be listened to as a kind of piano sketch for an orchestral treatment, and fascinating it is too. A pretty 'Les Fleurs Africaines' joins 'Solitude' and 'Warm Valley' to represent the salon element. Mingus's bass work is tremendously busy, and Duke has hard work keeping him in his place. This is undoubtedly the most bizarre trio record to be released for some time.

The characteristic flavour of Erroll Garner's piano, as British audiences have recently been reminded, cloys almost as soon as it delights, but as a public entertainer his stature is undeniable. 'One World Concert' (Philips), recorded in Seattle in 1960, has all the baroque floridity and loping energy of his best performances, and will serve anyone as a representative Garner disc, though it is a long way from the session with Charlie Parker on Dial in 1947. The appallingly-saccharine 'Happiness Is a Thing Called Joe' is balanced by a driving 'Sweet and Lovely', in which this unlikely vehicle is built into a riffing stomp with that faint suggestion of boogie in the left hand that is such a Garner trademark.

Big Jim Robinson was one of a group of native New Orleans musicians brought almost casually to light in 1943 to support Bunk Johnson, when Robinson was turned 50. Now, at 70, he qualifies as one of Riverside's 'Living Legends', and on 'Jim Robinson's New Orleans Band' demonstrates with Ernest Cagnolatti and Louis Cottrell that the quality of his music has not changed. Although the revivalist craze is over, it is still difficult to speak of this kind of playing without using ethically-loaded terms like 'simple' and 'joyous'. Robinson's solo on 'Take My Hand' – indeed, the whole track – is a masterpiece of unaffected relaxation. This is a disc where the whole is greater than the parts.

The Negro character of much popular music today no doubt explains the steady trickle of genuine blues records, of which the latest are 'Preachin' the Blues' (Stateside), 'A World of Blues' (London), and John Lee Hooker's 'Don't Turn Me From Your Door' (London). The first two are miscellanies; the former features Hooker, Memphis Slim and Jimmy Reed; the latter T-Bone Walker and five lesser-known singers. Hooker's disc is remarkable for the mysterious Mississippi monotony of his guitar, recorded here to better advantage than usual.

30 October 1963

Do Studios Kill?

Jazz depends so much on sympathetic playing conditions that when the introduction of magnetic recording tape and the LP disc made 'live' (as opposed to studio) performances more common it might be supposed that the quality of the music preserved would take an enormous step forward. The early jazzmen had to make their records either in the mornings before they went to bed or in the afternoons when they had just got up. The studios were barn-like and the recording officials quite uncomprehending. Often local conditions required performers to take their shoes off (to eliminate foot-tapping), cluster under an awning or stand yards away from the drummer, none of which was likely to promote ease of spirit. Cramping, too, was the arbitrary technical convention of the 78 rpm record that insisted that all jazz performances should be between two and a half and three and a half minutes long, a length we should now find damagingly short. That magnificently casual instruction of Louis Armstrong's, as reported by Louis Metcalf ('You take four, I'll finish with about six'), could never have been made in the recording studio. Bands such as King Oliver's that relied on numerous ensemble choruses for a crescendo of tension can only hint on their ten-inch records ('Snake Rag' for instance) what they must have been like in the flesh.

The predictable advance, however, cannot really be said to have taken place. There have been triumphs of historical preservation – Jelly Roll Morton in the Library of Congress, for example, or the 1941 scene at Minton's – but on the whole the greater flexibility of techniques that allow the embalming of 'Jazz at The Philharmonic' marathons (Verve has just put out a four-disc set) tends to prove either that what seemed so exciting was really no more than a tasteless piece of rabble-rousing, or that the majority of jazz concerts resemble that calm Sunday that goes on and on. Even artists most likely to be affected by audience participation – gospellers like Rosetta Tharpe, say – have not, on balance, produced better jazz outside the studio than in it. The more sensitive the equipment, the more co-operative the a-&-r man, the less seems to be happening. It is all very mysterious.

There are, however, exceptions. Two that have just been reissued are the Parker-Gillespie concerts at Carnegie Hall in 1947 and Massey Hall, Toronto, in 1953. The atmosphere of both was torrid and haphazard: according to Ross Russell, proprietor of Dial records, the Carnegie concert was the first attempt to present pure bop to a large and semi-formal audience. As it happened, the programme had been built round Dizzy Gillespie, who was not only better known but notoriously more dependable; in consequence, Parker, who has received no more than 'Guest Star' billing, arrived in a mean mood. (According to the sleeve, he had been asleep in a bath and had had to be rushed to the hall.) The result was staggering. The four pieces on 'Portrait of the Bird' (Columbia) show Parker at his most incandescently complex, on 'Dizzy Atmosphere' jetting flurries of perfectly articulated notes, and on 'Confirmation' achieving one of his most warmly beautiful solos, always perfectly in control of the situation, yet always startlingly adventurous. The other men – including pianist John Lewis – are scarcely noticeable in contrast. It is Parker's record and there is no better single example of his quality.

The Massey Hall night was different. Listening to 'The Quintet of the Year' (Vocalion) one realizes, despite Parker's still-formidable contributions, that in 1953 Dizzy was five years stronger and more practised while the Bird was five years deeper into self-immolation. Time and again it is Gillespie who takes one's breath away in his long choruses on 'Hot House' and 'Perdido', while comparison of the two versions of 'A Night in Tunisia' gives him as resounding a triumph in 1953 as Bird had had in 1947. The trumpeter's phenomenal technical control is completely justified by the audacity of his concepts, which are in turn governed by a higher level of taste than usual (note, for instance, the restrained start of his 'Hot House' solo). The accompaniment of Mingus, Powell and Roach make this, on balance, the better record. But one should really have them both.

13 November 1963

Ellington Panorama

Early Ellington records are like vintage cars. They are not as he or anyone else would make them nowadays, but historically they are still important and aesthetically they are still delightful. The 1927 'East St. Louis Toodle-Oo' with Bubber Miley has not been displaced by the 1956 version with Ray Nance: 'The Mooche', 'Rockin' in Rhythm' and 'Black and Tan Fantasy' are early models as viable in their context of the twenties as those of Henry Ford.

A chance to look at them again is offered by the first three discs of what promises to be a mammoth set from CBS ('The Ellington Era, 1927–1940, Vol. 1, Parts 1–3'). These offer a forty-eight-track conspectus from the Cotton Club days through the less familiar thirties, taking in the Jabbo Smith 'Black and Tan', 'Old Man Blues', some lovely Hodges soprano on 'Blues With a Feeling', Bigard's perfect Basin-Street chorus on 'Clarinet Lament' and Cootie's companion-piece 'Echoes of Harlem', Rex Stewart's half-valving 'Boy Meets Horn', and the slow gathering of the great 1940 band through 'Battle of Swing', 'Portrait of the Lion', and 'The Sergeant Was Shy'. 'Lazy Rhapsody' and 'Blue Tune' are reputedly from different masters, but I have not checked this.

This selection covers less than the first half of the Duke's recording career, and summarizes the pre-Strayhorn, pre-Latin-American, pre-Afro-Cuban, pre-concert-suite stage of his development. The pieces show his music still close to the conventions of the blues and the dance-hall, when the 'pictures' he drew were taken from the Savoy Ballroom rather than the Globe Theatre. No one wants him to repeat the past. No one, equally, would ever want to lose sight of such of it as this set represents.

A much more out-of-the-way collection presents the studio life of Jack Teagarden, the patent-leather-haired Texan who has rambled nonchalantly through thirty-five years of jazz without ever losing his southern accent or being permanently overshadowed by the city slickers. 'King of the Blues Trombone' (Columbia, three volumes) follows his career both as sideman and leader from 1928 up to four stinging tracks (three of them new masters) from his session with Bud Freeman's Famous Chicagoans in 1940. Highlights are 'Dirty Dog', a 1929 version of 'Makin' Friends', with Goodman and McPartland; 'Chances Are', with Fats Waller's piano ringing unmistakably through something called the Cloverdale Country Club Orchestra; 'Texas Tea Party', and that *carpe diem* Big Tea made so peculiarly his own, 'A Hundred Years From Today'. Teagarden's present-day manner (before his recent lamented heart attack) can be heard on 'The Dixie Sound of Jack Teagarden' (Columbia), a set of standards in the boneless Dixieland of the West Coast, with chief honours going to trumpeter Don Goldie and with a delightful 'Atlanta Blues' by Don Ewell.

Hooray for Christmas, as Bessie Smith calls rather cautiously on one of her tracks, and if all your friends like jazz it will present no problem. The inexpensive Realm label has put out two discs of 'A Lester Young Memorial', most of it dating from 1944, just before his disastrous war service. The first, with two lovely takes of

'Ghost of a Chance' in front of Freddie Green's rock-steady guitar, is the better.

The new Charlie Mingus, 'The Black Saint and the Sinner Lady' (HMV), is a furious, pretentious plumcake of sound such as Mingus delights to mix, including his own version of the Tristan love duet, here called 'Hearts' Beat and Shades in Physical Embraces'; it's incredible that eleven men can make as much noise as this. Hear it. Please yourself, however, about John Coltrane's 'Impressions' (HMV), where the master of the thinly disagreeable (particularly when aided by Eric Dolphy in 'India') sounds as if he is playing for an audience of cobras instead of that of the Village Vanguard in 1961.

Decca's noble reissue programme continues with 'Fletcher Henderson 1934' and 'Red Nichols and his Five Pennies' (both Ace of Hearts). The former is a clutch of sides featuring Henry Allen, Buster Bailey, Keg Johnson and Ben Webster not to be found in the CBS memorial albums; the latter covers the five years 1926–31, starting with the dapper 'Washboard Blues' (my copy was worn white) and ending when the Depression drove as many as thirteen men to shelter under Red's unamended title.

The tendency of the pure blues artist to move into the more lucrative stream of r-&-b is distressing, but there is still much rolling enjoyment in 'Broken Soul Blues' (United Artists) by Memphis Slim. In 'Chris Barber in Concert' (Pye) the listener is transported to the Royal Festival Hall in 1956, with Monty, Lonnie and all. Finally, what about the Beatles? 'With the Beatles' (Parlophone) suggests that their jazz content is nil, but that, like certain sweets, they seem wonderful until you are suddenly sick. Up till then it's nice, though.

14 December 1963

1964

The Billy Banks Sides

Every reviewer has a secret: what he would most like to find in his next exciting square package. I am preparing to risk being damned or dated if in consequence one day in 1964 I can withdraw from its wrappings an LP entitled 'The Rhythmakers 1932'. You will look in vain for this name in Charles Delaunay's *New Hot Discography* (1958). It was given to a group of musicians who met in the studio four times that year (under the aegis of Irving Mills) and cut, in all, fifteen numbers. The group was not always the same: the first two occasions saw Henry Allen and Pee Wee Russell fronting a formidable five-piece rhythm section cored by Eddie Condon and Jack Bland. The third and fourth sessions use a fuller instrumentation, bringing in clarinettist Jimmy Lord on the former date, and Tommy Dorsey and Happy Cauldwell on the latter. Russell had a spell on tenor, and Fats Waller replaced Sullivan on four sides. On the first three days Billy Banks sang the vocals, on the last Chick Bullock.

I value what was produced firstly because of the musicians used. The combination of Henry Allen and Pee Wee Russell was especially piquant: both are now often cited as moderns before their time, and the filigree duets of their eccentric voices reveals instinctive kinship. The five-piece rhythm, too, was a devastating concept, particularly when it included Pops Foster, Condon and Zutty Singleton, and the addition of Waller produced the power of a riverboat paddlewheel. I value it also because it recalls an age when a jazzman was a jazzman and could play pretty well anything with any other jazzmen: his music was a kind of lingua franca, like medieval Latin, and was not subdivided into East Coast or West Coast, modern or traditional, mainstream or thirdstream or any other speciality. It was a tough, careless language that accommodated the chortling minstrel-show atmosphere of 'Yes, Suh!' as easily as the heartbroken fantasy of 'Spider Crawl', or the satiric social realism of 'Mean Old Bed Bug Blues'. For this reason it can be recommended as an antidote to the present-day extremes of the corpse-walking of Miles Davis or the chuntering of the Coronary Society of Lower Basin Street.

I should not claim that the sides were flawless. Attractive though Banks's counter-tenor is, there is too much of him; Waller's solos are full of clichés; the bits of 'arranging' are tiresome. But the highlights – the last three choruses of 'Yellow Dog Blues' which Wilder Hobson transcribed in his book 'American Jazz Music' (1939) as a perfect example of collective improvisation; the explosive final eight bars of 'I Would Do Anything For You'; Allen and Russell on 'Oh Peter' and again on 'Bugle Call Rag', trailing long notes against each other while the rhythm beats away unhindered – all this cries for regeneration in microgroove, preferably with a few extra takes (the 'Oh Peter' with the Allen vocal, for instance) for good measure. I implore the record companies to give us this in 1964, instead of one of the six John Coltrane records no doubt already in production.*

11 January 1964

Wandering Minstrels

It is not difficult to imagine why, once a Negro jazzman has crossed the Atlantic, he is tempted to stay here. Our living conditions are probably not much worse than he would have had to accept in America anyway; we have no segregation laws; frequently some of our veneration for his music rubs off on him. Post-war Europe is in consequence sprinkled with American jazz talent.

'Americans in Europe' (two volumes, HMV) commemorates a concert given at Coblenz by as many of these as could be collected. They included Idrees Suleiman from Stockholm, Don Byas and Nelson Williams from Amsterdam, Albert Nicholas, Bud Powell and Kenny Clarke from Paris, and Champion Jack Dupree, then domiciled in Zurich, where nightlife ceases about 11.30 p.m. The sleeve claims that the occasion will become as significant in the history of jazz in Europe as Goodman's Carnegie Hall concerts were in the history of jazz in America. This is ridiculous overpraise: the tracks represent good-humoured music in various modes, but all with an easiness that suggests that its performers have somehow ceased to compete.

What we have is some highly listenable guitar from Jimmy

*In fact 'The Rhythmakers 1932' turned up in 1969, on Collectors' Choice 14.

Gourley with the Kenny Clarke and Bill Smith groups, the liquid Creole clarinet of Albert Nicholas, some not-too-serious blues singing from Jack Dupree and Curtis Jones, and a reminder of Don Byas's tenor, all of which make a nicely-varied entertainment. The most moving track is a solo 'Round Midnight' by Bud Powell; long, painstaking, slow, it is like a confession that omits nothing and excuses nothing, that one hears in silence and can think of no reply to.

One of the most famous expatriates who is still competing is the plentifully-recorded Coleman Hawkins, who turns in a nice quartet disc 'Today and Now' (HMV) with Tommy Flanagan, Major Holley and Eddie Locke. Picking such catchy standard folkies as 'Go L'il Liza' ('Little Liza Jane'), 'Swingin' Scotch' ('Loch Lomond') and 'Old Grey Bonnet', Hawk blows a seemingly endless stream of supple choruses, not perhaps wailing his mostest but sounding thoroughly at home. This is unfortunately not the case with 'Sonny Meets Hawk' (RCA Victor), where Hawkins sounds at a loss to match Rollins' obeisances to Ornette Coleman. It is sad to hear that celebrated gun-metal tone tortured into abrasive sobs and yelps in the interests of one doesn't quite know what: Rollins, who used to 'play angry', now plays silly. Some fragments of enjoyment may be rescued from the blues 'At McKies' and the duet that closes the quickie 'Just Friends'.

Every now and then there appears a record whose freshness and originality sets it in a class of its own (the last such I recall was the Philips Clarence Williams disc a couple of years ago): the latest is 'Fats at the Organ' (RCA Victor), fourteen tracks from 1926–7 made solo and with Tom Morris (cornet) and Charlie Irvis (trombone). Its appeal lies in the quaint contrast of the 'primitive' technique of the brassmen with Waller's light-flowing and sophisticated handling of an instrument one might suppose too cumbrous for jazz: the swelling legato breaks, predictable cymbal crashes and strutting twentyish gaiety of 'Take Me Home', 'Geechee' and 'Savannah Blues' have a prelapsarian innocence that is hard to parallel. The solos are more conventional: just Waller's brisk, rather stiff-moving clichés softened and dignified, the stately 'Lennox Avenue Blues' being a notable exception.

Archie Semple used to be a follower of Pee Wee Russell, though one would hardly think so from 'The Twilight Cometh' (Columbia), which exemplifies the present British trend for lush-hushed clarinets and breathes a set of standards confidentially over Dave Lee's apt piano. Better by far is the Realm reissue of the Braff-Russell 'Jazz at Storyville' made in 1952 in Boston just after Russell's near-fatal illness on the west coast. Over a stodgy rhythm Ruby and Pee Wee provide nightmare recollections of 'Squeeze Me', 'St. James's Infirmary', 'Anything For You' and others, vying with each other to produce the most way-out progression, which shows how ready Pee Wee was for his break with Dixieland. This reminds one, too, how in those days Braff seemed on the point of founding a really new white trumpet style.

8 February 1964

That Edwardian Rag

It is 1913. You are strolling along the promenade in the sun, wearing a boater and carrying 'The Pink 'Un' (or even 'The Green 'Un'): you have some gold sovereigns in your pocket and are wondering whether that is a cloud over the German Ocean or simply a heat haze. From nearby gardens unfamiliar music falls on your ears: not Sullivan, not Rossini, not 'Florodora', but that new darkie novelty, the cakewalk or ragtime or whatever they call it. You pass on your way.

A tiny kaleidoscope of what you might have heard has been put out by the Vintage Jazz Music Society as their first LP 'A Programme of Ragtime in Celebration of the Relief of Mafeking'. The title is frankly an excuse for an evocative but irrelevant sleeve; the contents are a number of orchestral, banjo and piano-roll pieces made between 1899 and 1916. Ragtime represented the initial attempt of the classical tradition to contain the new Afro-American impulse within its own techniques. Its characteristic device of syncopation was effected with an almost mechanical insistence against a regular bass, melodic variation being obtained not by improvisation but by the introduction of second and third themes. The result is a bizarre classicism, like plantation Scarlatti – witness the earliest and most attractive piece, 'Downtown Alley Cake-Walk', where the second theme might be some sporting-house professor's memory of 'The Arrival of the Queen of Sheba'. I would not pretend that this music of Charles Prince, Sousa, Arthur Pryor, Vess Ossman and the anonymous piano-rolls (why the mock Acker-Bilkery instead of proper sleeve-notes, by the way?) will be of more than historic interest to most listeners. But there is a jaunty wistful gaiety in ragtime that did not survive the First World War and is extremely affecting, and genuine examples are rare. This glimpse of a vanished musical tradition is as precious as it is unexpected.

I missed Jimmy Woods's first LP ('Awakening'), but his second, 'Conflict' (Contemporary), suggests that the hard boppers have a new alto star. With Carmell Jones and Harold Land in support, Woods whoops and wails his thin way through six originals, showing himself to be well in the astringent tradition of Coltrane and Dolphy. A pretentious sleeve-note ('It was a course in Sociopathic Behaviour at Los Angeles State University which clarified many of my thoughts on this subject') suggests that the music deliberately represents the anger and confusion of the modern American Negro; this is felt more in the acute-angled solos, the many arranged passages using the horns in long lines of unison or counterpoint. I came to look forward to the rich stretches of complexity laid down by Elvin Jones, to whom much of the record's success is due. Another altoist, Paul Desmond, has been called the Godfrey Winn of that instrument, but in 'Take Ten' (RCA Victor) his limpidity is never limp. Guitarist Jim Hall collaborates in standards ('Nancy', 'Alone Together') and a time novelty or two ('Take Ten'), with what Desmond calls some bossa antiqua thrown in for good measure. This disc upholds the reputation of a player who seemed in some danger of becoming a mannerist.

Those who saw The Bradford Singers will need no introduction to 'Alex Bradford and Chris Barber' (Stateside), ten stirring tracks of Bradford's gospelling with the Singers and the Barber Band in support. They do not quite come up to the early Rosetta Tharpe sides with the Sam Price trio, but the spirit is comparable, and I found at least one ('God Leads His Dear Children Along') excitingly moving.

Two blues issues of importance are a 1948–54 Lightning Hopkins set. 'Dirty House Blues' (Realm), and a collection of pieces by 'T-Bone Walker' (Capitol) from roughly the same period. Hopkins, an intensely personal performer, laments and gibes his way through twelve numbers including 'Everybody's Down On Me' and 'Freight Train'. It is surprising how such a rough vocalist can add such delicate guitar comments. T-Bone is smoother and less gripping (so, by now, is Lightning), but I have always cherished his fine 'They Call It Stormy Monday', which here appears.

An experiment in producing a piano trio composed of Bill Evans ('Conversations With Myself', Verve) results in a rambling series of light-weight performances of considerable charm. English listeners of a certain age will like to be reminded of 'The Young George Shearing, 1939–1944' (Decca), piano solos very much in Teddy Wilson's neo-Hines tradition with the occasional Waller pastiche; and everyone will welcome 'Django Reinhardt and Stephane Grappelly' (Decca), fourteen classic tracks from their irreplaceable Quintet that show more clearly than before how much the whole effect depended on Django. Grappelly's violin line is basically a Goodman-type clarinet. Django's single-finger solos and sudden explosions of strumming in the rhythm are unique.

4 March 1964

Monk

'A dramatic conversation in some other language, a fit of drunken laughter, a shout from a park at night' – yes, Thelonious Monk has at last received that American accolade, a *Time* cover, and this is the house style attempting to describe his music. At 44 he has arrived, an honoured guest anywhere in Europe and with a three-album-a-year contract with Columbia, but without sacrificing any of his personality.

This personality has for many years been a musician's legend, a bearded, brooding power behind the scene who disdained the daylight of success. 'Monk is the guy who started it all,' affirmed Art Blakey; 'The Monk', Parker conceded, 'is deep.' Following his debut at Minton's in the early forties, he was hired as an accompanist by Coleman Hawkins, but after 1945 obscurity descended ('he even had to pay to get into Birdland'), not helped by a baseless narcotics charge that lost him his precious cabaret card. It was ten years before he got going again, making records for Riverside in 1955: then his piano, his pieces and the small groups he preferred to work with began to be known.

Monk's goatee and funny hats suggest a kinship with Gillespie, and this is not as absurd as it might at first seem; Monk's thrashing feet and gnomic comments, together with his tendency to do a shuffle-dance, hands outstretched from the keyboard, all round the Five Spot (ending at the bar), constitute a kind of moonlight exhibitionism the reverse of Dizzy's (contrast Parker's public persona with either). His piano style is a mass of contradictions: rich, impish, angular, sad, it holds refracted in it surprisingly recognizable details from other traditions – Teddy Wilson's downward run, or James P.'s stride. The pianist he has most in common with is Duke Ellington: they have the same way of striking off-centre intervals and (unfortunately) the same unswingingness. Monk often lets the tempo go, especially when he is restructuring some familiar vehicle till it stands precariously on completely new foundations, his hesitantly-chosen chords crammed like suitcases with almost more than they can hold. As a composer he is responsible for at least one modern classic ('Round Midnight'), but few other pianists attempt to appropriate Monk's tunes to their repertoire. So much would get lost in translation.

Several Monk records have been issued recently: the only one I have received, 'Criss Cross' (CBS), is a good studio set of eight tracks made last year with tenorist Charlie Rouse, bass and drums. I am not enamoured of Monk's quicker tunes; however he treats them, they all stem from the barren screwy unison-riff tradition of the bop revolution, but the slower 'Tea For Two', 'Don't Blame Me' and 'Crepuscule With Nellie' are stirring and full of emotion. Monk plays with enormous force on 'Eronel', and Rouse's tenor encompasses in its choppy way the whole range from alto to baritone. The frequent and impressive lacunae Monk leaves in his piano lines usually reveal drummer Frankie Dunlop doing something interesting.

Someone must have thought the first Armstrong-Ellington record worth repeating, for now we have 'The Great Reunion' (Columbia), in which Louis's blow-torch vocals dominate Duke's rather bored-sounding piano. Let's face it, the two men have almost nothing in common, but 'Solitude' and 'I Got It Bad' showcase Louis's murderous ability to hit a tune on the nose.

How delightful is the reissue of 'Humph At the Conway' (Encore)! Humph's urbane emceeing of his own virile trumpet, Fawkes's clarinet and Bruce Turner's alto is the keynote of that Parlophone-Rhythm-Style British trad back in 1954 of which this is so admirable an example. Granted that their model is the Hot Five rather than George Lewis, there is still enough soul in 'Wally Plays the Blues' and enough fervour in 'Bucket Got a Hole In It' to interest 1964. And in a curious way the occasion sums up an era – Lyttelton's commanding personality, the happy audience whose records have at last come alive, the simple Ptolemaic jazz universe with Armstrong at the centre. Try it.

25 March 1964

New Orleans Preserv'd

Preservation Hall was opened in 1961 in the French quarter of New Orleans by a visiting West Coaster, Grayson Mills, in a deliberate attempt to provide a place for the older musicians to play in non-commercial surroundings. The furnishings are unpretentious: there are no waiters, no drinks, nothing to suggest the usual niterie conditions. The audience sits and listens, and sometimes contributes to the kitty. There is a $5 fine for requesting 'The Saints'.

The four-disc set 'Jazz At Preservation Hall' (London) was recorded by Nesuhi Ertegun in 1962, and features groups made up of veterans who in many cases must have been resigned to obscurity but who now form part of the Hall's weekly six-night rota. They are, respectively, The Eureka Brass Band (Volume One), Billie and Dede Pierce, Jim Robinson (Volume Two), Paul Barbarin, Punch Miller (Volume Three), and the George Lewis Band (Volume Four) – a magnificent assortment of New Orleans traditional jazz talent recorded under excellent conditions, for which one cannot be other than grateful. Having said this, one is bound to add that a little more variation in the front lines would have been welcome: the teams of Lewis/Louis Nelson and Cagnolatti/Louis Cottrell appear twice each, and Robinson is featured both under his own name and with George Lewis. A session with Albert Burbank or Kid Thomas would have added variety. My immediate impression, too, is that some artists have been more impressively recorded elsewhere – Billie and Dede Pierce, for instance, lose some of their individuality with Nelson and Lewis, though her two-fisted piano and fervent voice come over well on 'Love Song Of The Nile', and Lewis and Nelson shine on 'San'. The five Barbarin tracks ('Cag', Cottrell and 'Frog' Joseph) produce a phenomenal drive, aided by Lester Santiago's piano, but the Millers (Nelson, Lewis) make Punch sound thin and beat-up. The Robinson and Lewis groups are as agreeable as ever, but for once do not achieve the gay abandon one has come to expect in the ride-outs. This is all very fine, very genuine New Orleans jazz, but it comes a little too late in the day to set the Mississippi on fire.

The exception is the Eureka Brass Band. The seven tracks by this street marching band offer a completely new sound that is at times really exciting. Over a rhythm of bass drum, snare and sousaphone, the trumpet and clarinet of the Humphrey brothers, Percy and Willie, weave against the rich gruffness of two trumpets and two trombones, while the oddly Rusin-like tenor of Emmanuel Paul battles manfully for a hearing. The overall sound is crude and at times muddled, but if this is what a New Orleans street parade sounds like, then legend for once has not been misleading. 'Panama', 'Joe Avery's Blues', 'Bye and Bye' and 'Whoop'n' Blues' all bear out Thomas Sancton's lyrical sleeve-note: 'the innocence of children and the force of archangels'.

In contrast, two recent Blue Notes, Freddie Hubbard's 'Hub-Tones' and Dexter Gordon's 'Our Man in Paris' seem especially piquant. It's odd to find the sleeve calling Hubbard 'mainstream', but his supple, versatile manner sounds good by any name, whether floridly melancholy in 'Lament For Booker', mellowly romantic in 'You're My Everything', or beating up a fair storm on 'Hub-Tones'. James Spaulding is some degrees further out on alto and flute, and drummer Clifford Jarvis kicks the proceedings forward unsentimentally. Dexter Gordon, like Hubbard (or for that matter Muggsy Spanier), is a good punching player of no great originality without whom jazz would be immeasurably poorer. There is a constant exciting pressure behind his solos on 'Stairway to the Stars' and 'Willow Weep' that suggests reserves of force similar to the early Lester, despite several forays into the Coltrane territory. This disc is especially interesting because of the support given by Bud Powell and Kenny Clarke.

15 April 1964

Decline of Night-Music

'The history of jazz', writes Charles Fox in his leaflet accompanying 'Jazz In The Making, Vol. 2: The Swing Era' (Parlophone), 'might be described as the narrowing of a function.' Originally an integral part of all aspects of Negro communal life, jazz in the period under review became a nocturnal art for dancers only. This is very true. And one could add that another equally interesting set, 'Jazz Of The Forties' (Capitol, two volumes), shows the process going a stage further, a stage memorably summarized by Benny Green in 'The Reluctant Art' as 'After Parker you had to be something of a musican to follow the best jazz of the day'. What was all-pervading had become occasional; what was general, special; what was popular, esoteric.

This is a familiar progress, and on the Capitol set one can not only hear it happening but to some extent see why. The groups represented – headed by Al Casey, Benny Carter and Sidney Catlett for the swing era, with Gillespie, Davis, Tristano, Gonzales, Herman and Norvo on the other side of the barricades – produce average rather than outstanding performances, but this very unexceptional quality shows how thoroughly what might be described as the fag-end of the Henderson tradition needed revitalizing, having reached a point where its very vices – breakneck tempos, stratospheric notes, dissonant harmonies – began to sound like virtues.

Of course a piece like Miles Davis's 'Darn That Dream' (1950) represents a much richer and freer approach to scoring and instrumentation, but a broadening of technical resource is accompanied, as so often, by a narrowing of emotional appeal. Tristano's fascinating 'Intuition' (1949) exemplifies some early free-form blowing, but once was surely enough. Perhaps the most agreeable sides are those that hand on the killer-diller tradition of the thirties: Gillespie's 'Coast to Coast' and Herman's 'That's Right'. Or there are two Goodman sides in which the King of Swing is heard holding his own against insurrectionists Fats Navarro and Doug Mettome.

I am afraid that the modernist tradition in jazz – I am not for the moment thinking of gifted individuals such as Parker and Gillespie – strikes me, even in historical perspective, as no better than the modernist tradition in other arts – that is, as tending towards the silly, the disagreeable and the frigid. I am strengthened in this conviction by the Parlophone disc, which offers a varied selection from the thirties: Ellington ('Merry Go Round'), Meade Lux Lewis's 1935 'Honky Tonk Train Blues' (less good than the 1936, but still fine), Krupa's wonderful 'Blues of Israel' with the unregarded Nate Kazebier claiming immortality in twelve bars, 'Sweet Georgia Brown' by that driving Jimmy Noone group with Red Allen's old mentor, Guy Kelly, on trumpet, and a Billie Holiday ('Sailboat In The Moonlight') so typical that one almost cries to hear her acrid voice joined in a trio with Young's bone-hard tenor and Jo Jones's hi-hat sloshing away in the background. This is the flowering of a period that was bound to run to seed, perhaps, but was unequalled at its best.

Two recent Charlie Byrd records, 'Blues Sonata' (Riverside) and 'Prelude' (Realm), show this master of the acoustic guitar leading his counter-revolution against the 'sax sound' tradition of Charlie Christian. Byrd is one of the few jazz players who can use classical technique without sounding affected, and his echoes of other modes such as lute-music and Latin American are done in superb taste. On some of the Realm sides he is happily joined by Tom Newsom on flute: on the reverse of 'Blues Sonata' he offers standards such as 'Zing Went The Strings' on amplified guitar. All in all, two delightful discs. 'Dizzy Gillespie and the Double Six of Paris' (Philips) offers a unique combination of the French vocal team and Dizzy in vocalese versions of early hits such as 'Ow' and 'The Champ'. The Double Six resemble an inflation of Lambert-Hendricks-Bavan, with Mimi Perrin doing the bop solos, and most of the tracks have Bud Powell, Kenny Clarke and Pierre Michelot in attendance. Whether or not the two groups ever saw each other is uncertain, but this only makes Gillespie's fluent contributions more of a marvel.

In the welter of blues anthologies it would be a pity to miss 'Out Came The Blues' (Ace of Hearts), a sampler of rare tracks by such masters as Kokomo Arnold, Memphis Minnie, Peetie Wheatstraw and Sleepy John Estes strengthened by classic group offerings like the Bechet-Trixie Smith 'Freight Train Blues' and Rosetta Crawford's 'My Man Jumped Salty On Me'. Local honours go this month to 'Alan Elsdon Presents . . .' (Columbia), deliberately contrasting tracks featuring Johnny Barnes's alto and the Mick Emery Folk Group. I wonder how far up the chart the latter's 'Mule Skinner Blues' would get as a single.

13 May 1964

The New Russell

The appearance of 'New Groove' (CBS) by the Pee Wee Russell Quartet will at least satisfy the curiosity aroused by rumours that the veteran Dixieland clarinettist has 'gone modern'. The answer is that the cautious harmonic adventures herein preserved are hardly modern any longer, and that Pee Wee was always a modern anyway. What it does show is this restless and unpredictable artist in the entirely new context of a heavily-arranged chamber quartet with Marshall Brown (valve trombone), Russell George (bass) and Ron Lundberg (drums). Stylistically, this is the post-1951 Russell, a hollow feathery tone framing phrases of an almost Chinese introspection with a tendency to inconclusive garrulity that would have been unheard of in the days when Pee Wee could pack more into a middle eight than any other thirties pick-up player.

This may sound a prelude to hostile dismissal: on the contrary, this is a rich and curious record that will earn many replayings. Brown, who is credited with challenging Pee Wee to play a modern book, is a notable musical educationalist (he organized the Farmingdale band heard at Newport in 1957), and has achieved a full and at times contrapuntal sound somewhat in the manner of the Mulligan Quartet. His devices are conventional – arranged intros and codas, solo and accompanying voices (frequently the bass, as on the pretty 'Round Midnight'), fours and breaks – and his phlegmatic brass tone contrasts in texture and temperament with Russell's clarinet. One can agree, in fact, that it is all thoroughly well done. The question that arises is how far it was worth doing.

The repertoire here offered is wide and unusual. 'Pee Wee's Blues' reworks a theme rather better exploited on the earlier 'Portrait of Pee Wee' (Counterpoint), and 'Taps Miller' has enough of Russell's old verve and fire to satisfy the unregenerate (particularly the second thirty-two bars of his solo). 'Round Midnight' and 'Chelsea Bridge' are two composer's set-pieces, while with Tad Dameron's 'Good Bait' and Coltrane's 'Red Planet' we are into the modern scene past the point of no return. Every track is done with both competence and confidence – especially invigorating is Lundberg's brushwork – but the emotional temperature hardly ever rises above warm. Pee Wee's pre-war adventures remain unobliterated.

The confusion surrounding Charlie Mingus's 'Town Hall Concert' (United Artists) – was it a concert? a recording session? even a rehearsal? – is reflected in the ragged and fragmentary nature of the music, which constitutes snippets from what must have been an embarrassingly puzzling occasion. There is some good Clark Terry to be gleaned from 'Clark in the Dark', and Charlie Mariano's alto shines on 'The Search', a tune bearing some resemblance to 'I Can't Get Started'; otherwise this is the usual Mingus brew of exasperation and enchantment presented with all the random exuberance of the jungle at moonrise. It is a tribute to his compelling quality that this disc should be worth recommending despite its patchiness.

Ella Fitzgerald's 'These Are The Blues' (Verve) and 'American Folk Blues Festival 1963' (Fontana) offer a piquant contrast in blues singing. Ella treats her ten standards ('How Long', 'See See Rider', 'Downhearted' and others) with her customary technique of refraction and control, but it is doubtful whether it is really suited to the blues, which are all the better for a little rugosity. Ella's very flawlessness gives an impression of indifference, while the double tempo of 'Trouble In Mind' comes over as downright insensitive. Better tracks such as 'St. Louis' and 'Hear Me Talkin'' restore the balance, however, as do Roy Eldridge, Wild Bill Davis and the rhythm section of Brown, Ellis and Gus Johnson. The Festival side is a live package recorded in Bremen last October, featuring a number of artists who made an all-too-brief appearance here. Their styles range from Victoria Spivey and Lonnie Johnson (can he really be eleven years older than Armstrong?) to Muddy Waters and Memphis Slim. The classic mode of the two older artists is singularly moving, and after them it is the instrumental work that is most noticeable – Sonny Boy Williamson's airy harmonica, for instance, and Matt Murphy's guitar. The record's success means that the tendency for all the artists to sound like each other has been firmly avoided.

Assiduous readers of this column will remember my appeal in January for a reissue of the Rhythmakers sides of 1932. While the home front has so far proved indifferent, I am glad to say that from Australia has come 'Fats Waller With The Rhythmakers' (Swaggie Jazz Collector Series). This seven-inch LP contains 'Yes, Suh', 'Anything For You', takes 2 and 3 of 'Yellow Dog' and 1 and 2 of 'Mean Old Bed Bug'. Those readers who wrote supporting my original appeal should pester the specialist jazz shops without delay – or try Swaggie direct at Box 125, P.O. South Yarra, Victoria.

10 June 1964

All What Jazz?

Comes inevitably the month when the new records seemingly offer nothing but platitude, prolixity, pretension. Jazz, the reviewer thinks, is dying – or is it himself? If he were twenty years younger, would Miles Davis sound like Bix? Or Monk like Jelly Roll Morton? Or the Jazz Misanthropes like the Chicago Rhythm Kings? Perhaps all he needs is a holiday. Experiment, at any rate, gets a morose reception. Last December Johnny Dankworth anticipated Christmas with a Dickens suite: now he catches Shakespeare year with 'Shakespeare And All That Jazz' (Fontana), settings of Shakespearean or pseudo-Shakespearean word-pieces featuring Cleo Laine. The Dickens venture was successful, showing Dankworth's dandyish, witty, occasionally tender talent to advantage. This Shakespeare one is not: leaving aside charges of 1564-and-all-that opportunism and the poetry-and-jazz fallacy, to make a number of reciting all the play titles is sub-W. S. Gilbert, to set Sonnet XL ('Take all my loves, my love, yea, take them all') to Ellington's 'Sonnet to Hank Cinq' is barbarity. Arthur Young's four settings from the thirties re-done by Ken Napper merely arouse nostalgia for Marion Mann and the Bobcats.

Cleo Laine's sultry, slightly-adenoidal contralto is in good form, and one or two pieces succeed – the Minnie-the-Moocher-like 'Dunsinane Blues', for instance, or Dankworth's own 'Shall I Compare Thee To A Summer's Day', in which by a subtle extension of the metre the line 'By chance, or nature's changing course, untrimm'd' comes over with devastating poignance. The accompaniment, led by Ken Wheeler's attractive trumpet, has all mod cons. But the truth is that by letting Shakespeare's words into this exercise in frivolity Dankworth blows the idea away like a dandelion-clock.

The same is true for the present Gallic habit of swinging Bach, popularized by the Swingle Singers and further exemplified by Jacques Loussier on 'Play Bach: Numéro Quatre' (London). Alec Templeton's original delicate musical joke 'Bach Goes To Town' contained within the confines of a mock-fugue all one needed to say on the subject: these tasteless expanses of real Bach themes distracted with aimless bits of syncopation seem the acme of pallid vulgarity.

Then what of Brubeck? A suddenly telescopic view of his career is afforded by the simultaneous appearance of 'Jazz At Storyville' (Vogue), a reissue of tracks from the early fifties, and 'Time Changes' (CBS), his latest screwy-tempo album, which also contains his first orchestral piece, 'Elementals'. My opinion of Brubeck (not lately revised) is that despite his battery of unvarying devices (the reiterated triplets, the automatic crescendos, the blind-man's-buff modulations), his records may be relied upon to contain a few of those moments when the proceedings drift away on a long ripple of understanding between him and Paul Desmond that evokes an answering wave of applause. In the Vogue disc this happens rarely: what one chiefly notices is how the absence of a bass shows up Brubeck's rhythmic deadness. The new album has little fresh to say on the time-signature theme, while 'Elementals', showing the Quartet struggling like flies in the syrup of an Eastman School of Music Orchestra, is no more than a series of gestures in the direction of atmosphere – menace, romance, Stan Kenton, Latin America, and a kind of seaside bandstand noise that accompanies Paul Desmond.

What comfort the month has afforded comes from scratching among reissues. 'They Tore My Playhouse Down' (Good Time Jazz) links two little-known West Coast pianists, Burt Bales and the legendary veteran Paul Lingle. Both play in the lilting vein of mingled ragtime and Jelly Roll, an unemphatic mode of great stamina and intense musicality that suggests it might well go on for ever. Lingle is rougher than Bales (he plays a Monkish 'Yellow Dog'), but both refresh.

The tracks contained in 'King of Swing' by Count Basie (Encore) were made in 1953, and, under the title 'Dance Session', heralded the return of Basie to the roll of great bands. Hefti, Wilkins, Mandel and Wess were the writers, Wess, Newman and Coker the main soloists with, of course, Basie himself and the driving drums of Gus Johnson. Realm also offers Kenny Clarke and Cannonball Adderley in 'Bohemia', some lusty and varied pieces with Nat Adderley and Horace Silver, vintage 1955, well worth the trifling sum this LP label costs. This kind of past gives hope for the future.

18 July 1964

Mingus, Mingus, Etc.

The trail of discontent and hurt feelings left by Charlie Mingus and his group during their European tour earlier this year – delayed starts, insulted audiences and damaged property – reminded me of an anecdote that describes how the Ellington band when in St Louis once couldn't get anything to eat between shows. The segregated restaurants were too far off. They sent a white man to a drugstore for sandwiches, but the proprietor refused to make them when he heard they were for a Negro band. Meanwhile the second house began, and the Ellingtonians, still hungry, had to get back on the stand, where Duke flashed his winning smile and his world-famous soloists bowed to the applause just as for the first house. The moral? I wouldn't dare draw one. It's just that the two incidents seem connected somehow.

Mingus and Ellington are connected in other ways. 'It's absurd to put Ellington in polls,' the turbulent bassist declares on the sleeve of his new LP entitled (typically) 'Mingus, Mingus, Mingus, Mingus, Mingus' (HMV). 'He should just be assumed to be in the first place every year.' This admiration suggests that Mingus himself is fast approximating to a kind of Kennedy-era Ellington (odd that Duke's second name should be Kennedy) with some characteristics of the earlier model: he has a strong musical personality, best expressed by an orchestra rather than an instrument; he is concerned with expressing the Negro character and environment. There is even the suggestion that they think in the same way – that is, in pictures and stories (Mingus: 'A composer is a chronicler': Ellington: 'In my writing there's always a mental picture').

Listening to this LP I found Mingus suffering rather than profiting by the comparison. The 78-rpm record schooled Duke to make an effect quickly, then stop; Mingus's pieces go on too long and sprawl all over. In 'Better Get It In Your Soul', for instance, the piece is virtually over when Mingus suddenly starts up in a different tempo on bass. For a few choruses we have barrelhouse piano and tenor-against-riffs in a mood quite unrelated to thc earlier 'church' atmosphere. Again, Duke the entertainer would never show the contempt for audiences Mingus shows: most of these numbers have appeared before under different names, while 'Celia' and 'I X Love' sound like two halves of the same piece, which in turn openly resembles the earlier 'Nouroog'. Ellington is sophisticated: I can't recall his recording anything downright absurd. Mingus is not: he made 'Passions of a Man'.

Yet for all this, every Mingus record is a tremendously exciting experience, and this one is no exception. His rowdy pieces ('II BS', 'Better Get It', 'Hora Decubitus') are a chorus of instrumental cries – agonized, blubbering, grotesque – concerted over ferocious drumming and impelling bass. In the slow numbers ('Theme for Lester Young', 'I X Love') the same basic technique produces slow ambling hardly-related lines of melody, notably the alto of Mingus's Johnny

Hodges, Charlie Mariano, while Mingus strums a guitar-like accompaniment. The impression is one of tumultuous, hypnotic richness, unmemorable and unique.

It was heart-warming to see Louis Armstrong beating the Beatles with 'Hello Dolly!': his LP of that title (London) is a clutch of a dozen standards, some of them ('Jeepers Creepers', 'Blueberry Hill') pretty threadbare by now, but all exhaling a simple freshness that is irresistible. Vocals predominate: to hear Louis's colossal voice tearing words up by the roots ('mel-o-dee') is still an awesome experience, but his trumpet is tender and spritely, leading with grace and precision ensembles that are comfortable as old jackets. Listening to his 'Moon River', a piece of slop if there ever was one, I came to the conclusion that it is Armstrong's staggering and economical sincerity that makes this kind of number succeed. Indeed, it brought tears to my eyes. What it does for the teenagers I hardly dare hope.

There is good jazz to be had from the World Record Club: 'Meet Me in Chicago' joins the bands of Art Hodes and Jimmy McPartland in a double date featuring Russell, Freeman, Brunis, Dickinson and Floyd Bean. If this kind of music was overrated in the thirties, it is underrated now: strong, careless, uncluttered, it here shows the trombones to specially good advantage.

This month I found myself liking a Coltrane record: 'Coltrane Live at Birdland' (HMV) has some excellent tripartite discussions between Coltrane, Tyner and Jones, notably on 'Afro-Blue', and there is a passage on 'Your Lady' when Jones and Coltrane exchange unaccompanied statements that are eloquent with a new kind of authority in jazz. Claims that jazz has been thereby extended, however, seem thin when Coltrane spends so long rocking backwards and forwards as if in pain between two chords.

15 August 1964

How Do We Stand?

That genial, unopinionated American contemporary, *Down Beat*, was 30 years old this July, and took the occasion for a long look at the music it exists to document. Such a handsome, 102-page issue might be expected to constitute a landmark of a booming international industry. Certainly there is an optimistic introduction by

Ellington himself, and an onwards-and-upwards account of the four decades of its publication with studies of representative figures (Goodman, Parker, Davis, Coleman). But it is clear from a final discussion between four expatriates (Dexter Gordon, Leo Wright, Kenny Drew and Ray Pitts) that all is not well in the American jazz scene.

Their comments make it clear that the trouble is not artistic, or racial, but simply economic: 'I think there are only some 800 out of 40,000 members of the union in New York who have steady jobs of some kind . . .' 'One week I walked up to the unemployment office to draw my check and walked into a great musician, and he'd been drawing checks longer than me.' 'Like this past summer, I was playing at Montmartre for three months straight, which doesn't sound like a really long time, but I've never been booked into a place in the States for three months, never in my entire career . . .' Coupled with this is reported a slackening in the morale of players: 'They are losing a lot of enthusiasm, and a lot of them are allowing themselves to fall into a state of mental apathy and melancholia.' The spirit of emulation, of competition, that produced the blowing sessions of the thirties and forties has gone. What's the reason for this depression in so outwardly-popular a music? The musicians thought the principal reason was the decline of the club: 'When a guy can sit all night looking at television or listening to his records, why should he go out and spend $5-$10 in a club?'

This point is taken up from the other end at the close of an article on Ornette Coleman and the future: 'Jazz is a music that has functioned, until the present, almost exclusively beneath the aegis of the popular entertainment business . . . When fundamental changes began to take place in the late fifties, it soon became clear that the new materials of jazz would have little relevance to the casual listener. And it is this casual listener who sets the economic standard of the entertainment industry.' So there you are: like all other arts, jazz is intellectualizing itself out of the market. For some, temporarily, Europe is a solution. Ellington remarks that when he first went to England in 1933, he found 'they had had a magazine more or less devoted to our kind of music for several years' (*The Melody Maker*, 1926? *Rhythm*, 1927?), and the feeling persists that, to be appreciated, the jazz man must come to Europe: 'They are not listening off the top. They are listening to the emotions, the modifications . . .' Europe is, in short, a more civilized place, more receptive to jazz because more receptive to all art.

But what future has jazz in America? According to *Down Beat*, as jazz becomes increasingly a composer's music, the club will have to be replaced by the concert hall. Gunther Schuller, André Hodeir, Larry Austin, George Russell and Charlie Mingus may be engaged in producing a new American music that, like Indian classical music, will reflect a whole civilization: the present confusion and uncertainty are inevitable signs of an age of transition. Not everyone, however, would agree. A later correspondent writes: 'Ornette Coleman, John Coltrane, Cecil Taylor, Eric Dolphy and their ilk are the reason that jazz clubs are closing down all over the country.' The implication is that if the new jazz men are not listened to in clubs, they won't be listened to in concert halls, either.

In the meantime, scratching about in the dust-bowl of late summer issues produces three nuggets. 'The Blues of Otis Spann' (Decca) provides twelve solidly-traditional tracks from Muddy Waters' pianist that quickly dispense with the Muddy Waters manner in favour of the subtler, more glancing approach of older piano-and-vocal men such as Memphis Slim and Champion Jack Dupree. Spann is something of an eclectic performer, and I would not guarantee to pick him out from half a dozen others, but lovers of good rolling piano blues and unaffected vocals should hear this.

'Movement' by the Joe Harriott Quintet (Columbia) is made up of 'free form' pieces mixed with fairly conventional smallband stuff. Personally I relegate free form along with action painting to a limbo of absurdity, but Harriott and the plump, smudgy tone of Shake Keane's flugelhorn make agreeable music that can be enjoyed in any mode. 'Pee Wee Russell Plays Pee Wee Russell' (World Record Club) presents eight sides from 1958 Stereocraft that have something of the swing and dash typical of the pre-Guiffre Russell. By the end of the session ('The Lady's In Love') things are moving nicely, thanks to sympathetic support from George Wettling and the great Walter Page, and the shades of the concert hall appear to recede a little.

9 September 1964

Way Down Yonder

It is a pity that no settled market exists for 'Jazz Odyssey, Vol. 1; The Sound of New Orleans, 1917–1947' (CBS) as it would for its literary equivalent. If all universities, colleges and public libraries were to buy it as they would buy a comparable edition of pre-Shakespearean drama or Border ballads, the publishers would receive the reward they deserve but which, I fear, they are unlikely to get from the general listener.

For its main interest is undeniably historical. Of these forty-eight tracks by native New Orleans performers, no less than thirty-nine are pre-1930, which means a fair helping of imperfect copies of acoustic recordings, and the need for a tolerant ear. Volume One (sixteen tracks cut in New York) is the most immediately enjoyable, being a magnificent lucky dip for the new collector including Armstrong's 'Dallas Blues' (a lyric marriage of trumpet and orchestra), a new master of Sissle's 'Dear Old Southland' with Bechet, and 'The Entertainer' from that uncharacteristic New York session Bunk Johnson held with musicians of that city.

Volumes Two and Three overlap to some extent with Decca's 'Jazz Sounds From The Twenties' last year. Chicago pressings of Oliver, Morton, Dodds, Blythe and Noone, and from New Orleans Fate Marable, Johnny De Droit, the NORK, and the entire recorded output of Sam Morgan's Jazz Band, eight sides from 1927 in which the young Jim Robinson can be heard easing along this legendary combination that seems to have had the loose free-wheeling quality associated with the George Lewis groups. There are also good sides by Manone and Sharkey Bonano (especially the latter's 'Panama'), but all in all it is the listener's degree of historical imagination that will decide whether or not he buys the complete set.

The appearance of Louis Armstrong in 1947 at the head of a small group was one of the most spectacular comebacks in jazz. If younger readers object that he had never been away, I can assure them that ten years previously his reputation had been virtually a minus quantity. 'The mighty have fallen so low', a reviewer wrote in about 1937, 'that it is no longer polite to mention it.'

Today the pendulum of taste has swung to the other extreme: we accept mugging, set solos, mediocre support, short-winded trumpet and long-winded vocals all with tears in our eyes. 'Satchmo At Symphony Hall' (Ace of Hearts, two discs) is a fair sample of his post-war output: recorded in Boston in 1947 with the original Bigard-Teagarden-Cary-Catlett group, it has a full complement of muddled ensembles, fluffed notes, comedy vocals and bass solos, but there is a splendid Catlett 'turn' on 'Steak Face' (one really sees what Whitney Balliett means about him) and some flashes of Louis's quality on 'Sunny Side' and 'Black and Blue', which incidentally shows him still singing the now avoided ('My only sin Is in my skin') lyrics. Great good humour prevails, which, as Gertrude Stein might say, is a comfort.

A celebrated British performer announced recently that jazz would now last only as long as Johnny Hodges and Buck Clayton, but the former's 'Cue For Saxophone' (Vogue) and 'Mess of Blues' (Verve) are less compelling than usual. The former 1959 collection under Strayhorn's name has Shorty Baker and Quentin Jackson, but only 'Rose Room' shows Hodges being more than mellifluously deft. On the second disc he is joined by Wild Bill Davis on organ, but the result is hardly more than nice. These little blues pieces sound as if he turns them out in his sleep, and the result certainly doesn't equal the team's earlier 'Blue Hodge'.

Another historic set, Gene Krupa's 'Drummin' Man' (CBS, two discs), recalls many memories of Roy Eldridge's reign with the band, and demonstrates how completely the swing seam had been worked out by 1945. 'The Great Isham Jones' (RCA Victor) is more fascinating. Jones, a society bandleader of modest origins (he once worked in a mine) was a prolific composer of songs such as his theme 'I'll See You in My Dreams', and these sixteen tracks from 1932–4 show his lean and individual vernacular as an arranger which from time to time (*vide* 'Dallas Blues') trembled on the edge of jazz. In 1936 Woody Herman took over the group as an openly-hot organization. The interest here, however, is the elegant and nostalgic sweep of ballroom sentiment.

Don't miss Charlie Byrd's 'Byrd at The Gate' (Riverside) on the grounds that Byrd discs have been numerous lately; this is a melodious and charming set with contributions from Clark Terry and that careless unbothered tenor Seldon Powell. If you are in London, look at Paul Oliver's wonderful exhibition, 'The Story of the Blues', in the main entrance lobby of the American Embassy before 30 October. All kinds of photographic and other archive material can be found here, probably for the only time in your life.*

7 October 1964

* Happily published in *The Story of the Blues* (Barrie/Cresset, 1969).

Shout It, Moan It

A distinguished friend of mine, who once played banjo with the Dixieland Rhythm Kings and now edits fifteenth-century English verse, recently gave me a copy of Bessie Smith's first record. As I watched the blue American Columbia label race round, and heard Bessie's deep voice fluctuate over Clarence Williams's elegant piano on that February day in 1923, I realized that this then unknown 'comedienne' might well have come over with the Third American Negro Blues Festival that was with us last month – might, that is, but for her mythopoeic death in 1936. Lonnie Johnson, five years her senior, was here last year.

But would she have succeeded? Impious question: yet there are two blues audiences today, and Bessie would have appealed to only one of them, the white antiquarians, for whom Horst Lippmann annually exhumes Sleepy John Estes, Sonny Boy Williamson and their ilk. Today's rhythm-and-blues following would find her insufferably tedious. Bessie specialized in slow, dragging numbers that she could proclaim in homiletic fashion, eliciting 'amens' from the audience; on the rare occasions when she picked up the tempo she was gay, boisterous, and quite free from the relentless qualities of 'beat'.

But for all this, popular music today – popular in the real sense of the word, that which makes the most money – is founded squarely on the blues, but the blues of the shouters, not the moaners. It is as if the sudden translation of jazz to the realms of chromatic art-music had called out its most rudimentary elements in compensation – the three-chord trick, as somebody called it, of the twelve-bar blues. From every quarter come whanging guitars, querulous harmonicas, slugging off-beats, and a pretty dreary business it is for the most part. The city Negroes, oscillating between the monotonous Chuck Berry, the lachrymose Ray Charles and the celestial fakery of Ruth Brown, have come perilously near creating a new kind of glossy commercialism out of what originally had been earthy and honest. And of course the whites have followed suit.

Among the most notable issues in this genre have been the Storyville 'Portraits in Blues'. 'Lonnie Johnson With Otis Spann' shows this veteran with the light, sad voice calling his slightly-sweet songs above Spann's clean, rolling piano: a breath from an earlier world. 'Sonny Boy Williamson' has been acclaimed as Sonny's best yet, and it certainly exemplifies his highly personal vocalizing and mouth-harp playing. His appearances here show how his tremendous rhythmic sense and natural authority dominate his audiences, and this counter-balances the breathless, bitty air of his dual performance. With 'Big Joe Williams' we are back in the familiar country of ringingly strummed guitar under half-smothered, half-shouted Southern aphorisms, with the occasional falsetto holler and the extra bars thrown in for good measure.

'The Best of Muddy Waters' (Pye) has a range of familiar favourites, from the classic country 'Louisiana Blues' to the arrogant citified 'Hoochie Coochie Man', with the emphasis on the first style. A companion disc, 'The Best of Little Walter' (Pye) brings to the foreground Muddy's harmonica player, who proves to have a plangent tone to complement his cheerful voice. Other solo albums are Jimmy Reed's 'Boss Man of the Blues' (Stateside) and 'The Best of Ruth Brown' (Atlantic), the former some run-of-the-mill pieces by the popular singer and harmonica player, the latter the usual Grand Guignol tear-jerkers that are such an odd sidelight on urban Negro taste.

On the instrumental side, Ace of Hearts presents fourteen tracks from 1936–7 by that individual group, The Harlem Hamfats. This is good casual music, dignified by the limited sonorities of Herb Morand's trumpet and Odell Rand's fuzzy clarinet: it doesn't quite reach the standard of the group's later sides with Rosetta Howard, but has a welcome skiffly insouciance.

From 1955 comes a reminder of some sombre elegance compiled by Miles, Mingus, Britt Woodman and others: 'Blue Moods' (Vogue) has quintet versions of 'Easy Living' and 'Alone Together' that are a credit to all concerned. So, in a different way, are the ten tracks on 'Chris Barber's Band Box' (Encore): this is the 1959 gang, still with Sunshine, and such springy items as 'Hot House Rag' and 'Swanee River' recall what a beautiful little band it was.

Four unrelated sessions from Britain in the thirties make up an odd Ace of Clubs disc by Ellington ('Hyde Park'), Carter, Jimmy Dorsey and Una Mae Carlisle. The last three use British musicians, who cope commendably with the Carter orchestrations of 'Scandal In A Flat' and 'You Understand', and in the persons of Bertie King and Dave Wilkins provide the jam for Una Mae's Wallerish songs at the piano. The Dorsey clarinet in 'St. Louis Blues' has a welcome union of sincerity and grace.

There is a strange resemblance between the excruciating facetiousness of 'Satchmo At Pasadena' (Ace of Hearts) and 'The Dizzy Gillespie Story Vol. 3' (Realm), though we didn't see it at the time. Dizzy's take-off of Louis on 'Confessin'', thorough though it is, merely underlines that one mugging trumpeter is very like another. *Plus ça change* and all that jazz.

4 November 1964

From the Festival Platforms

Any notion that Miles Davis is a studio performer overly dependent on balance, tape surgery and individual mikes is dispelled on 'Miles Davis in Europe' (CBS). Recorded at the Antibes Festival last year, these five tracks, like those at the Blackhawk some time ago, show Davis absolutely revelling in cut-and-thrust opportunism. Not that this makes me like him any more; the fact that he can spend seven or eight minutes playing 'Autumn Leaves' without my recognizing or liking the tune confirms my view of him as a master of rebarbative boredom. But the applause is there for all to hear; clearly for those who like Miles's particular brand of hard bop, this is an adventurous and energetic dish of it. George Coleman, Herbie Hancock and that young drumming sophisticate Tony Williams join the leader in standards such as 'Joshua', 'Walkin'' and 'Milestones'.

Another occasion recalled is 'Thelonious Monk: Big Band and Quartet' (CBS), this time at New York's Philharmonic Hall last December. Again I need the applause to convince me that Monk's screwball flippancy has any emotional significance, even when scored for nine pieces by Hall Overton; for seven-eighths of the time, neither band nor leader swings, and the insistent ripostes of Frank Dunlop's drums sound hollowly detached from the ensembles they might be expected to stimulate. The orchestrations are harmonically fruity, however, and Phil Woods and Charlie Rouse take most of the solo honours.

'Miles and Monk at Newport' (CBS) pleased me rather more. Anyone who saw Pee Wee Russell recently, manœuvring his clarinet like someone driving against one-way traffic, will cock an ear at two tracks from Newport 1963 he made with Monk's quartet. Personally I was disappointed. Monk's strong, decided chording makes Russell sound timid and bothered, like an old lady wavering between alternatives; in contrast Charlie Rouse on both 'Nutty' and 'Blue Monk' blows with a hard jauntiness. The other side, Miles at Newport in 1958 with Coltrane, Adderley and Bill Evans, is just as exciting, though rather a ragbag of manners – Coltrane playing sheets-of-sound, Adderley leaning towards Parker, and Miles going fast and fervent on 'Ah Leu Cha'. Jimmy Cobb's drums are over-recorded, but all the soloists are sufficiently powerful to surmount them.

'Stitt Plays Bird' (Atlantic) might have done better in a month that didn't include 'Charlie Parker – Historical Masterpieces' (MGM, three volumes). Supported by John Lewis, Jim Hall and Connie Kay, Sonny turns in nine Parker standards pleasantly enough, but his tone lacks that free cutting edge that gave Bird wings, and which is markedly in evidence on the MGM set of 1948–9 airshots originally issued on Jazz Cool. The title is somewhat inflationary: these are fairly run-of-the-mill Royal Roost jobs with Davis or Dorham, Al Haig and Roach, not at all well recorded, but eloquent of the brisk and oddly humorous musicianship that characterized Parker even when he was not – and on these sides he frequently is – rising above his fellows.

The latest Armstrong reissue is 'Town Hall Concert Plus' (RCA, Victor), offering 'Back O' Town Blues', 'Ain't Misbehavin'' and 'Rockin' Chair' as well as 'Snafu' and 'Long Long Journey' with a Leonard Feather all-star group. Some of the Town Hall trumpet is so good it must be Bobby Hackett. Another worthy trumpet record is 'The Happy Horns of Clark Terry' (HMV), on which Phil Woods and Benjamin Webster, as the label calls him, participate, backing Terry in a Duke-slanted set including 'Do Nothing', 'Impulsive' and 'Return to Swahili'. Or you can have a whole raft of Miles, Dizzy and Fats Navarro on 'Trumpet Giants' (Stateside), 1949–51 scene, with Sonny Rollins twice discernible in the middle distance.

The Vintage Jazz Music Society has produced another assortment of ragtime pieces made between 1902–14, and if you liked the bittersweet lingering taste of the first, then the orchestras such as Prince's Band and the Peerless Orchestra will delight you on 'When Grandma Was a Teenager'. Mike Bernard's piano is also featured. Almost as remote to us today are Al Cooper's Savoy Sultans ('Jumpin' At the Savoy' (Ace of Hearts), the modest nine-piece house band that scared visiting celebrities to death. Something, though not much, of their quality comes through, altoist Ruby

Williams and trumpeter Sam Massenberg decorating the Basiesque ensembles of 1938–41.

Basie himself continues to span the years with 'Basie Roars Again' (Encore), the much issued 'Two For The Blues',/'Sixteen Men Swinging' set from 1954 and now 'Easin' It' (Columbia) a garland of blues-based Frank Foster originals well worth the wearing. Mingus followers should try 'Mingus Plays Piano' (HMV), meditations at the keyboard of unexpected couthness and charm. And my fellow reviewers sent me back to 'The High And Mighty Hawk' (Vocalion) for a second listen to Hawkins's seventeen choruses on 'Bird of Prey Blues'. Verdict? Woeful negligence. It's great.

9 December 1964

1965

They'll None of Them be Missed

Making resolutions for oneself is easy enough: making them for other people is even easier. So here's to a ban in 1965 on that irritating habit of present-day jazz, the quotation.

You know what I mean: the soloist is giving out on some accepted vehicle or other, when all of a sudden he interpolates a phrase or two from something quite different – another tune, a nursery rhyme, a national anthem. Everyone laughs as if he has done something clever, but has he? What should we think of the actor who interpolated a line of 'Gunga Din' in 'To be or not to be'? That he was guilty of silly bad taste to get a cheap laugh, of course. And that is what I think of, for instance, J. J. Johnson when he quotes from 'The Surrey with the Fringe on Top' in the twelve-bar blues, or Charlie Parker playing 'Pop Goes the Weasel' in some context which till then had been a serious one.

And let's have no more bass solos. I don't mean the bass break, when for a few seconds a whole band such as Luis Russell's cuts out to expose Pops Foster's bronze-painted fiddle beating away like the engine of a liner. I mean these arid stretches of thirty-two or even sixty-four bars when some fervent bassist, aware that his instrument was 'set free' by the late Jimmy Blanton, demonstrates its half-audible limitations while the rest of the band rest their lips. Why? The bass is not an elephantine guitar; to make it sound like one is to use the foundation stone for the cornice. Bassists are great quoters, too. Both these nuisances break the emotional flow between player and audience, the first by its frivolity, the second by its tedium. The tension, the interest, dies away and has to be worked for all over again.

Neither of them is encountered in the handsome issues in Riverside's 'Classic Jazz Masters' series wherein antiquarian material is presented in depth. 'Honky Tonk Train' is a boogie-woogie anthology of sixteen pieces from 1927 to 1932 by such players as Cow Cow Davenport, Will Ezell, Henry Brown and Blind Leroy Garnett; it is nice to have the original Lux Lewis 'Honky-Tonk Train Blues' that sent John Hammond searching all over America for its portly originator, but I was most struck by Jabo Williams and his 'Jab Blues'. A companion album, 'Georgia Tom and Friends', dates from much the same period, and presents sixteen distinctly secular tracks by the now-veteran gospel singer Thomas A. Dorsey. These are songs about the Negro and his environment during the Depression, sometimes dismal, sometimes rowdy, at times ('Hip Shakin' Strut') taking the listener right into this vanished milieu.

Another notable retrospect is 'The Rare Bix' (Parlophone), 1927–9 sides with Trumbauer and the Broadway Bellhops. From Bix's Goldkette period, these are mostly pretty commercial efforts, with some dire girlish vocals from Irving Kaufman and Martin Hurt, but the Beiderbecke horn leaps in from time to time to good advantage, notably on 'Hour of Love' and 'Borneo'. The best side, 'Humpty Dumpty', was issued in Philips's 'Thesaurus of Classic Jazz' in 1961.

Among middle-period reissues is a startling Volume Six to 'The Charlie Parker Memorial Album' (Realm), a mysterious and somewhat muddy tape reputed to have been made at a party in about 1950 with Wardell Gray, a guitarist (Billy Bauer? Bill De Arango?) and other rhythm. The tenor, Gray or not, wails lustily. The same label has also put out 'Fats Navarro Memorial, Vol. 2', pick-up groups from 1947, and 'Joe Turner Sings The Blues, Vol. 1', material by this great Kansas shouter from 1945 to 1947, four tracks with Frankie Newton, Don Byas and Pete Johnson. And then there is 'The Best of the Dizzy Gillespie Big Bands' (Verve), a hearty clutch of pieces, 1956 and 1957, when Dizzy was holding together a splendid organization of both punch and sophistication and featuring, at times, Quincy Jones, Phil Woods, Ernie Wilkins, Benny Golson and Wynton Kelly. At times the saxes are as smooth as Goodman's.

16 January 1965

Ask Me Now

A contemporary, writing of the recent visit of tenorist Ben Webster to Ronnie Scott's amused me by ending his piece with an assurance to the effect that Webster played nothing that a layman would not understand. The implied patronage of this U-certificate had me hoping he would enjoy Webster's successor: Sonny Rollins, who nowadays can puzzle even the experts – Humphrey Lyttelton, for instance, who to the question 'Did you like it?' could only answer 'Ask me in 25 years.'

I should be prepared to answer now. Since his two-year retirement (1959–61), Rollins, as his present records demonstrate, has been thrashing around chaotically, producing sounds of such repellent harshness that the listener feels he is being pelted with slivers of granite. Not that he was ever noted for mellifluity: he came to fame in the middle fifties as the possessor of a sour sombre gutty tone very much at variance with the cool ellipsis favoured by the heirs of Lester Young. Listening to him was brutally stimulating, like a Finnish *sauna*. His solos were like iron, like untreated concrete, full of anger and *non serviam;* he pushed the limits of bop experiment further and further out to produce solos that reduced tunes to stuttering fragments which he then proceeded to reassemble. The effect was invigorating.

How far his present Ornette-derived manner, like his Mohican haircut and Zen allegiances, is part of a consciously-adopted *persona* is uncertain. His latest record, 'Now's The Time' (RCA) is something of a respite from them: true, his rubbery, staccato, totally unswingy intonation is well to the fore on the title tune and on 'Blue 'n' Boogie', but on the second side 'St. Thomas' (a kind of samba – Rollins is of Virgin Island ancestry), 'Round Midnight' and 'Afternoon in Paris' are handled forthrightly with moments of sonorous splendour. The eight tracks are variously peopled: Herbie Hancock makes three appearances on piano, and Thad Jones's cornet invades a version of Monk's 'Fifty-Second Street Theme'. Another first-ranking saxophone record, 'Classic Tenors' (Stateside), has eight Hawkins and four Young tracks dating from 1943. The four Hawk numbers with a trio including Eddie Heywood are immense – 'Sweet Lorraine' and 'The Man I Love' are probably as good as any pieces he has ever recorded. The other four and the Young tracks are made with small, rather noisy groups, led in each case by Bill Coleman, and feature barren riff-based tunes which are something of a handicap. However, the two stars and Coleman (and Dickie Wells, if you like him) keep the record safely in credit.

Earl Hines, now in his sixtieth year, can always be relied on for full-scale piano entertainment, and on 'Spontaneous Explorations'

(Stateside) he takes a blues or two with one original and six standards to exploit his still considerable talents. 'New Baby' has most of the Hines pyrotechnics – cross tempos, melodramatic runs and trills – and 'A Sunday Kind Of Love' a kind of elegant charm, but Hines's solos do not build, as, say, Garner's do, producing instead a rich and somewhat indigestible baroque. Harmonically, Hines is a child of the twenties, and I noticed an Ellington echo or two along with an actual quote from, of all things, 'Honky Tonk Train Blues', but his richly ornamental technique is a luxury in these, as in any, days.

With 'Louis Armstrong At the Crescendo' (Ace of Hearts, two volumes) we have perhaps the most typical of the post-war All-Star concerts. Here is 'Sleepy Time' to start and finish with, Bigard, Young and Kyle, and twenty-two tracks from the repertoire of the mid-fifties. How shocked we were that the All-Stars were not a conscious resurrection of the Hot Five! But if you can get over that, and the drum and bass solos, and the Velma Middleton numbers, there is plenty of consolation, notably a sequence of four tracks on side four, 'Someday', 'St. Louis', 'Back o' Town', and another blues that sustains a pretty good level of Louis's mixture of righteous jazz and vaudeville entertainment.

Followers of Charlie Mingus may not be as surprised as I was by the glimpse of his aquarelle beginnings afforded by 'Jazz Composers Workshop No. 1' (Realm) and 'The Charlie Mingus Quintet Plus Max Roach' (Debut). These date from 1954 and 1956 respectively: the first, with La Porta, Ted Macero and George Barrow, show Mingus's love of polyphony in embryo, mixed with ruminative, foreboding no-tempo efforts that seem to me quite negligible. But the wish to experiment, to be different, is there. The second disc, recorded in the Café Bohemia, New York, has Eddie Bert on trombone, Barrow again on tenor, and Mal Waldron. These are more uniform pieces, more audience-orientated, and wildly misnamed: a tidy little piece entitled 'Haitian Fight Song' sounds as combative as a tea-cosy, but otherwise pleasant enough.

The latest treasure from the Decca re-issue bag is 'Bennie Moten and his Orchestra: K. C. Jazz' (RCA), containing fourteen tracks dating from 1926–9. There is none of the conclusive individuality one might expect from this forerunner of the Basie band, but in 'Slow Motion' and 'Trouble In Mind' enviable relaxation is attained. A ripe record.

15 February 1965

Some Tenors

The news that Don Byas is playing salon tenor in a French Alps nightclub seemed a little sad to me, and a little ironic. So many American jazzmen have stayed in Europe because they feel their work is valued here for what it is. Yet for Byas the wheel has come full circle: 'They don't like me to play jazz.'

What they like him to play probably bears some resemblance to five quartet tracks dating from 1964 found on 'Don Byas on 52nd Street' (Realm). They are simple, fairly straight statements of ballad themes, and have great charm: I didn't expect 'London-Donnie', credited to L. Herman, to be 'The Londonderry Air', but there it is, given full and respectful value, and if it isn't jazz it's at least pleasant to listen to. The reverse has four tracks with that acolyte of bop, Little Bennie Harris, composer of 'Ornithology', who contrasts muted work in the early Miles manner on 'How High' with a more forthright open horn on 'Byas a Drink'. On both sides Byas plays the easy Hawkins-derived tenor for which he is famous, but lighter and less turgid than Hawk is on occasion.

Hawkins himself of the same period – the middle forties – can be head on 'Swing!' (Fontana) in the rattling good company of, variously, Teddy Wilson, Eldridge, Clayton, Shavers, Byas, Tab Smith, Carney and some stalwart rhythm men. Fourteen tracks – the disc runs to over fifty minutes – offer a selection of at first unpromising standards such as 'Just One Of Those Things' and 'Three Little Words', but there are numerous bustling performances dominated by Hawkins' swooping tenor and wired together by the laconic Wilson. All the trumpets are good – Shavers especially so – and 'Battle of the Saxes' has Byas, Smith, Carney and finally Hawkins trumping each other's aces on the theme of 'China Boy'. I don't want to overpraise this record, but it does show why these men have their reputations.

It spoilt me somewhat for 'The Modern World of Stan Getz' (Columbia), for, impeccable and driving as it is, Stan's Lester Young sound seems just a little mechanical beside Byas and Hawkins. These tracks date from 1950–1 and were made with different American and Swedish rhythm sections, one of them featuring Jim Raney; although the vehicles are ballads, one is left with an impression of unremitting forcefulness. A good record in any other month.

That notable label Blue Note had a Silver Jubilee recently – 1939 to 1964 – and to commemorate the fact have put out an 'Anniversary Album' made up of tracks from some of their more successful modern sessions between 1947 and 1953 – Miles's 'Tempus Fugit', Monk's 'Round Midnight', Clifford's 'Easy Living', Bud Powell's 'Night In Tunisia', and some baroque percussion work by Art Blakey and Chano Pozo. This is a worthy sampler for anyone dabbling on the edges of modernism, and a monument to the company's dedicated enterprise, but I hope they won't forget their early triumphs with classics like Albert Ammons' 'Boogie Woogie Stomp' and Bechet's 'Blue Horizon'. A companion disc would be appropriate – featuring, may I suggest, that magnificent Kaminsky-Cless-Hodes 'Yellow Dog' from 1944. The latest Blue Note offering is Freddie Hubbard's 'Breaking Point', in which the title-piece yokes atonality with a jolly calypso. Hubbard, altoist James Spaulding and two-fisted pianist Ronnie Matthews struggle to make something of it, but they are sunk by a long bass solo and the track never coheres. 'Blue Frenzy' is a twenty-four-bar blues waltz, and 'D Minor Mint' beats up a fair storm, but on the whole the picture on the sleeve is aptly chosen: this music has the fragmentary lacerating quality of broken glass. Its pleasanter moments are when Hubbard's austere command inclines in the direction of more melodious themes, such as 'Mirrors'.

Howlin' Wolf's 'Smoke Stack Lightnin'' is an amazing performance, a piece of pure jazz Gothic, creating with no more properties than an echo chamber and his own remarkable voice an impression of Coleridge's demon lover wailing for his woman. 'Moanin' in the Moonlight' (Chess) contains this track and eleven others, none its equal but all having some of its quality. This is one of a first batch of five Chess records to be distributed by Pye, and suffers from tone distortion sometimes found on this label. British rhythm and blues can be heard on 'Good Mornin' Blues' (Columbia) by the Chris Barber Band with Ottilie Patterson, while 'American Folk Blues 1964' (Fontana) shows this year's team in action in Hamburg – Hopkins, Williamson, Estes, Howlin' Wolf, the late unfortunate John Henry Barbee and the egregious Sugar Pie Desanto. Followers of Charlie Byrd will find 'In!' (Fontana) delightful, tracks taken from some Offbeat discs in the late fifties where his acoustic Spanish guitar deals with some of his own pieces such as 'Lay The Lily Low'. And the Beatles' 'The Things We Said Today' is only one reason for hearing 'Woody Herman's Recorded Live' (Philips), relaxed, exuberant, ripely scored. Warning: vocals are by Joe 'Bebop' Carroll.

17 March 1965

The Parker Legend

The tenth anniversary of the death of Charlie Parker cannot but provoke a look, however brief, at what in another context would be called the state of Parker studies. One's suspicions are neatly summarized by a letter in a recent *Melody Maker* protesting against the habitual rave accorded to every Parker issue: 'I cannot believe that he was in such tremendous form on every single record date.' Nor is there any indication in the Charlie Parker Memorial Issue of *Down Beat* that the chaotic adulation of *Bird: the Legend of Charlie Parker*, edited by Robert Reisner (MacGibbon and Kee, 1962), has begun to settle into a more considered pattern.

The popular view is still that Parker was a genius who from 1945 to 1954 poured out an undifferentiated sequence of brilliant recordings to which we can only go down on our knees. This may be so. Methodical study of Parker's output is rendered difficult by the confused discographical situation obtaining once the Savoy Memorial Album finishes in 1948. But it would be useful to have this Birdolatry corrected occasionally by normal critical standards – to know whether Parker got better, or changed, and, if so, in what direction. I have never seen any mention of his clichés, which were as numerous and obtrusive as Spanier's. And again, how true is it that his encounters with Sidney Bechet in Paris in 1949 and 1950 equipped him with a Bechet bag, on which he drew increasingly?

Certainly a track like 'I Remember You' from 'The Pick of Parker' (Verve) suggests that in his later, or Granz, period Parker had come to realize that plainly stated themes and fully valued notes could be as artistically satisfying as the ellipses of bop. On this, and on its session-mates 'Confirmation' and 'Now's The Time', he uses a warm mellow tone instantly reminiscent of Bechet and Bechet's other pupil Johnny Hodges, and his improvisation has dispensed with frenzy while retaining urgency.

Again, we have now surely heard enough of Thelonious Monk to evaluate his limited repertoire when it appears once more on 'Thelonious Monk in Europe, Vol. 2' (Riverside). Here, and elsewhere, it can be said that every Monk record is over once Rouse and the leader have had their say, for who can sustain interest in Ore's stumping bass or Dunlop's flutter-bump drumming, or the last chorus which is a mere matter of form? We should be able to admit, too, that however Monk's music can be described musically, emotionally it is flippant, 'nutty', surprising and never far from humorous. Now this is all right, but these qualities carry no more weight in jazz than in any other art, and despite his originality Monk remains a funny-hat man to whom it would be idle to ascribe profundity.

In fact this is a good month for secondary examples of primary figures: another bop foundation member rebreaks surface with 'The Return of Bud Powell' (Columbia), a record made since his reappearance on the New York scene last autumn. One's instinctive hope that Bud is his own man again is only partly gratified; he goes at his numbers ('I Remember Clifford', 'Just One Of Those Things', 'Green Dolphin Street') with energy and dash but repeatedly a hinted clumsiness makes him sound not quite on top of his material. J. C. Moses' drumming is heavy and unsynchronized.

'Charlie Mingus: To-night At Noon' (Atlantic) goes back to 1961 and 1957, featuring Roland Kirk on 'Peggy's Blue Skylight', 'Invisible Lady' and 'Old Blues'. John Coltrane's 'Black Pearls' (Stateside) also dates from 1957 when he was playing with Miles Davis, along with Red Garland and Paul Chambers; here Garland and Donald Byrd contribute smart, collected solos on the title-piece, 'Lover Come Back', and a whole-sider, 'Sweet Sapphire Blues', but Coltrane's experiments have not worn well. 'Getz Au Go Go' (Verve) recalls an evening in Greenwich Village last summer when Stan was blowing helpfully behind the flat, disconsolate vocals of Astrud Gilberto (Joao's wife) and doing a solo or two into the bargain. This is a wistful, enchanting chain of numbers, not unlike some other Getz discs, but quite unlike anyone else.

The new West Coast alto Ernie Anderza teams with Jackie Wilson on 'Outa Sight' (Fontana) to produce an agreeable medley of pace numbers and ballads ('What's New?', 'All the Things You Are'). Anderza's steep intervals and protracted falsetto don't detract from his fundamentally warm and friendly approach, and Wilson pounds harpsichord as well as piano to good advantage. One can fault Anderza for thinness of tone, but not much else. A valuable blues reissue, 'Big Bill and Sonny Boy' (RCA), presents fourteen Chicago

Bluebird recordings from the middle thirties when these artists were still entertaining coloured audiences. Broonzy is passionate ('Good Jelly') and jocular ('Keep Your Hands Off'), Sonny Boy Williamson (the original who died in 1948) a forceful singer and harmonica player. Besides being good jazz this music is repeatedly valid social comment.

7 April 1965

Fast and High

I suppose one of the major differences between listening to jazz today and twenty-five years ago is the changed attitude to technique. Today playing very fast, or (for a horn man) very high, is more or less taken for granted as part of the equipment of a good player, like having an instrument at all. Twenty-five years ago it was regarded as bad taste. When Armstrong claimed to have hit 280 high C's followed by a high F his admirers shuddered as they did when Harry James played 'Flight of the Bumble Bee'; Muggsy Spanier's retort to the club owner who wanted him to 'play some high notes' ('Aw, go get a piccolo player') was treasured as an epiphany of integrity. For a player to have a better-than-average technique, like Goodman or Tatum, was thought to be dangerous (it might tempt him to 'exhibitionism') or at best a little irrelevant, like having been to a good school. All the emphasis was on feeling, emotional communication, sincerity.

In an age when the high C sounds like the middle register this may seem perverse, yet it came to my mind when listening to 'Bud Powell: The Vintage Years' (Verve). These sixteen solos, chosen from sessions in 1949, 1950 and 1951, undoubtedly make up the most thrilling piano record for several years, yet at times one is almost impelled to snatch the piano away from him, so to speak, as Ben Webster snatched the tenor from Charlie Parker ('it ain't *supposed* to sound that fast!'). On 'Tea For Two' (Powell is reputed to have made ten masters of this) the unremittingly breakneck approach provokes not enjoyment but memories of the later Bud who was not in control of himself and could only be stopped by the bass player flashing a light in his eyes. The same is true of 'Just One Of Those Things', made a few days before a nervous breakdown. But there are many calmer numbers ('Celia', 'I'll Keep Loving You') where Bud's luxuriant poise and control are sheerly delightful, and one realizes that within this bop pioneer is a romantic sensibility that just enjoys pretty chords. I cannot agree with Berendt when he says that Powell followed the 'horn' rather than the 'pianistic' tradition of piano playing. Both seem to me to be adequately represented. This is a great record, and an ironic comment on last month's 'The Return of Bud Powell' (Columbia). *The* Bud, alas, will never return.

Other notable piano records recently issued include Pete Johnson on Joe Turner's 'Jumpin' The Blues' (Fontana), originally made for Arhoolie in 1948. Of course this is principally blues shouting in the familiar Kansas City style and very good it is, too, but Johnson is always driving the ensembles and has two solo tracks ('Rocket Boogie 88' 1 and 2) on which, as the sleeve says, the good times roll. Then there are Bill Evans and Oscar Peterson, both recent visitors to these shores, but both sounding very lightweight beside Bud and Pete. Recently Cecil Taylor, a more adventurous but less celebrated pianist, took Evans to task for being 'so uninteresting, so predictable and so lacking in vitality'. I must say that 'Sunday At the Village Vanguard' (Riverside) seemed to me precious rather than valuable, though these six tracks from 1961 are excellent examples of Evans-La Faro *rapport*. Peterson's 'We Get Requests' (Verve) is also on the delicate side, ballads of the 'Quiet Nights' and 'The Days of Wine and Roses' type, including a chord-progression curiosity called 'You Sure Look Good To Me', but the fur flies on 'Goodbye JD' at the close of the second side. Ray Brown and Ed Thigpen make their usual masterly contributions to this highly professional performance.

The Douanier Rousseau of jazz is here again on 'Monk' (CBS) and in better form than on his concert dates. True, I don't know how he gets away with a solo like 'I Love You', which sounds like your sister trying over sheet music from Woolworth's, but 'Teo' is a dark, close-knit cooker with Larry Gales's bass to the fore, and there is plenty of spidery charm on 'Pannonica' and 'Liza' to make this a worthwhile buy.

After Moscow, Tokyo, and the Benny Goodman Quartet's 'Made In Japan' (Capitol) offers ten-and-a-bit tracks of the customary Goodman elegance with some better-than-average piano from Dick Shreve, who is eloquent (no other word) on 'Like Someone In Love' and 'Close Your Eyes'. Goodman has played all this ten thousand times before, but it's still worth recommending to the new generation, who no doubt think he came up the river from New Orleans on a steamboat.

New issues featuring two of my favourite instrumentalists are 'Blue Rabbit' (Verve) with Johnny Hodges and Wild Bill Davis, and Charlie Byrd's 'Guitar Showcase' (Riverside). Rabbit sounds very comfortable except in a storming 'Things Ain't', while Byrd takes his material from Tin Pan Alley for once. And I can't forbear to mention the only poetry-and-jazz track I have ever enjoyed: Christina Rossetti's 'When I am Dead, My Dearest', sung by Belle Gonzalez on 'Poets Set In Jazz' (Jupiter). Eddie Blair's trumpet is suitably rain-wet and Victorian.

5 May 1965

Sidney Bechet from New Orleans

Positive as I am that Sidney Bechet is one of the half-dozen leading figures in jazz, I sometimes hesitate when asked to name a record by him that will bring any unbeliever round to my way of thinking. For his particular power resides, after all, in generalities – the majestic *cantabile sostenuto*, the authoritative vitality – and these exist despite innumerable individual records that reveal gobbling irrelevancy, mannered quotes from minor classics, sticky balladry, instant Dixieland, frightful travelling companions. Pressed, I suppose I should nominate 'Nobody Knows The Way I Feel This Morning' (1940), 'Blue Horizon' (1944), or 'Maple Leaf Rag' (1932). But I can think of many more that never rise above flamboyant triviality.

At least my third choice is on 'Bechet of New Orleans' (RCA Victor), sixteen tracks from the Victor catalogue of 1938–40, with two 1932 Feetwarmers sides thrown in, but otherwise it is a mixed bag. 'Shake It and Break It' has some splendid high-pressure Bechet, and there is a beautifully-poised solo amid the genial polyphony of Jelly Roll's 'I Thought I Heard Buddy Bolden Say'; among the sidemen, the young Shavers plays some strong open horn on 'Texas Moaner', while Earl Hines erupts imperially on 'Save It Pretty Mama'. These apart, however, the collection is hardly more than average – Bechet's average, of course, which is still worth the money.

But it might well be remembered that the Mezzrow-Bechet King Jazz saga of 1945 and 1947 is still available on the Danish label Storyville. These five discs are not so much records as one man's –

Mezzrow's – philosophy of life, expounded haltingly by himself in link-tracks, and flowingly by Bechet, Lips Page, Sammy Price, Catlett, Foster and several others in a luxuriance of blues numbers, but it is also a monument to Sidney Bechet, a long conspectus of his mature talent. These unique sessions, made for love rather than money, must always have a powerful claim on the attention of any Bechet admirer.

Another New Orleans clarinettist, Jimmy Noone, is revived on 'Jazz at the Apex Club' (Ace of Hearts), a dozen sides from 1928–30 when Noone was at the height of his reputation. Noone is in the smoother Creole tradition of Bigard and Edmond Hall, and his combination with the alto of Joe Poston (reminiscent indeed of Mezzrow and Bechet) is somewhat eccentric, but in five tracks with Earl Hines this little group achieves explosive drive and spirit – 'Every Evening', 'My Monday Date' and 'Apex Blues' being classic examples. At times it is Earl himself who seems to dominate the proceedings, since in 1928 he was playing fresh, brilliant piano that no one could equal.

In the summer of 1960 the British blues scholar Paul Oliver toured the south and west of the United States persuading the blues singers he found to talk and sing to his tape-recorder. From this material he made up *Conversation with the Blues* (Cassell), a rich source-book of how blues men think and talk and live, but he has also made a vivid anthology with the same title for Decca, featuring Otis Spann, Roosevelt Sykes, Whistling Alex Moore, Mance Lipscomb and many others. It is a strange, exciting record, on which fumbling, incoherent speech contrasts sharply with the precise vivacity of the music, and is fully the equal of earlier field recordings by Alan Lomax and others.

Ten piano solos from Monk on 'Thelonious Alone in San Francisco' (Riverside) are about six years old, and illustrate how little his style has changed despite his sudden international fame. Versions of 'Pannonica', 'Blue Monk', and 'Ruby, My Dear' team with ballads, such as 'Remember' and 'There's Danger In Your Eyes, Chèrie' (an oddity if there ever was one), and lovers of his lumpy, off-beat piano will find plenty to enjoy. I should like it better if he made me tap my foot sometimes, but still.

It sounds as if Cannonball Adderley has rid himself of the Bird label only to find Benny Carter's mantle hovering over his shoulders. On 'Know What I Mean?' (Riverside) he has lost a lot of his boisterousness, but this may be the result of collaboration with Bill Evans, who dominates from the piano and composed 'Waltz For Debby' and the title-piece. MJQ-ites Percy Heath and Connie Kay keep the atmosphere intact, and altogether this is very pleasant music, but old Cannonball fans have been warned.

And one can say much of what I said earlier of Bechet about Mahalia Jackson. No one would contest her thrilling power of voice, either in those static preliminary cadenzas or in the steady rocking reiteration of her simple gospel pieces, but all too often she was fouled up with celestial choirs, electric amplification, sickly choice of material. On 'Mahalia' (Columbia) there are some fine tracks dating from the late forties and early fifties such as 'I'm Glad Salvation is Free' and 'Move On Up', on which she is accompanied by piano and organ only. 'No Matter How You Pray' (also Columbia) is rather more draped and opalescent – the equivalent, shall we say, of Bechet in France.

9 June 1965

The Tenor Player With 50 Legs

'I wish someone could tell me what's so great about Coltrane,' said Jimmy Rushing plaintively in an interview with the Toronto *Globe and Mail* recently. 'I don't think he can play his instrument.' This accords very well with my own opinion that Coltrane sounds like nothing so much as a club bore who has been metamorphosed by a fellow-member of magical powers into a pair of bagpipes. This month, however, sees the issue of two Coltrane discs, each of which was greeted with five stars in America: 'My Favourite Things' (Atlantic) and 'A Love Supreme' (HMV). As about three years separates them (1961–4) it is tempting to look for development.

The earlier collection offers the title-piece, a waltz tune with strong Middle East affiliations, 'Every Time We Say Goodbye', 'Summertime' and 'But Not For Me'; the latter is a kind of religious suite of four movements with titles such as 'Acknowledgment' and 'Resolution'. In all of them similar features recur. There is, first, the Coltrane tone, whether on tenor or soprano sax – a thin, keening noise, sometimes sour as an oboe, at times expiring in an upper-register squeak, possessed continually by an almost Scandinavian unloveliness. Then there is the way themes are flagellated rather than played: in accomplishing the not inconsiderable feat of making an ugly record of 'Summertime', Coltrane shreds each chord to nothingness at breakneck speed, and the same ferocity recurs in the section 'Pursuance' in the later record.

It is of course absurd to suggest he can't play his instrument: the rapidity of his fingering alone dispels that notion. It would be juster to question whether he knows what to do with it now that he can play it. His solos seem to me to bear the same relation to proper jazz solos as those drawings of running dogs, showing their legs in all positions so that they appear to have about fifty of them, have to real drawings. Once, they are amusing and even instructive. But the whole point of drawing is choosing the right line, not drawing fifty alternatives. Again, Coltrane's choice and treatment of themes is hypnotic, repetitive, monotonous: he will rock backwards and forwards between two chords for five minutes, or pull a tune to pieces like someone subtracting petals from a flower. Apart from the periodic lashing of himself into a frenzy, it is hard to attach any particular emotional purpose to his work.

As for development, there is a lot of pretentious guff on the sleeve of 'A Love Supreme', a signed statement by Coltrane that this album is 'an attempt to say "THANK YOU, GOD" through our work'. Let us hope this is the whim of the A. & R. man, for otherwise it would point to a degree of self-seriousness most inimical to an artist. The nicest part of both these records is the ballads and the fourth section 'Psalm' of the later collection; the latter has something of the manner, if not the spirit, of the delightful 'Alabama' from 'Coltrane Live At Birdland'. In such pieces Coltrane seems to display an increasing awareness of how to dispose his music for aesthetic or emotional effect – the only worthwhile kind of development.

'Louis, like the Mississippi,' said Murray Kempton, 'pure like its source, flecked and chocked with jetsam like its middle, broad and triumphant like its end.' 'Louis Armstrong In The '30s/In The '40s' (RCA Victor) is mostly the flecked and chocked sort, for my money: six 1933 tracks include 'World On A String', 'St. Louis Blues' and 'Swing You Cats', sometimes fine, but often just playing-off of 'amazing' trumpet against anonymous orchestra. The forties ('Do You Know What It Means', 'Jack-Armstrong Blues', 'It Takes Time') show a clouded, thinner tone, but a release from exhibitionism and a consequent enrichment of emotional content. Here we approach the elder Louis who claimed that 'a straight lead is better than any solo'.

Paul Desmond and Jim Hall have put out a charming record. 'Bossa Antigua' (RCA Victor) – the title is a joke ('old thing'), the sleeve-note by Desmond another ('John P. Marquand of the alto'), and, really, isn't the whole thing a send-up of Getz and his guitarists? But it is delicious listening all the same, which is more than can be said of 'Bob Brookmeyer and Friends' (CBS); lovers of the leader's chamber-trombone, Getz, Hancock and Gary Burton, may find extenuating circumstances in these rather formal little pieces.

I was keenly interested to receive 'Lucky Roberts and Willie "The Lion" Smith Piano Solos' (Vogue), specimens of Harlem 'stride' piano by two of its old masters. Knowing that Roberts, the Lion, James P. Johnson, Duke Ellington and Fats Waller were all keyboard mates makes it easy to see this brand of piano as distinctive – not hot, not earthy, not swinging; for the most part, I should say, the descendant of the album of 'pieces' on the upright piano in the parlour in better-class Negro homes. This is an extremely valuable historical issue. Contemporary have put out again 'Sonny Rollins Way Out West', the 1957 collection by a plainer, more direct Rollins than today, featuring such numbers as 'Wagon Wheels'. Finally, there is some lovely Braff (at present in this country) in 'Midnight Concert in Paris' (Philips), pick-up stuff with Pee Wee and Vic Dickenson. The same day (15 April, 1961) Algeria revolted, and not a ticket was sold. But you can hear it now.

12 July 1965

The Dixieland Bag

A title such as 'The Best of Dixieland' (RCA Victor) sends a shudder down the spine. It is distressing that an adjective of the most impeccable lineage (the very first jazz record, included here, was 'Livery Stable Blues' in 1917 by the Original Dixieland Jazz Band) should now denote no more than a dreary repertoire of worn-out trudging numbers verging at times on juvenile funny-hat comedy. But there it is. The word is practically synonymous with 'traditional' –and bad traditional at that.

It is too late in the day to disentangle the various strands that make up the modern Dixieland image. It ought to be possible to say that Dixieland is a white tradition, for instance, and that Armstrong, Allen and Bunk Johnson are therefore out of place on this record, but from whom did that pioneer Dixieland revivalist, Muggsy Spanier, derive, if not from Oliver and Armstrong? And where has the corny 'Saints' routine come from, if not from the parallel but quite different New Orleans revival, that began with the white Lu Watters band and is still going strong in that haunt of New Orleans Negro veterans, Preservation Hall? And who can trace the slow degeneration of Condon's lingua franca of the thirties, appropriate to coloured artists such as Waller, James P. Johnson, Bechet and Hot Lips Page, to the musical somnambulism his name conjures in the sixties?

With all this in mind, it is not surprising that 'The Best of Dixieland' is a mixed bag. The best tracks are the most familiar ones – the ODJB, Muggsy's 'Sister Kate' (as fresh as the day in 1939 it was made), the Armstrong-Teagarden 'Rockin' Chair', Bunk's 'Saints'. Two carnivals of polyphony, 'High Society' and 'Milenberg Joys', were made by white New Orleans men in 1956, with solos by Pecora, Fountain, Larry Shields and Tony Almerico, and the rest is Turk Murphy, Scobey, The Dukes. For all the forebodings it arouses, this is ultimately a heart-warming record, and can be recommended to beginners for that reason.

At the other end of the scale, but equally commendable, is 'Shades of Blue' (Columbia) by the Don Rendell-Ian Carr ensemble. This British group set out to play the blues 'in form or feeling', not scrupling to utilize fancy time signatures, bossa nova, and flirtations with free form, and while they didn't come within a mile of it for my money, they have certainly produced crisp, professional and swinging music. Rendell is the best British tenor to my mind, and Carr's flugelhorn is velvetly practised. The title-piece 'Shades Of Blue', is by Neil Ardley, of New Jazz Orchestra fame, and is a really very pretty minor-key blues. Colin Purbrook's piano also scores.

One of the most celebrated sessions supervised by Norman Granz was the Art Tatum-Ben Webster Quartet in 1956, seven ballads in which the poised, allusive Webster tenor brushed-in its easy lines against Tatum's sweeping meticulous piano. These great men are not without their mannerisms – I should like to write an essay on 'The Downward Run in Ellington, Wilson, Tatum and Thelonius Monk' – and the atmosphere at times suggests 'Music For Sliding Your Arm Along The Back Of The Sofa To', but 'All The Things You Are', 'Where Or When' and 'Have You Met Miss Jones' are plain delight, a perfect antidote to a surfeit of Dolphy, Coleman or Sonny

Rollins. Another Granz record is 'Highlights From Jazz At The Philharmonic' (Verve), containing some extremely interesting tracks and solos from 1946–53. 'JATP Blues' has Parker, Young, Hawkins, Clayton and Willie Smith: 'I Can't Get Started' features one of Lester's most beautiful recorded solos; 'Tenderly' is contributed with great panache by Peterson. Drawbacks are Al Killian ('in the manner for which he was paid' as the sleeve says icily), and Lester's awful drummer brother Lee Young. Surprise is Willie Smith on alto on four of the six tracks, doing all but cut Parker himself. A worthy but somewhat daunting array of Young is offered in 'The Great Lester Young' (two volumes Liberty), twenty-four tracks made for Aladdin during 1945–7. They feature small groups rich in talent, but it is Young who dominates, shaping utterly individual solos on 'Funny That Way', 'Foolish Things' and 'Driving Me Crazy'. Lionel Hampton's concert at Amsterdam in 1954 appears again on 'Live!' (Fontana), offering subtle, sensitive versions of 'Star Dust' and 'Lover Man' with hardly any flagwavers, while the second volume of 'King Oliver's Dixie Syncopaters' (Ace of Hearts) covers 1926–8 and 'Sugar Foot Stomp', 'Black Snake Blues', and others. Sometimes I wonder if Oliver was all he was cracked up to be.

Note for my Coltrane correspondents: the master played forty-seven minutes of 'A Love Supreme' at the Antibes International Jazz Festival recently and was rewarded by a packed audience with lukewarm applause and a few boos. A time when fifty million French men weren't wrong. Wild Bill Davison is planning to settle here in the autumn.

9 August 1965

The Idols of the Twenties

Readers of John O'Hara's *Appointment in Samarra** will remember the curious scene near the end where the hero, Julian English, drinks an enormous highball from a flower-vase and plays his favourite jazz records. After a while he goes out to the garage and kills himself. The interesting thing is that the records he plays are not by Armstrong, Ellington or even the Chicago Rhythm Kings, but Whiteman's 'Stairway To Paradise' and Goldkette's 'Sunny Dispos-

* This novel was published in 1935, and set in 1930.

ish'. Enough to make anyone seek oblivion, you may say, and I thought at one time that O'Hara (who certainly knew his jazz – witness *Butterfield 8*) was being satiric.

The lush pictorial album accompanying 'The Original Sound of the Twenties' (CBS, three discs) has a yearning essay by Roger Whitaker that makes me not so sure. The twenties, and particularly the music of the twenties – 'loud, clear, jolly, sentimental, brash, bubbly, lifegiving and altogether and forever unforgettable' – are plainly full of emotional punch for their contemporaries. Perhaps Julian English's swan song was meant seriously. The three discs, which are available separately, are divided into Whiteman/other bands, pianists/male vocalists, and female vocalists. From the jazz point of view the first is the best – Whiteman is pretty awful, but the reverse has Ellington's 'Diga Diga Do', Armstrong's splendid 'St. Louis', and the Dorsey Brothers 'My Kinda Love', not to mention Cass Hagan's 'Varsity Drag' which sounds straight out of 'The Boy Friend' – but the appeal of the other tracks will depend on the listener's age and taste. The girl singers – Sophie Tucker and Kate Smith in particular – are forthright rather than seductive, and the men – Cliff Edwards, Buddy Rogers, Rudy Vallee – are of the almost forgotten pre-crooning world and sound incredibly cheerful and decent in consequence. And there are so many surprises: who would expect Gershwin to rattle out such an insensitive version of 'Someone To Watch Over Me', or for the whole thing to be rounded off by Bessie Smith proclaiming 'I've Got What It Takes (But It Breaks My Heart To Give It Away)'? One star: add another for every year of age after, well, 59.

But popular music is odd. To compare this set with the Beatles' 'Help!' (Parlophone) demonstrates how its appeal has shifted from the Edwardian ballad and comic-song tradition overlaid with syncopation to the genuine blues overlaid with the hybrid and plangent romanticism that is the Lennon-McCartney hallmark. Will this Original Sound Of The Sixties be the standard of the eighties? I hope so. All the same, nothing on 'Help!' equals the slick inventive patter of the Rhythm Boys (Barris, Crosby, Rinker) on Whiteman's 'Louise'.

Encouragement should be given to the RCA Victor Race series, that begins with three EPs drawn from the Victor-Bluebird catalogue by Ishman Bracey (1928), Leroy Carr (1935) and Walter Davis (1938). Bracey is a new name to me, but shows himself a fine country blues man, especially on 'Trouble Hearted Blues'. Langston Hughes' gospel version of the Christmas story 'Black Nativity' (Fontana), is, while admittedly unseasonable, full of moving work by the wonderful Marian Anderson, Alex Bradford, Madeleine Bell and the rest of the cast. The rocking side of gospel is always exciting; it is the 'Sweet Little Jesus Boy' type of number that tends to cloy.

Coleman Hawkins, Dickie Wells and Garnet Clark would no doubt have been surprised to learn that the sides they recorded in the thirties would eventually be reissued as 'Django and His American Friends, Vol. I' (HMV). There were many good coloured musicians in Paris in those years, notably Hawkins (whom Jack Hylton had brought over to co-star with Armstrong, who ducked out), Bill Coleman and Benny Carter, and it is not till the classic three-trumpet sides under Wells ('Bugle Call Rag' and so on) that Django gets his head. This is odd, for Django already had a great reputation in Paris at the time, and the 1935 Quintet records were spreading it further. However, the record is well worth having if only for Clark's Hines-like piano and the elegant Coleman. An outstanding blues issue is 'Victoria Spivey' (Xtra), being the Folkway's 1962 session. Victoria Spivey has a strong, rather sardonic voice, and accompanies herself with an utter lack of ornament on the ukelele while she delivers songs that have a convincing smack of reality about them, sometimes, as on 'Six Foot Daddy', telling a story. On five tracks she transfers to piano. Like all great blues singers, she has her own individual 'tunes' within the harmonic framework, and these, along with her swinging, unforced approach, make this a memorable disc.

On 'Ellington 66' (Reprise) the Duke again demonstrates his ability to produce custom-built silk purses. Perhaps the numbers are a little syrupy, but as long as the orchestral thunder opens intermittently to reveal the supreme soloists, Hodges on 'Red Roses', Cootie on 'Charade' who are we to grumble? This is one of the great orchestras. In deference, perhaps, to the title two Beatles numbers are included.

15 September 1965

How Billie Scores

A perennial jazz controversy is whether Billie Holiday's talent declined. The sleeve of 'The Incomparable Billie Holiday' (Verve), unquestionably the best record to come my way recently, says this notion is a fallacy, whistling up Miles Davis to support the view that what she lost in technical control she gained in emotional depth. Certainly the work represented here – eight sides from a 1946 JATP with an anonymous supporting polyphony that may have included Clayton, Young and Hawkins; four pieces from the Webster-Edison session of 1957, and four other excellent tracks from the early fifties – shows that on her day Billie was always liable to greatness. Some nights, according to Carmen McRae, she sounded as if she were through. 'Then the next night she sings her ass off, pardon my expression.' But I have always wondered whether Billie's much-vaunted technique of 'using her voice like a horn' produced her best work. To me she is best when singing a tune because she likes it and words because she believes them, while a few good sidemen take care of the improvising in the background. When in 'The Man I Love' on the first side she sings 'We'll build a little home', the shiver the listener feels is produced not by any significant-form attitude that regards the tune and lyrics as raw material to be improved but by an absolutely straight treatment that convinces him that Billie means simply that when she meets the man she loves they will be happy ever after. She could always get this effect, just as she could always seem strained when searching for some counter-melody ('I'll Get By' in 1937, for instance) or melodramatic when torching for night-club audiences. Her voice deteriorated: her faults and virtues changed less through her career than is popularly supposed.

Johnny Hodges is another controversial figure, this time because he doesn't decline. In other words, is perfection boring? 'Joe's Blues' (Verve) is another set with Wild Bill Davis, this time with Lawrence Brown thrown in for good measure, and is very much the mixture as before – two riff blues, some Ellingtonia ('Warm Valley', 'Solitude') and some ballads, including a light-stepping 'Somebody Loves Me'. There is some excellent guitar work by Grant Green. Wild Bill Davis turns up again on 'Free, Frantic and Funky' (RCA Victor) in the interesting company of Seldon Powell and Jerome Richardson, plus some dirty flute playing from one Bob Brown.

We are in a Hines wave at the moment, following the Fatha's visit, and 'The Grand Terrace Band' (RCA Victor) presents sixteen sides from 1939–40, notably 'Father Steps In', 'Grand Terrace Shuffle' and 'Deep Forest'. Though much vivacity is evidenced, the band seems characterless to me, rather like the Mills Blue Rhythm Band: now riffing in the style of Basie (with some remarkable Lester imitations from Budd Johnson), now growling with the Duke. Hines stands head and shoulders above his men, who include trumpeters Walter Fuller and Shirley Clay, and Omer Simeon. 'Omer Simeon' (Ace of Hearts) represents an earlier stage in the career of Jelly Roll Morton's favourite clarinettist, consisting of sides with Reuben Reeves and Alex Hill and his own trio dating from 1929–30. The Creole clarinet tradition is a bit gentle for some tastes, but Reeve's fierce trumpet and some astonishingly Hines-like piano by William Barbee (Orin Blackstone says it *is* Hines) redress the balance.

'A Little Juicy' (Philips) by the Billy Mitchell Quintet has some good solo work by Mitchell and Thad Jones over a pouncing, bouncing rhythm section led by Richard Wyands. Something of an anthology of modern manners, the record is funky on 'Brother Peabody', Coltraney on 'Juicy', and has a muscly bossa nova.

On 'Cooking' (Fontana) sides made by Zoot Sims at the Ronnie Scott Club in 1961 are reissued. This is a rather tousled Zoot, squeaks and all, laying about him on 'Stompin' at the Savoy' and 'Somebody Loves Me', but achieving greater conviction on 'Gone with the Wind'. Stan Tracy provides the usual noble support. I don't know who buys records like 'The Definitive Jazz Scene, Vol. 2' (HMV), but it is delightful listening once one gets over the first track on each side (Ray Charles and John Coltrane): Shirley Scott's organ on 'Blues Ain't Nothin' but Some Pain' is nicer than Wild Bill's, Hampton's 'Moon Over My Annie' comes from the Terry-Webster session last year, and there are good tracks by McCoy Tyner and Tommy Flanagan. Talking of pianos, it is interesting to see how Basie maintains his extraordinary authority as a band pianist in 'Basie Picks the Winners' (Verve). His contributions are made with the utmost poise and concision, and I really don't recollect anything like his solo lead in 'I'll Get By' – quiet, stalking, resonant.

'The Spiritual and Gospel Festival, 1965' (Fontana) was recorded live in Bremen, and was probably more fun to watch than to listen to, except for the Original Five Blind Boys of Mississippi. Sidney Bechet's 'Rockin'' (Fontana) is a set of muddy 'This is Jazz' airchecks with Spanier and Nicholas plus two other secondary sessions from 1949. For Bechet fans, perhaps, but whom does that leave out?

13 October 1965

The Big Fellers

I freely confess that there have been times recently when almost anything – the shape of a patch on the ceiling, a recipe for rhubarb jam read upside down in the paper – has seemed to me more interesting than the passionless creep of a Miles Davis trumpet solo. 'ESP' (CBS) is an immense improvement. The slow Davis solos – on 'Iris', '81' and 'Little One' – are declaimed with enormous authority, keen and kingly, like incidental music of genius for a Swedish film of *Hamlet*. This is the latest Davis group, with Wayne Shorter, Hancocks, Carter and Williams, and the last-named has a long spell on 'Agitation'. Davis is his usual bleak self, his notes wilting at the edges as if with frost, spikey at up-tempos, and while he is still not my ideal of comfortable listening his talent is clearly undiminished.

Another successful big-timer this month is Dave Brubeck – free for once from fancy time signatures, he and Paul Desmond set about a bunch of Matt Dennis tunes on 'Angel Eyes' (CBS) with forthright enthusiasm. 'Let's Get Away From It All', the opening track, has Desmond playing with that cool flaccidity reminiscent of some Chicago-style reeds, and Brubeck follows with an unaffected swinginess. Having dispensed with some of his heavier mannerisms he sounds at times ('Will You Still Be Mine?') quite ordinary. Desmond is lyrical on 'Angel Eyes' and 'The Night We Called It A Day', pushing on 'Will You Still Be Mine?' Another talent refreshed.

'The Real Earl Hines' (Atlantic), a New York Concert in March, 1964, is a more baroque affair. Listen to the audience laughing with delight at Hines's lovely runs on 'Tea For Two', his running fight with drums and bass on 'Satin Doll', his five-minute trill on 'St. Louis Blues' – this is pianistics with knobs on. Earl has a tendency to take each chorus separately, to show off a different facet of his talent, which spoils continuity, but one might as well listen because there's no one else like him. Budd Johnson solos tenderly on tenor, in 'Someone To Watch Over Me'.

The screeching dreariness of John Coltrane is not for me, and of 'The John Coltrane Quartet' (HMV) I can say only that the group of Coltrane, Tyner, Garrison and Jones treat 'Chim Chim Cheree', 'Nature Boy' and two Coltrane originals, 'Brazilia' and 'Song of Praise', in their accustomed manner. The last-named is one of Coltrane's slow, not unmelodious meditations against chiming piano and sawing bass. Woody Herman's 'My Kind of Broadway'

(CBS) is a bunch of show tunes done in a neo-Basie manner with spirit though small originality. 'Autobiography', by Nat Adderley (Atlantic) has some punchy cornet on 'Little Boy With The Sad Eyes' and 'Stony Island', but in general the atmosphere is too coloured by Seldon Powell's genteel flute and a deal of Latin-Americanism.

I'm afraid I poached Bob Dylan's 'Highway 61 Revisited' (CBS) out of curiosity and found myself well rewarded. Dylan's cawing, derisive voice is probably well suited to his material – I say probably because much of it was unintelligible to me – and his guitar adapts itself to rock ('Highway 61') and ballad ('Queen Jane') admirably. There is a marathon 'Desolation Row' which has an enchanting tune and mysterious, possibly half-baked words. On the reissue side, Verve offers 'Ben Webster's Big Sound', fifties tracks with assorted groups including Oscar Peterson, Hawkins, Edison and Mulligan. 'Sunday', 'Tenderly', 'Chelsea Bridge' and 'Makin' Whoopee' are all dealt with authoritatively, and the blues 'Late Date' beats up a fair storm. 'The Best Of The Dizzy Gillespie Small Groups' (Verve) has some excellent though rather unrelated performances with Getz ('It Don't Mean A Thing'), Rollins ('Wheatleigh Hall') and Leo Wright ('Night In Tunisia'), dating from 1953–61. Dizzy has always been rather emotionless for my taste, and my reply to the sleeve's contention that a tempo of over ninety bars a minute sorts out the men from the boys would be that it is the boys – like Dizzy – who can cope. Technique by itself is as boring in jazz as anywhere else.

RCA Victor continues its admirable exhumations of the early Ellington with 'The Duke Steps Out', in this case offering alternative takes of 'Ring Dem Bells', 'Old Man Blues' and 'Blue Bubbles' along with other Ellingtonia from 1927–32. 'The Best Of The Modern Jazz Quartet' (Stateside) presents again those memorable sides from the middle fifties – 'Delaunay's Dilemma', 'Queen's Fancy', 'Django' – that constituted such an astonishing innovation, stylistically, at the time.

A fine John Lee Hooker LP on Chess ('John Lee Hooker') gives another sample of this brooding back-country talent, with 'The Journey', 'Dreamin' Blues' and 'Worried Life Blues' as the highlights. Finally, there are three more issues in RCA Victor's Race Series – Elder Charles Beck, with his trumpet and 1939 congregation (very exciting, this); Julius Daniels, and the fruity-voiced

Doctor Clayton, with Blind John Davis on piano. These are EPs, but a good little one is better than a big bad one, as they say.

10 November 1965

A Far From Indifferent Guy

We are slowly verifying what we always suspected, namely that Django Reinhardt is dateless. His commanding, sinuous line, at once melodic and rhythmic, springs out of the NAAFI-like 1940 backgrounds of 'Djangology' (Music for Pleasure) as immediately as Bechet from a 1923 Clarence Williams blues group. If he were alive today (his death from a stroke at 43 took away Europe's one jazz master), there is no reason to suppose he would sound in any way different.

There was always a kind of arrogance about Reinhardt. He landed in America without a guitar, imagining the different makers would fight to give him one; when in 1939 he arrived for a recording session with Stewart and Bigard they had to find him a broken-backed instrument before he could play: as 'Django And His American Friends, Vol. II' (HMV) proves, he was in magic form. This second record, made with American Negro visitors such as Carter, Eddie South, Coleman and the Duke's men, is, not unnaturally, the best; besides Django, it has the ravishing 'Eddie's Blues', the Stewart-Bigard sides, and the renowned 'Big Boy Blues', with New Orleans clarinettist Frank Goodie.

'Spirits' (Transatlantic) is the first Albert Ayler record I have heard, and if you take it as a further example of experimental American Negro art music it is quite acceptable, or at least no crazier than some European art music. If Ayler's tenor sounds at times like a cello being scraped with a wet rubber galosh, Norman Howard's trumpet achieves a kind of benediction at the close of the eleven-minute 'Witches and Devils' that is charged with emotional feeling.

By contrast with all this squeaking and gibbering, 'Sonny Rollins On Impulse!' (HMV) signals something of a return from recent extremes: on 'Three Little Words' he is smoothly amazing and the calypso 'Hold 'Em Joe' has a punchy swing that I could have wished for in 'Green Dolphin Street' and 'Blue Room'. That magnificent pianist Ray Bryant snatches a solo here and there.

'Inspired Abandon' (HMV) by Lawrence Brown with Johnny Hodges presents Ellington men and material with sharper attack than sometimes. It amazes me that Nance, Hodges and Brown can still produce a gripping version of 'Mood Indigo', but grip they do and cornettist Nance is also outstanding on 'Little Brother' and 'Stompy Jones'. Cat Anderson, Harold Ashby and Gonsalves all contribute, while Brown does his standard 'Do Nothing' and Hodges is ubiquitous. Two sides, according to the sleeve, were made after Ella Fitzgerald had sent in a gift case of whisky.

'The Blues At Newport 1964 – Part 1' (Fontana) presents the grassrooters Doc Reese (Texan work songs), Robert Pete Williams ('Levee Camp Blues' as on the earlier disc made at Louisiana State Prison) and Fred McDowell singing to bottle-neck guitar along with the more seasoned Sleepy John Estes, who has Hammie Nixon and Yank Rachel in attendance for 'Mailman Blues', 'Drop Down' and other standards. That other Louisianian, Mahalia Jackson, has rather better material than usual on 'In The Upper Room' (Columbia), with fewer choirs, organs and introductory flourishes and more stomping gospel build-ups on 'If You Just Keep Still', 'Run All The Way', and others.

A magnificent month for reissues is headed by 'Bird Symbols' (Verve), sides from 1946–7 including 'Bird's Nest' and 'Cool Blues' with Garner and a clutch of ballads ('Embraceable You', 'Out of Nowhere') where Parker reigns supreme. Two old Hendersonians, Dickie Wells and the late Chu Berry, appear separately on 'Heavy Duty!' (Vocalion), those four-trombone Felsted pieces from 1958 and 1959, and 'Sittin' In' (Fontana), Chu's two Commodore sessions with Eldridge and Hot Lips Page respectively. These are splendid samples of Chu's keening tenor, but eight 78 rpm's on a twelve-inch LP is pretty short measure.

Further into the dark backward and abysm of time, more multifoliate Riverside Classic Jazz Masters have appeared, notably 'Fletcher Henderson Orchestra 1923–1927', which demonstrates through eight of its sixteen tracks how tall the corn grew in this band in the pre-Armstrong or 'Muffle Jaws' era. Then there is 'Gertrude "Ma" Rainey – Vol. 1', covering 1923–4 and so earlier than the three London ten-inch LPs; I arose from it confirmed that Ma Rainey's talent was mellower, more musical and at times more enjoyable than her pupil Bessie's. Reproduction, however, is dire. Equally precious is 'Scott Joplin, 1899–1914', piano rolls of that early prelapsarian mode called ragtime that combines the jaunty and the wistful in heart-stirring proportions. Finally, anyone not already possessing Jelly Roll Morton's Commodore piano solos may – must – now buy them on Fontana. They are all ten here from December, 1939, the twilight valediction of a great player broken in health but not spirits, in whose rags and blues the ghosts of New Orleans a quarter of a century ago are still very agilely walking.

8 December 1965

1966

How Am I To Know?

What is a good critic? In an art such as jazz, one is tempted to call him the anticipator – the man who praised Parker in 1945, Coltrane in 1955, and is now rooting for Ayler: an aesthetic punter continually bringing off 100-1 shots. Less extravagantly, he may be thought of as the listener who hears the good in everybody, who can slip it logically on to the long string stretching from Archie Shepp back to Buddy Bolden. His critical motto (assuming he had read the poem) would be 'Whatever is, is right'.

Nice work, certainly, if you can get it. But the fact is that the jazz scene is so complex today that the sensibility that could respond to all of it would be rare indeed. Gone are the days when jazz was a single simple manner, stirring the world and bringing Ravel and Milhaud into thrall. Its complexity is due to the fact that in two or three generations it has proceeded (note I do not say progressed) from folk-art to cult-art, from something everyone can understand to something nobody can understand, and in fact both of these are going on simultaneously, for the man who gave Armstrong his first job back in New Orleans, Kid Ory, is still playing intermittently on the West Coast.

Then, again, it has got tied up with the civil rights movement, so that pre-Kennedy jazz is somehow politically suspect: the message of a good deal of today's output can be summed up in the words of a speaker at a New York nightspot not so long ago: 'You want to know how to help us, white folks? Drop dead. That's how you can help us.' And lastly, of course, it is still, basically, a racket – flourishing in the underworld of the entertainment industry where, to quote Charlie Parker, 'bread is your only friend', and the gimmick is supreme.

The danger, therefore, of assuming that everything played today in jazz has a seed of solid worth stems from the fact that so much of it is tentative, experimental, private, the doodlings of men educated far beyond their night club environment, the efforts of artists wishing to prove themselves not only individually but racially. And for this reason one has to fall back on the old dictum that a critic is only as good as his ear. His ear will tell him instantly whether a piece of music is vital, musical, exciting, or cerebral, mock-academic, dead, long before he can read Don De Micheal on the subject, or learn that it is written in inverted nineteenths, or in the Stygian mode, or recorded at the NAACP Festival at Little Rock. He must hold on to the principle that the only reason for praising a work is that it pleases, and the way to develop his critical sense is to be more acutely aware of whether he is being pleased or not. There is the lodestone that will guide him through the jumble – musical, social, chronological – of jazz in 1966.

The year at any rate got away to a flying start with the magnificent 'Pee Wee Russell – A Legend' (Fontana), including six of the eight sides Russell made in 1941 and 1944 with Sullivan and Stacy respectively. The later, better session is here complete, and contains some of the finest middle-period Russell on record: 'D. A. Blues', in particular, must be the most passionate extended encounter Pee Wee ever had with the twelve-bar form. His timing is perfect, his phrasing oratorical without being melodramatic, his tonal distortions involuntary, and all is conceived in that vein of unique, hard-hitting lyricism the Commodore crew made their own.

The bag is made up with odd Condon-crowd sides from the same era, including the thrilling Spanier 'Snag It', but they have been issued here already. A pity all eight trio quartet sides are not here, but even so this is a superb collection.

The impresario Norman Granz ('Jazz At The Philharmonic') earned himself so much criticism by his noisier stage shows and the way in which he brought the technique of pattern-bombing to jazz recording that the listener is only now realizing that some of his recordings were in fact very good. Two more anthologies of these – 'Art Tatum Alone And With Friends' and 'The Legendary Lester Young' (both Verve) each gives an extended conspectus of the maturities of two widely-differing great artists, Tatum, the piano eccentric, and Young, the founder of a whole new way of thinking on the tenor.

For my taste, Tatum is rather like a dressmaker who, having seen how pretty one frill looks, makes a dress bearing ninety-nine, but tracks included are 'S'wonderful' with Benny Carter, 'Makin' Whoopee' with Hampton, a driving 'This Can't Be Love' with Eldridge, and a nice 'Trio Blues' with Callender and Jo Jones. Pres's album is similarly eclectic, ranging from 1945 to 1956 through accompanists Nat Cole, John Lewis, Oscar Peterson and Teddy Wilson, producing with the last-named a sinewy 'All of Me' from their 1956 session. Also recommended: 'Wardell Gray Memorial Album, Vols. 1 and 2' (Stateside), sides made between 1949 and 1953; 'Willie "The Lion" Smith – A Legend' (Fontana); and the Modern Jazz Quartet's 'Patterns' (United Artists), which, despite occasional tinges of 'Listen With Mother',is frequently charming and quite inimitable.

9 February 1966

The Bessie Smith Story

Everyone knows at least one thing about Bessie Smith: that she died from injuries after being refused admittance to a hospital on account of her colour. That is the legend that has come for many to epitomize the racial situation in America. In fact there is no evidence for it. Bessie was rushed to hospital in Clarksdale, Mississippi, and one of the town's best surgeons operated on her, but to no avail. She died on the afternoon of 27 September 1937.

The reissue by CBS of the four-disc 'The Bessie Smith Story' gives the listener a chance to test another Bessie legend: that she never made a bad record. Here, too, some reservations should be made. The awkward country girl, 'tall and fat and scared to death', who was acclaimed by her people as the Empress of the Blues in less than ten years, had a voice of enormous power and dignity, and a natural gift of rhythmic phrasing. Some of her records, such as 'Reckless Blues' or 'Young Woman's Blues', are beautiful in a way nothing else in jazz equals. But the change of taste that abandoned Bessie as a primitive could see what we prefer to ignore: that her voice was sometimes merely harsh and loud, that she could be monotonously repetitive, that her accompaniment could be grotesquely facetious.

Was her decline, too, a legend? As the thirties drew to a close some of her material grew tasteless. But the isolated post-depression session with Frank Newton, Chu Berry and Jack Teagarden produced four sides as buoyantly memorable as any we have. Some of her phrases ('I'm twenty-*five* years old . . . I'm always like a *tiger* . . .') burn into the memory with all the old excitement. This collection, comprising about a quarter of Bessie's recorded output, commemorates a unique and imperious talent which at its best commanded a sombre tragedy as rare as it is moving.

'The New Wave in Jazz' (HMV) offers five tracks from a Black Arts Theatre concert last March at the Village Gate, ranging from post-Bop to the squeak-and-gibber school of Albert Ayler. The well-known publicist LeRoi Jones contributes a sleeve-note which, while at times portentously silly ('New Black music is this: find the self, then kill it'), makes large claims for this mode as an epiphany of the emergent Negro spirit. As entertainment (remember the word?) it varies: the Tolliver-Spaulding-Hutcherson version of Monk's 'Brilliant Corners' is elegant, and the Shepp 'Hambone' really rather funny. Coltrane and Ayler are more taxing.

Numerous other notable issues can be mentioned briefly only. Sonny Rollins is twice featured, a reissue of the 1956 'Saxophone Colossus' (Stateside) and a bunch of solos off the editing-room floor called 'The Standard Sonny Rollins' (RCA Victor). The latter has a lovely 'Travelin' ', with an arco and a plucked bass, but it fades out. The former is a classic performance of the early Rollins, including his famous 'Blue Seven'. I found the collection 'Andy Kirk: Clouds of Joy' (Ace of Hearts) less exciting than I expected of this Kansas City group: they are in fact rather early sides, 1929–31, and it is only when Mary Lou Williams or her husband, John Williams, breaks through that distinction is achieved. 'Snag It' is an exception, beautifully handled in the Oliver tradition. A livelier excavation is 'Cab Calloway: The King of Hi-de-Ho' (Ace of Hearts). Again from the 1930–1 period, they represent the vanished tradition of the all-singing, all-dancing leader whose antics proclaim the hotness of his music, but the band itself has good outings on 'Aw You Dog' and 'Bugle Call Rag'. It is surprising how a Negro personality as ebullient as Calloway's can be so devoid of jazz interest.

'Kings of Swing' (MFP) is much better than its title, being in fact some good white small-group stuff from the thirties, including a different master of the Freeman-Berigan 'Tillie's Downtown' from the old Parlophone 78, that strangely delightful 'Last Round-up' by Krupa's Chicagoans, 'Dr. Heckle and Mr. Jibe', and others, A treat for the money. 'Misterioso' (CBS) presents eight tracks by the Thelonius Monk Quartet from tour performances, all of which I found lively and swinging, and much less bogged down by bass and drum solos than of yore. 'Gettin' Sentimental' from the Jazz Workshop is especially good. There is nothing much new to say about Johnny Hodges and Wild Bill Davis, who on 'Con-Soul and Sax' (RCA Victor) do their double act as efficiently as before.

Terry Gibbs's 'It's Time We Met' (Fontana), with tenorist Sal Nistico, is, for all its monotony, a real old-fashioned hot record, and is commended as such. Eddie Condon's 'We Called It Music' (Ace of Hearts) rounds up some 'March of Time' period pieces from middle and late forties, when the Condon spirit was becoming a little watered by second-line talent. Finally, 'The Roots of Lightnin' Hopkins' (Verve) is the Folkways record that brought Lightnin' back to the limelight, described by Sam Charters in his book *The Country Blues*. Lightnin' has never done better.

9 March 1966

Must We Swallow the New Wave?

'Merely a raucous and inarticulate shouting of hoarse-throated instruments, with each player trying to outdo his fellows in fantastic cacophony' – yes, if it's the New Wave you are talking about, you took the words right out of my mouth. Only, of course, it isn't, or wasn't. This was Sigmund Spaeth in 1928, proclaiming that 'Jazz Is Not Music', and the reactions of other critics of the period ('staccato tempi', 'curlicues', 'rasps', 'cries' and 'laughs') are eloquent of the perennial unadaptability of human taste. This, of the stately and classic music of Armstrong, Morton and Ellington! It makes you despair of human perception.

It also makes today's critic pretty wary of approaching such releases as 'Mohawk: The New York Art Quartet' (Fontana), which is one of four New Wave discs on this label, the others being 'Ted Curson: Tears for Dolphy', 'George Russell: The Outer View', and 'Dollar Brand Trio: Anatomy of a South African Village'. In some ways the leader of the Quartet, John Tchicai, has first claim on our attention: he is in fact Danish, of African-Danish parentage, and did not reach the United States until 1962. Perhaps for this reason his music is not muddled up with racism: there is a placid, almost slack air about his alto playing that is eloquent of his remark, 'If one wants to go outside of that question, it's possible.' The music he plays with trombonist Roswell Rudd, bassist Reggie Workman and drummer Milford Graves is uncompromising avant-garde: it is atonal, out of tempo, seemingly themeless, spending itself in slow exhalations of discord ('Sweet V') or twittery flirtations with excitement ('Banging On The White House Door'). It has not the aggression of Shepp or the Gothicism of Ayler. It leaves the impression that Tchicai could introduce, if his pieces were more integrated, a kind of New Wave pastoralism unheard from other quarters that would be by no means unpleasant.

Ella and the Duke have lived 113 years between them, but 'Ella At Duke's Place' (Verve) evinces a smooth and vivacious command that is timeless. The full band is here, notable not so much for solo spots (though Gonsalves, Hodges et al, have their say) as for the hand-tailored orchestrations of Jimmy Jones. The first side ('the pretty, the lovely, the tender, the hold-me-close side') is the drawback: tunes like 'Passion Flower' and 'Azure' are full of Ellington's dated exoticism, which Ella has a job to stop from sounding corny; the second is livelier, with a warbling 'Cottontail', an intriguing 'Brown Skin Gal' and a nicely swinging 'What Am I Here For'.

Near the Ellington territory is 'Wings and Things' by Johnny Hodges and Wild Bill Davis (Verve): and we might be excused for neglecting all further issues by this duo, which seem to come out weekly, but in fact this is a cooker, possibly owing to the presence of Lawrence Brown, who seems to spur Rabbit to a tougher approach. The title track and 'Spotted Dog' are both long blues that deploy all talents to the full, and the romping 'Imbo' and Hodges' 'The Nearness of You' contrast admirably. Definitely a buy.

Fans of Gerry Mulligan (among whom, on the whole, I don't number myself) will be interested in 'If You Can't Beat 'Em', Join 'Em' (Mercury), Mulligan treatment of a series of popular themes with a rhythm section led by Pete Jolly's piano. He is a brave man who seeks to patronize 'A Hard Day's Night' and 'Mr. Tambourine Man'. 'Collaborations' (Verve) is an anthology of 1957–60 pieces, mainly by small Granz groups but with the concert Jazz Band's 'Blueport'. The gawky Mulligan baritone is blended acceptably with such stalwarts as Edison, Getz, Webster, Hodges, Sims and Peterson.

This month has brought an above-average number of records which the reviewer would neither dream of knocking nor of paying good money for. Typical of these 'Ain't Misbehavin'' (MFP), some of Fats Waller's London recordings including two Continental Rhythm band numbers and some rather fine spirituals on the organ. 'The Blues Never Die!' (Stateside) offers Otis Spann singing and playing piano with the Muddy Waters group; a little noisier than Decca's 'The Blues of Otis Spann' but full of solid beat and feeling. 'Here's Art Tatum' (Ace of Hearts) collects a series of solo or trio items from the middle forties when Tatum's talent had not effloresced into the full baroquerie of his later days. These standards ('Honeysuckle Rose', 'Moonglow', and so on) bring out in my view the mechanical aspect of Tatum's technique, those downward runs struggling with the Hines-Wilson tradition ('Rosetta') and the breathtaking nimbleness that inspired, for good or ill, the unhappy Bud Powell.

I am bound to report that there is a new Miles Davis, '"Four" and More' (CBS), taken from live concerts in 1964 and featuring 'Walkin'', 'Four', 'So What' and others. Most of the tunes are quick and show off Miles with his current Hancock-Williams quartet, and the emcee remarks, 'I know you agree it's been wonderful.' On the contrary: for me it was an experience in pure duration. Some of it must have been quite hard to do.

6 April 1966

The Documenter of Jazz

Pride of place this month goes to a book. With *Jazz Records A-Z, 1932–1942* (5gns.), the doyen of British discographers, Brian Rust, adds nearly 700 pages to his earlier volume, *Jazz Records A-Z, 1897–1931*, bringing his definitive record of who played what and when up to the imposition of the ban on recorded music by the American Federation of Musicians on 31 July 1942. It is a significant date. As Mr Rust himself states in his preface, it closed the era of swing music. When the ban was lifted two years later, jazz had split into what seemed two irreconcilable camps, be-bop and trad revival, and things were never quite the same again. Although Mr Rust does not say so, one suspects that he will now let the Danish discographer Jorgen Grunnet Jepsen continue the tale with his *Jazz Records 1942–1962* (four volumes at present published), now that 'an ever-freer form' has, in his own words, 'ceased even to be recognizable as jazz at all'.

Such undertakings are, after all, labours of love, and Mr Rust has long been known for his enthusiasm for Golden Age music. In the decade treated in this volume, jazz records were more sought after in Europe than America, where the Depression had struck more damagingly, and at one time British companies were even commissioning American representatives – John Hammond, for instance –

to arrange sessions in America for British labels. Nor has Mr Rust ignored the first struggling efforts of British groups to reproduce the styles and strains of the American masters: Teddy Foster, Nat Gonella and the Six Swingers, for example, are here *in extenso*. All jazz lovers owe Mr Rust their deepest gratitude for his industry and enterprise.

Though once upon a time I resisted bop, I find myself letting New Wave flow over me. Whereas the earlier music seemed derived from the thin and eccentric riffs of the little bands of the thirties, Kirby or the Goodman and Ellington units, there is a rich absurdity about the present revolution that is rather appealing; furthermore, as it cannot possibly be called a *travesty* of jazz (at least, no more than of any other kind of music), one is freed of resentment and can afford to be tolerant. I found George Russell's 'The Outer View' (Fontana) of considerable fascination. Issued in America in 1963, this collection is by his Sextet with Russell on piano and Don Ellis leading on trumpet, and is characterized by the confident unexpectedness that marks all Russell's music. The most striking piece is 'You Are My Sunshine', a slow-motion rendering of this rookie favourite with an eerie vocal by Sheila Jordan, but the title piece, with its alternating out-of-tempo 'breaks' and scampering accelerations for all players, ending with triumphant brass chordings, is almost its equal.

With 'Four For Trane' by Archie Shepp (HMV) we are on more familiar ground, with Shepp and Tchicai dingeing away at four Coltrane originals in that disintegrated and disagreeable manner one has come to expect. 'Naima' shows off Shepp most acceptably in what for him is probably a meditative mood. The Terry-Brookmeyer Quintet continue to paddle the mainstream with 'The Power of Positive Swinging' (Fontana), an excellent collection of tracks showing their spirited and synchronized cohesion: significantly, the two thirty-two-bar commercial bits, 'Gal In Calico' and 'Just an Old Manuscript', carry the most free-booting solos. 'Hawg Jawz' is a string of low-down blues clichés that stops too soon, probably through selfconsciousness, but it was nice.

Talking of the blues, 'Blues: Southside Chicago' (Decca) is another anthology of current exponents such as Eddy Boyd, Shakey Horton, Poor Bob and Robert Nighthawk. With samish accompaniments based on Henry Gray (piano), Joe Young (guitar), Willie Dixon (bass) and Clifton James (drums), these singers slam through fourteen pieces very much in the modern urban tradition, unremarkable but satisfying. Champion Jack Dupree on Decca's 'From New Orleans to Chicago' has greater poise, greater variety, and greater delicacy; there is an unusual track where Jack plays guitar. This collection is not perfect, but Dupree's rolling piano and suddenly clamant voice have that indispensable timing of all good blues singers.

A classic set by the young Miles Davis, now known as 'Birth of the Cool', has been reissued by Capitol. These 1949–50 pieces by that famous Miles-Mulligan-Konitz-Winding-Evans-Roach bunch, 'Jeru', 'Move', 'Godchild', 'Boplicity' and the rest, established once for all a new mood in jazz, and are unassailable for that reason. It is incredible to realize that Davis and Mulligan, for instance, were 21, the age of third-year students: the music has a relaxed, mature quality, a richness of voicing, that speaks of experience rather than youth. Essentially ensemble pieces, they hold solos by Miles that he has never surpassed. Another notable reissue is 'Tintinnabulation' by Lionel Hampton (Verve), a selection of Granz tracks with Peterson, Getz, Wilson, Tatum and so on, dating from the middle fifties. Rather stale tunes ('China Boy', 'Dinah'), rather killer-diller approach, but with a great deal of enjoyment to be quarried nonetheless.

4 May 1966

The Bubbles Waller Blew

If you were a friend of Fats Waller, you called him 'Tom'. His preference for the name given him in 1904 by his Baptist pastor father over the sobriquet that travelled with him from Harlem's buffet flats to the stage of Carnegie Hall was indicative of his growing desire to escape his public persona, to 'play more organ . . . write more . . . do some writing of classical music'. He never achieved this escape, not even posthumously. Dying, like Dylan Thomas, at the age of 39, he has left a mass of records to preserve his reputation, but they are almost entirely those engaging musical bubbles blown by 'Fats Waller and his Rhythm' between 1934 and 1942.

Nobody, not even Armstrong, Bechet, or Bessie Smith, left a more characteristic opus, nor perhaps one based on a more limited formula; a commercial tune, first played on the piano, then sung by Waller with varying degrees of respect, then a chorus split between trumpet and tenor, and a final, much less respectful vocal with the band playing hell-for-leather behind. Interspersed with the solos was a great deal of stylized jiving from Waller to his sidemen, often based mockingly on the lyrics he had just sung. What was so good about these performances was not so much the music, which could be threadbare (Waller was a king of cliché), nor the Waller humour (for Fats, like most famous humorists, was desperately unfunny two-thirds of the time), but the irresistible drive and bouncing jubilation that pervaded them.

Panassié declared that they were the only records he had heard where the musicians played as if they were in a nightclub. Their dynamic was Waller's personality and his ringing authoritative muscular piano that undersprung every performance he gave. His records were not remarkable for the quality of the instrumentalists, for Autrey and Sedric and the rest were scrappy players at best, but for the constantly-varying vivacity, tenderness, satire and righteous jazz that made every Waller performance a new experience, no matter how often you had heard the routine before.

It would be wrong, therefore, to speak of a Waller revival, for in fact he has never gone away, but '34/35 Fats Waller' (RCA Victor) adds another sixteen pieces to the repertoire currently available – fine ones, too, including the driving 'Serenade to a Wealthy Widow', with Mezzrow and O'Brien, 'If It Isn't Love', with Bill Coleman, two 1929 piano solos, and the occasional delightful trifle such as 'Lessons In Love' and 'Breakin' the Ice'. Who, finally, can resist the swift transition at the beginning of 'Dust Off That Old Pianna' from clowning to the fleetest of hot piano? No doubt Waller could have given us more than he did. But this is no reason for being anything but thankful for what we have.

There is much to enjoy on Benny Goodman's 'Countdown' (Verve), tracks dating from 1937–40 and stemming mostly from broadcasts of that time, previously issued on MGM's 'Treasure Chest' albums. One side is chiefly band numbers, such as 'Madhouse' and 'Dear Old Southland', and the other chamber groups, mainly based on the original trio. It is curious how narrow and pinched Goodman's ensemble sound is beginning to seem, but the master himself and his principal soloists are in fine form.

Riverside's 'Louis Armstrong in New York, 1924–25', comprises sixteen pieces mostly in support of Alberta Hunter (here called 'Josephine Beatty'), Trixie Smith and Grant and Wilson: a little archaic, interesting more for Bechet and Buster Bailey on the Hunter tracks, but with fine Louis on the later year's works. How plangently that Coot Grant line comes over, 'You can read my letters, you can't read my mind'! 'The New Orleans Jazz of George Lewis' (Verve) has a rather sluggish first side from 1956, with John Robichaux good on 'Riverside Blues', but mannered elsewhere, and a better reverse from 1958, featuring a majestic 'West End Blues'. The band never recovers its earlier sailing quality, but seems better pitched than sometimes.

A last one for the Old Nostalgians' Annual Dance: 'Jack Hylton and his Orchestra' (Ace of Clubs) – '42nd Street Medley', 'Heartaches', the lot. Much better than you might think.

1 June 1966

A Loss to Jazz

Some Eric Dolphy records have accumulated lately, testifying to the talent of this remarkable young instrumentalist who died of diabetes or heart failure or both in Berlin two years ago. Men who stand between traditions are always interesting, and this altoist who achieved distinction on the bass clarinet and became a virtuoso on the flute now seems to link the Parker era and the New Wave. He was an eager, charming young man who used to answer bird calls on his flute to get the quarter-tones, and his playing in general has little of the anger of Civil Rights jazz.

The most striking track by him of late is 'You Don't Know What Love Is' (on 'Last Date', Fontana), where he produces a meditative flute passage against arco bass (a favourite combination), magical in slow tempo, and displaying magnificent control, despite a tendency to twitter, when the beat picks up. This was recorded in Holland with a local rhythm section in the month he died, along with 'Epistrophy' – the edgy Monk line suits Dolphy – and 'Miss Ann', in which Dolphy tries hard to sound harsh but fails to get the effortless tonal distortions of his successors.

By contrast 'In Memoriam Eric Allan Dolphy 1928–1964' (Fontana) was originally issued in America three years ago and called 'Conversations'. Dolphy settles to a thirteen and a half-minute discussion on bass clarinet with Richard Davis on bass in 'Alone Together', and their understanding and response are remarkable. However Dolphy uses the long range of his instrument to escape inherited forms, he continually appears to fall back on conventional symmetries and harmonies of the bop tradition. Other tracks include a sprightly 'Jitterbug Waltz' and Dolphy on flute and a sort of calypso called 'Matador' with three reeds, a flute (Prince Lasha), bass and drums.

Another commemorative sleeve encloses 'Eric Dolphy and Booker Little Memorial Album' (Stateside), a pair of side-long pieces recorded at the Five Spot in 1961 with Mel Waldron, who sounds curiously ill-at-ease with this advanced stuff. 'Potsa Lotsa' is a lively affair featuring Eddie Blackwell's drums, and 'Booker's Waltz' spots Little, with Dolphy gobbling away for good measure on the bass clarinet. An incoherent player, one feels in the end: a well-intentioned, brilliant, charming but unfinished talent that now never will mature.

I can thoroughly endorse the sleeve of John Coltrane's 'Ascension' (HMV), which says 'This record cannot be loved or understood in one sitting.' In fact I played it twice, but the double-sided carpet of bellowing and screeching laid down by Shepp, Hubbard, Marion Brown, Pharaoh Sanders, Tchicai, Dewey Johnson and the Master himself, patiently propelled by Tyner and Jones, held little appeal. Soloists appear and submerge like Titanic passengers. Yet what solace does a record such as 'The Jazz Side of Harry James' (Verve) hold for the traditionalist? These fifteen tracks date from 1959–62, representing the end of the Basie-Herman tradition as exemplified by Ernie Wilkins and Neil Hefti: sharp, harsh, stiff-jointed pieces, with hammering drums, the leader's trumpet either muted or stuttering and flaring against ensembles. 'Cottontail' is headlong, 'End of Town Blues' sombre and growling; James is helped by Willie Smith in the solos, but for the most part the impact is *tutti fortissimo*.

Going backwards, 'It's Duke Ellington' (Ember) reissues some famous 1946 tracks such as 'Overture to a Jam Session', 'The Beautiful Indians' and 'Happy Go Lucky Local'; Hodges scores in 'Magenta Haze' and 'Sultry Sunset' – how hard he blew twenty years ago! From the thirties comes 'Bluebird Blues' (RCA Victor), a delicious dip into the riches of one of the most famous of 'race' catalogues: Tommy McClellan, Sleepy John Estes ('Lawyer Clark Blues'), Arthur Crudup ('Death Valley Blues') and others provide endless variations on age-old themes.

11 July 1966

Basie: the First and Best

It is startling to reflect that more than twice as many years separate us from Count Basie's first recordings as separated the Count himself from the Oliver-Armstrong-Gennett sessions in 1923. In a way the sets can be compared: both brought to perfection a certain style of playing and at the same time contained the seeds of its overthrow. The seed was in Oliver's case, of course, Armstrong; in Basie's, Young.

When the Basie band came to New York in 1937 it was, despite its magnificent potential, a little rough and scuffling, and some of its original members had to return home, but its tradition was a mature one and Basie himself was well into his thirties. A year later it was the apotheosis of the shouting Kansas City orchestra, with its head arrangements, simple building tension, and supreme soloists. This was the band that made Basie's name: Clayton and Edison in the trumpets, Young and Herschel Evans in the reeds, the audacious simplicity of Basie's piano and the propulsive power of the Green-Page-Jones rhythm section. By 1939 it had got a little tired, and though there has been much good music since, things have never been the same.

'Jumpin' At The Woodside' (Ace of Hearts) is a fair memorial of this wonderful eighteen months. One can't help thinking how much better it would have been if the tedious 'Cherokee' and such lightweights as 'Time Out' had been dropped for the fiery session-mates 'Sent For You Yesterday' and 'Swingin' The Blues': a collection of this period without a single Rushing vocal is in any case delorable. How about the under-issued 'Evenin'', from the Jones-Smith Inc. session? However, here is the title-piece: I have never heard a band whoop in the last ride-out as this one, and how striking the accompaniments are – the menacing trombone figure behind Clayton, the harsh falling single note behind Young repeated like an accusation. 'Every Tub' is the band's most storming 'head', yet even with the excitement of the open trumpet and Basie's logical single-note line there are subtleties such as the slight change of reed figure between second and third ensemble chorus. What a band it was! With 'Topsy', 'Doggin' Around', 'Texas Shuffle' and 'Blue and Sentimental' in addition, this is a massive collection. One can only hope that Basie has forgiven the promoter who paid him a flat $750 for twenty-four sides and tied him up for three years.

Another monument of the thirties is 'Benny Goodman: The Small Groups' (RCA Victor), sixteen sides from the BG chamber groups, 1936–8. Here are 'Dizzy Spells', 'The Blues In Your/My Flat' (originally two takes of the same number), the two-part 'Bei Mir' with Elman and Martha Tilton, 'Vibraphone Blues' and many others. One can't say Benny either began or ended the chamber tradition, but he supplied a kind of headlong precise excitement that was new to jazz. The big news of three years ago was that Pee Wee Russell had 'gone modern' and was playing Coltrane numbers with far-out companions. The Pee Wee Russell Quartet, with trombonist Marshall Brown, has disbanded since, but 'Ask Me Now!' (HMV) recalls its heyday. The eleven pieces are neatly arranged to showcase Pee Wee's wandering lines, and some of his plain statements (Ellington's 'Prelude') are engaging studies in false simplicity, but there is a general lack of grip that explains the group's demise.

The Earl Hines vogue continues unabated, with 'Stride Right' (Verve), wherein Earl and Johnny Hodges divide nine tunes from the repertoire of both – 'Rosetta', 'C Jam Blues' and so on. 'Caution Blues', Hines's old 'Blues In Thirds', goes beautifully, and Hodges' 'Fantastic' and 'Tale of the Fox' exhibit his familiar yet ever-new charm. On the whole it is Rabbit who swallows Fatha: Hines's piano is much less knotted and florid than elsewhere. Kenny Burrell supports ably. Good big band reissues are found on 'Great Big Bands' (MFP) and 'The Great Big Bands – 1: Ellington' (Capitol), the first offering an Ellington-Henderson-Carter mélange from the thirties ('Merrygoround', a different master of 'Queer Notions') and the second a bunch of sides from 1953–5, one of the Ellington-is-finished eras that in retrospect have a lot to offer. Clark Terry shines like a good deed in a naughty world.

Sixteen more Fats Waller pieces 'of the best period', as Wilde would say, make up 'Valentine Stomp' (RCA Victor), and very nice they are – 'Bran' New Suit', 'Why Do I Lie?', a new 'Black Raspberry Jam', and of course the title number, immortalizing Hazel Valentine of Harlem's Daisy Chain in 1929. There's been plenty of Waller recently, but can one have too much? Billie Holiday's 'Easy To Remember' (Society) has a long latterday 'Fine and Mellow'. On the archive front, two notable Riverside classics are 'Lovie Austin and her Blues Serenaders' and 'Piano Blues 1927–33', the former giving this group's entire output with Ladnier and Dodds, and the latter exhuming precious tracks by Jabo Williams, Rudy Foster ('Black Girl

Makes Thunder'), James 'Bat' Robinson and others. Their music sounds so old, unhappy and far-off it's hard to realize their intentions were of the sprightliest.

21 September 1966

Can the Real Thing Come Along Any More?

The condition of jazz today is such that the announcement of a new star produces not so much the reaction 'And how is he new?' as 'How can he be new?' What novelty has been left unexplored in the name of jazz? Does he bellow like a bull, squeak like a slate-pencil, cough like a raven? Old stuff. Does he play three instruments at once, saw a violin left-handedly, hit the piano with his elbows? All been done before. Does he simply puff down his instrument without vibrating the reed to give us the piquant sensation of silence? Fifties trick. And so it goes on.

It is something of a relief, therefore, to find that Charles Lloyd, about whom Continental critics went overboard earlier this year with a splash that resounded from Oslo to Frankfurt to Amsterdam, does not attempt to push the boundaries of the music any farther back, at least for the moment. On 'Dream Weaver' (Atlantic) this tall, bespectacled flute and tenor player shows himself to be something of a Coltrane man, capable both of the master's meditation ('Autumn Prelude') and his hard-driving frenzy ('Dervish Dance'). If he has an individual quality I should say it is a tinge of romantic lyricism; Coltrane might say of Lloyd what Gertrude Stein said of Hemingway: 'You do something first, then someone else comes along and does it pretty.' Despite Lloyd's manifesto, 'I want to extend music beyond its previous boundaries, while retaining the lyrical, earthy feeling that has been part of jazz since the beginning', it is Keith Jarrett, pianist in his Quartet, who strikes the listener as more markedly original. On 'Dervish' he does a sheets-of-sound in terms of piano, seeming at times to strum physically on the strings inside the lid, while on 'Bird Flight' he has a delightful passage of little sinuous runs dealt swiftly right and left from the middle register. Bassist Cecil McBee and drummer Jack Dejohnette also get plenty of elbow-room. As a soloist Lloyd is energetic, as a composer deliberately difficult. He may yet justify his Continental acclaimers.

A remarkable gathering is found on 'Once Upon a Time', by Earl Hines (HMV), where Fatha mixes with some veteran Ellingtonians and, of all people, Pee Wee Russell and Elvin Jones. On 'The Blues In My Flat' Nance does the Hampton vocal with Russell in effortful twittering support; 'Hash Brown' swings enormously on a rhythm base of Aaron Bell and Sonny Greer; 'Black and Tan Fantasy' provides splendid Russell and Hines solos with Greer in florid attendance. On the whole the music is too much of a gallimaufry to succeed, and Hines is rather subdued, but as a mainstream curiosity it is justified.

The reissue of 'Miles Ahead' by Miles Davis with the Gil Evans Orchestra (CBS) recalls one of the most celebrated records of the fifties? 'I tell you', Dizzy Gillespie said, '*everyone* should own that album.' The placing of the sad plangency of Davis's flugelhorn against a shifting background of scored brass, French horns and woodwind produce a much pleasanter surface texture than usual with this soloist, and one can see how, like the companion album 'Porgy and Bess', it won instant popularity. Though only one piece – 'Blues For Pablo' – is actually by Evans, he is the presiding genius, and the album marks a peak of integration of soloist with ensemble. The only trouble from my point of view is that, as jazz, it is practically non-alcoholic. No such charge could be levelled against 'Blues I Love to Sing' (Ace of Hearts) by Jimmy Rushing with early Count Basie Orchestras. This is a companion volume to the wonderful 'Jumpin' At The Woodside', reviewed last month. Rushing has an invigorating voice, like pouring sunshine, almost entirely without mannerisms to distract from its boundless energy, and the band was at its best, with Basie, Evans, Young and others breaking through. 'Lester Young Leaps Again!' (Fontana) is a reissue of two 1943/44 Keynote sessions, the first with Guarnieri, Slam Stewart and Catlett and the second the Kansas City Seven team with Clayton, Wells and the rhythm. Some critics have said that this is the best Young on record, and certainly his lean, unhesitant, surprising tenor shows what a new star was like a quarter of a century ago. Nobody had to tell you: he told you himself.

19 October 1966

Goodman's Guitar Man

When critic John Hammond smuggled Charlie Christian through the kitchen and on to the stand of the Victor Hugo in Los Angeles in

August 1939, he was unwittingly setting one of those legendary scenes that jazz abounds in. The leader, Benny Goodman, was having dinner. Arriving back, he was furious to see this 20-year-old gangling, unpolished Negro planted, amplifier and all, among the Sextet: he might have ordered him out. Instead, he called for 'Rose Room'. It was a wise decision. That was the longest 'Rose Room' Benny ever played, forty-five minutes of trading new exciting phrases with a jazz stylist of complete originality. It was not only that amplification brought the guitar at one stride into the solo line: Christian's long-running single-note phrases and seemingly-inexhaustible vocabulary of riffs were utterly contemporary – even, perhaps, a hint of things to come. At the end of 'Rose Room' the Goodman band had a new guitarist.

For Benny it was a lucky break. The loss of Krupa and Wilson had shattered his small-group pattern; now it was remodelled, abandoning the old standards such as 'Body and Soul' in favour of originals based on these fluent dynamic repetitions Charlie kept feeding out – 'Gone With What Wind', 'Air Mail Special', 'Flying Home' and the rest. For Charlie it was not so happy. Promotion to the big time and $150 a week brought with it chicks, drink, drugs and a reawakening of tuberculosis. Most of the time he sat playing the chords with the band, then dashed down to Minton's to play with the young boppers. By the end of 1941 he was in hospital. Somehow Benny never did get to see him. In March, 1942, he died.

'Solo Flight' (CBS) is a second harvest of those few years (the first, with 'Waitin' For Benny', was issued some years ago) – a new master of the title-piece and 'Honeysuckle Rose' with the band, 'Flying Home', 'Boy Meets Goy', 'Shivers' and 'Rose Room' itself from smaller groups, plus ten others. Here the emphasis is slightly on the 1936 book, and one can see how irritating Goodman must have found his new acquisition at times: in 'Star Dust', for example, after a stately chorus apiece from Benny and Hampton, Christian inserts the best-known banality from 'Pretty Baby' with disastrous effect. In fleeter numbers such as 'Shivers' and 'Royal Garden', however, solos and ensemble alike flower into the inimitable free-wheeling freedom that was Charlie Christian's characteristic contribution to jazz.

It is saddening to learn that a subsidized group is touring Southern high schools to teach children to like jazz – apparently an uphill job, for 'when the group demonstrated the bop era, the lecturing proved more difficult'. Shades of Louis Armstrong's first long pants! What would the kids say to John Coltrane's 'Meditations' (HMV), the Master's latest religious suite, the first side of which is the most astounding piece of ugliness I have ever heard? Coltrane is joined here by Pharaoh Sanders, Elvin Jones by one Rashied Ali. The other movements are easier to take and, in all, the work has a wild audacity one can't help admiring. At the other end of the spectrum is 'The Original Dixieland Jazz Band' (MFP), twelve tracks recorded in England in 1919/20. Despite the sleeve's claim that their music was improvised, this 'Tiger Rag' sounds much like the 1917 version; later pieces, especially 'Mammy o' Mine', sound on the verge of freedom from ragtime syncopation. Considering they could never have heard an Armstrong solo, they were pretty good.

Benny Carter's 'Additions to Further Definitions' (HMV) – the year's worst title? – shows this admirable soloist cutting session-mates Bud Shank, Collette, Teddy Edwards and Bill Hood, aided by Barney Kessel. 'Come On Back' is a sweeping blues, and on 'Rock Bottom' the five reeds show their powers individually and collectively. The brassless ensembles are somewhat feminine, though. 'Basie's Beatle Bag' (Verve) offers twelve Chico O'Farrill arrangements, eleven of Lennon-McCartney tunes, with good spells of Lockjaw Davis and Marshall Royal, but Basie clearly does not know what magic he is meddling with. A better buy is 'Count Basie Plays, Joe Williams Sings' (MFP), an assortment of pieces from the late fifties, some with organ backing. Not all are blues, but 'Low Down Dirty Shame' is outstanding in a better-than-average selection.

'Parker Panorama' (Verve) shows two of the less attractive facets of the Bird's recording career: with Machito's Lat-Am outfit and (on the second side) with strings. 'The Bird' (1949), just Parker and rhythm, is a restorative, as is the unregenerate trombone of Tommy Turk on 'Visa'. Everyone should own at least one Erroll Garner concert disc, and 'Campus Concert' (MGM), made at Purdee University, has as much vitality as any, 'Lulu's Back in Town' and 'These Foolish Things' taking especially well to Garner's tramping treatment.

Finally let me recommend 'Hot Jazz, Pop Jazz, Hokum and Hilarity' (RCA Victor), Jelly Roll sides with George Mitchell and Johnny Dodds, plus a batch of wholly uncharacteristic tracks with Henry

Allen and the Russell Orchestra. Animal noises, yes, but Allen's nervy trumpet foreshadows much.

16 November 1966

From Clifford to Connie

I never liked bop. It seemed to me a nervous and hostile ('something that they can't steal because they can't play it') music, at odds with the generous spirit of its predecessors. But it had its masters. One of these was Clifford Brown, the trumpeter whose brief career (he died in 1956, aged 25) is now commemorated in a handsomely-boxed two-disc set 'The Immortal Clifford Brown' (Mercury). Many of these fifteen sides are by the celebrated Brown-Roach Quintet, and all date from the last years of his life, embodying the relaxed broad attack Brown brought to a feverish narrow mode.

On the other hand Coleman Hawkins's 'Cattin'' (Fontana) presents fourteen tracks from 1944, and is heavy with the end of a tradition. Despite Earl Hines with Cosy Cole's All Stars, and Jack Teagarden's casual domination of George Wettling's New Yorkers, not to mention Sid Catlett's drumming, there is a certain sogginess about this repertoire that a host of talents cannot redeem. For the most part Hawkins takes his place as one more soloist in a rather tired period, ready as the rest for a shot in the arm from Minton's. Bop was historically inevitable.

Samuel Charters, author of *The Country Blues*, has been at work in the middle West, to produce 'Chicago/The Blues/Today!' (Fontana), a three-disc set exemplifying present-day South Side club music by Junior Wells, J. B. Hutto, Otis Rush, Johnny Young, and others. They are all much of a muchness, the Mississippi tradition of Robert Johnson and Elmore James amplified to a slamming coarseness, but containing many delights – Buddy Guy's guitar with Junior Wells, Jimmy Cotton's harmonica, the passionate vocals of J. B. Hutto. But they contrast oddly with 'Jazz Gillum 1938/1947' (RCA Victor), a much more musical set by a singer often mistaken for Broonzy, who features in some of the ensembles. Most Gillum pieces have a tune – perhaps 'New Vicksburg', or 'Keys to the Highway' – and all instruments are, of course, free from amplification; Chicago thirty years back sounds curiously innocent in consequence.

Should you buy Ellington's 'Concert Of Sacred Music' (RCA

Victor)? My impression is that it's pretty empty, jazzwise; out-of-tempo doodling and gospel singers, with occasional flashes from Hodges, Anderson and Hamilton, just the sort of pretentiousness to fill a modern cathedral. Much better big-band stuff is 'The Great Big Bands Vol. 2 – Woody Herman', one side from 1948–50, rather frenzied ('Early Autumn', 'Lemon Drop'), the other 1955 ('Sentimental Journey', 'Captain Ahab'), a less-known Herd but more relaxed and swinging. Hermann on alto and clarinet presents a judicious blend of Hodges and Bigard.

The trouble with 'Bud Freeman Esq.' (Fontana), made over here with Dick Katz and rhythm, is that the dean of white tenors is far too respectful to his British session-mates, allowing them pretty well chorus for chorus so that he himself never gets going. Katz's loud piano is nearer salon than saloon, and only occasional titles ('I Could Write a Book') show Bud at his best. Go rather for Stan Getz's 'Crazy Rhythm' (Verve), Norman Granz sides with all sorts of people from Eldridge to J. J. Johnson, 1954–8: driving stuff on 'Pernod' and the title-piece, two good blues, and a delightful 'Jordu'. This is the best Getz for some months.

Finally, let me, after several months, mention 'Nothing Was Sweeter Than The Boswell Sisters' (Ace of Hearts) vivacious close-harmony singing from 1931 with the Dorsey Brothers, Berigan, Venuti, Lang, Manny Klein and others. It's a blend of charming period vocal arabesques (not so odd as today's, most of them) and down-to-earth hot playing, both fitting each other admirably. Probably the surprise disc of the year.

5 December 1966

1967

Credo

'Of course, to a purist like yourself . . .' Me? To the purist all things are poor, making him worry whether the banjoist is standing or sitting, or denounce Louis Armstrong, and as I staggered into 1967, hearing that Ornette Coleman had been voted *Down Beat's* Musician of the Year, I took stock of my position. True, I don't like fancy time signatures, or want any African or Latin-American or Indian or Caribbean tinges, or bass solos, or New Wave nonsense, or free form fatuity; in fact, the whole thing has gone to pot since 1945, or even 1940, but this is no more than saying that I like jazz to be jazz. A. E. Housman said he could recognize poetry because it made his throat tighten and his eyes water: I can recognize jazz because it makes me tap my foot, grunt affirmative exhortations, or even get up and caper round the room. If it doesn't do this, then however musically interesting or spiritually adventurous or racially praiseworthy it is, it isn't jazz. If that's being a purist, I'm a purist. And the banjoist can stand on his head for all I care.

The Christmas recess seemed suddenly to be filled with piano records, some of them first-rate, like 'Oscar Peterson Salutes the Count and the Duke' (Verve). Peterson salutes the Count much more effectively, to my mind: stomping slamming versions of 'Easy Does It' and 'Lester Leaps in', backed by Herb Ellis, Brown and Rich, made in 1956. The Duke tracks are shorter and three years later, part of a marathon 106 recordings in seventeen days with Brown and Thigpen, and they seem slighter and more coasting in consequence. Peterson in 1966 can be heard on 'Put On a Happy Face' (Verve), seven pieces recorded at The London House, Chicago, with all the customary dash, precision and finesse.

Patriarch Dave Brubeck has a new disc 'Time In' (CBS) eight originals in much the usual vein except for some slightly mocking funk in 'He Done Her Wrong' and some Biblical pastoralism in '40 Days', 'an excerpt from a work in progress'. Brubeck is a delightful pianist, and Desmond an admirable alto, and neither does anything here to enhance or damage his reputation. 'Dave Brubeck's

Greatest Hits' (CBS) brings together 'Take Five', 'Raggy Waltz', 'Camptown Races', 'Unsquare Dance' and others for the uninitiate.

'Mama Yancey Sings, Art Hodes Plays Blues' (Verve) is mostly attractive for the glimpse it provides of Hodes, nimbler now and with fewer rumbling rolls; he hasn't quite the magical timing of Jimmy Yancey, who could make one note do the work of ten, but his playing is beautifully relaxed. Estella Yancey has a strong, nasal, unvarying voice, showing few signs of age and exhibits the classic approach. Much has been heard of Denny Zeitlin and 'Live At The Trident' (CBS) shows him to be less an original than an extremely competent devotee of Bill Evans, perhaps with a crisper touch, but equally self-indulgent when it comes to romantic wanderings. Bill Evans himself turns up on 'Intermodulation' with Jim Hall on guitar, six lengthy offerings, included the latter's 'All Across the City'. Pretty, but oh-so-background.

I feel I should mention The Spontaneous Music Ensemble's 'Challenge' (Eyemark Records), the first British free form disc according to the sleeve, though I went to sleep during it. Five first-class musicians, Clark Terry, Kenny Burrell, Herbie Hancock, Ron Carter and the leader, get together in Ed Thigpen's 'Out Of The Storm' (Verve), (the drummer-composer's first disc in his own name, which displays a somewhat literary and picturesque approach). Clark Terry has a fine low-down solo on 'Storm' and a silly one (mouth-piece only) on 'Elbow and Mouth'.

20 February 1967

The Ellington Reputation

There are times when one wants to attack the whole Ellington mystique, to expose him as an indifferent pianist whose orchestral tastes lie in the direction of alternate vapidity and pretension and who has been carried along since the twenties by a succession of magnificent soloists and his own charm, intelligence and energy. True, this would mean ignoring the famous Ellington band ethos – a mixture of the Athenaeum and A. S. Neill – and discounting the creativity which keeps him (at an age when professors are forcibly retired) scribbling new works that edge old favourites out of the band book. It may not be a bad thing, either, to be immovably pre-Parker in one's musical thinking. But when did he last make a record as good as, say, 'Harlem Airshaft'?

The second three-disc instalment of 'The Ellington Era, 1927–1940' (CBS), however, stresses, if it does nothing else, that the second fifty Ellington records have more personality, variety and historical interest than anyone else of the period could muster for their first choices. Moving from the irascibility of Miley ('Move Over') to the virtuosity of Williams and Stewart ('Tootin' Through the Roof'), this set has inevitably to rest on lesser-known pieces or unfamiliar versions of old favourites. 'Beggar's Blues', 'Sweet Chariot' and 'Old King Dooji' are admirable, and there is an interesting version of 'Rent Party Blues'; the thirties was a soggy time for Ellington, though, as evidenced by 'Reminiscin' in Tempo' (Hammond reviewed it as 'The Tragedy of Duke Ellington'), and 'In a Sentimental Mood' and 'No Greater Love' do not really bear resurrection.

Ellington's reputation has benefited a good deal from discs such as 'Things Ain't What They Used To Be' (RCA Victor), sixteen tracks from 1940–1 by the Johnny Hodges and Rex Stewart small bands, but although he is the pianist in both, the genius of the music stems in each case from the leader. Following the vogue for a 'band within a band' (Goodman's Trio, Crosby's Bobcats, Dorsey's Clambake Seven), Ellington unwittingly released at least one major talent (Hodges), as the title piece 'Goin' Out The Back Way' and 'That's The Blues Old Man' testify. The Stewart sets are somewhat less coherent, but 'Subtle Slough', 'Menelik' and 'Mobile Bay' show off his remarkable range of tone. Both groups are supported by the bass of Jimmy Blanton.

'Coltrane Live At The Village Vanguard Again' (HMV) returns us sharply to the sixties, offering two pieces: 'Naima' and 'My Favourite Things', by the Master supported by Mrs Coltrane, new recruit Pharaoh Sanders, Jimmy Garrison and a couple of drummers. Frankly, I should not mention it – so much of the blended insolence and ugliness known as New Wave seems epitomized therein – if at least one journal didn't term it five-star material and assure its readers that 'its scalpel cuts through the layers of dead tissue that insulate us from reality'. To these unregenerate ears Mrs C. is no substitute for McCoy Tyner (though she is not well recorded), but the scalpel image is good: rusty, at that. No doubt most people know what they think of this kind of thing by now. Strong traces of earlier Coltrane, by the way, can be found in 'The Maynard Ferguson Sextet' (Fontana); nice trumpet and flugelhorn on 'Sandpiper' and 'April Fool', but the cookers (and why must one be 'Summertime'?) seems as derivative as Red Nichols used to be.

Fred McDowell's 'My Home Is In The Delta' (Bounty) is an example of Mississippi singing at its finest. On the blues side (the other is spirituals with Annie Mae McDowell) his voice trails, whimpers, blusters and mumbles in loose harness with his guitar expressing a kind of melancholy monotony that is like a way of life, using as vehicles 'Waiting For My Baby', 'Diving Duck Blues' and 'The Sun Rose This Morning'. 'Spoon Sings and Swings' (Fontana) catches Jimmy Witherspoon at The Bull's Head, Barnes, in pretty rowdy company, but on 'Nobody Knows The Way That I Feel' and 'Lotus Blossom' he and Dick Morrissey's tenor achieve very listenable music. 'A Collection of Beatles Oldies' (Parlophone) is more a short history of this musical phenomenon from 'She Loves You' to 'Eleanor Rigby', and would prove admirable demonstration material for Marx's theory of artistic degeneration: WEA lecturers please note.

Though somewhat impatient with Jack Teagarden during his lifetime (he always seemed to be getting in the way of better soloists), I find his posthumous albums magnificent, and 'Jack Teagarden' (RCA Victor) is well up to form, comprising a long conspectus from Jack's first record ('She's a Great Great Girl' with Roger Wolfe Kahn in 1928) to Freeman's revived 1957 Cum Laude group. There's a new master of one of my favourites, Condon's 'I'm Gonna Stomp Mr. Henry Lee', where Teagarden fluffs the words and Sullivan is not quite so filigreed: the MCBB's 'Tailspin', 'Ridin' But Walkin'' and other classics mingle with admirable unknowns such as Pollack's 'My Kind of Love'. All in all, a splendid bag.

15 March 1967

The Funny Hat Men

I sometimes wonder whether, despite all evolutionary claims, Negro jazz men do not constantly divide into crowd-pleasers and conservatory men – Bolden and Jelly Roll Morton, Armstrong and Ellington, Gillespie and Miles Davis. And the distinction is always cropping up, sometimes unexpectedly: take the business of hats, for instance. Wearing a funny hat is surely the essence of Uncle-Tommery, yet what else unites Dizzy, Monk, and now Archie Shepp? 'You've got to dress up for it . . . I like hats, I change them all the time,' he says on the sleeve of 'Archie Shepp Live in San Francisco' (HMV). It gives the music a new slant: these death-to-all-white-men wails, this portentous gibberish recited in the accents of Sir Henry Irving against two bowed basses, this semi-farcical resurrection of the Webster breathing-down-your-neck manner – all this is suddenly seen as no more than an act for the folks, and as such jolly enough. What would happen to the New Wave, though, if its bassists and drummers played as horribly as its horn men?

Art Farmer on 'Baroque Sketches' (CBS) stands revealed as the second kind: like the Swingle Singers, and Benny Goodman before the war, he has discovered that Bach goes to town, and wants to help him along. 'Aria' ('Air On the G String') and 'Jesu' ('Jesu Joy of Man's Desiring') come as varying degrees of a shock, but Farmer's fat flugelhorn and the polyphonic ensembles are rich and robust. Other Baroque originals are Albeniz, Chopin and the Broadway hit show 'Sweet Charity'. The pieces are short and brisk and for the most part enjoyable, but the whole project is undertaken on the principle that 'Bach and Chopin were both improvisers of genius'.

Like the second instalment of Ellington, the CBS 'Billie Holiday: The Golden Years, Vol. 2' leaves a faint but persistent impression of barrel-scraping. This group of forty-eight tracks from 1935 to 1942 reiterates that Billie's pre-war career fell into three groups: the initial Wilson/Cozy Cole, the central Lester Young, and the later scored-saxes. This set begins nicely with such classics as 'Sunbonnet Blue' and 'Let's Call The Whole Thing Off', and progresses through different takes of 'I'll Get By' and 'Mean To Me', but its culmination in such depressing concessions as 'Mandy Is Two' and 'It's The Same Old Story' suggests that Billie Holiday's career was concave, rising during the fifties to a second peak under Norman Granz. Once again, how unfailingly good Teddy Wilson is! Another kind of singer is represented on 'Women Of The Blues' (RCA Victor), a representative selection from Sippie Wallace, Alberta Hunter, Mamie Smith and other examples of that vanished race, the female blues exponent. Most of these tracks date from the twenties, and have varying accompanists such as Henry 'Red' Allen, Johnny Dodds, and the youthful Rex Stewart.

No sooner have I declared Duke Ellington an indifferent pianist than he comes up with the best recorded solo of his career, 'The Second Portrait of the Lion' on 'A Musical Exchange' (RCA Victor), made in June 1965, at the Pittsburgh Jazz Festival – hard-hitting stride stuff with no champagne or velvet, and no holds barred either. The Lion himself is featured on 'Contrary Motion', Earl Hines with 'Somehow', and Mary Lou Williams on 'Angle' and 'Joycie'; Billy Taylor and Charles Bell also appear, and there is a good deal of fun to be had spotting who's who in the combined efforts such as 'Sweet Lorraine' and 'Rosetta'. This was certainly one of the rare occasions when the big names justified themselves.

'The Popular Duke Ellington' (RCA Victor), made last year, consists of tunes of creaking familiarity, but there is plenty of rather effortful Cootie Williams, now of course back with the band, as on 'Black and Tan Fantasy' and 'The Mooche'. Another medley of Ellington hits with a difference is 'The Duke Ella's Way' (Verve), tracks recorded by Norman Granz in 1957. Ray Nance plays a delightful first chorus on what Ella persists in singing as 'Drop Me Off *In* Harlem', and there is the trumpet chase (Terry, Baker, Cook, Anderson, Gillespie and Nance) on 'A Train', as well as lots of gold-painted Fitzgerald vocals and the Duke's 'Portrait of Ella Fitzgerald'. Conservatory man or crowd-pleaser, Duke always ends up on the credit side.

12 April 1967

Ornette Again

People who say Ornette Coleman isn't jazz, Hugues Panassié once pronounced sternly, should have said the same earlier on about Miles Davis, and for the same reasons. Which is one way of saying, I suppose, that they stand in an evolutionary relation to each other, like green apples and stomach-ache. I am reminded of the French critic's dictum by the simultaneous appearance of 'Miles Smiles' (CBS) and 'Free Jazz' by the Ornette Coleman Double Quartet (Atlantic). The latter disc, the less recent, bears on its sleeve a reproduction of a Jackson Pollock painting, and until the last ten minutes or so of its forty-minute length is a fair musical representation of it, a patternless reiterated jumble. The Coleman-Cherry-La Faro-Higgins four is balanced by a quartet of Hubbard, Dolphy, Haden and Blackwell, and the record's technique of free form doesn't preclude facetious banalities such as a quotation from 'Jingle Bells'. On the credit side, there are no wilful distortions of tone such as is found in many New Wave groups, and when listening to Coleman I found myself repeating Blake's couplet 'If the sun and moon should doubt They'd immediately go out.' There *is* something lyrical and confident about Coleman that attracts even the most hardened. This is more than can be said of Davis, who in the company of Shorter, Hancock et al is his usual snarling staccato disagreeable self, with the exception of the corpse-walking 'Circle'. To me this is heartless and uninteresting jazz, and the only pleasure to be had from it is Tony Williams's drumming – light, attacking, unexpected, especially on the cymbals.

'The Blue Bechet' (RCA Victor) complements the recent 'Bechet of New Orleans', and once you get over the disappointment of its not being all blues is a fascinating cross-section of an irreplaceable vitality. The selection kicks off with three 1932 Feetwarmers pieces, including the rare 'New Baby', then seven 1940 tracks such as the magnificent 'Nobody Knows The Way I Feel This Morning' (rendered inexorable by Catlett's drumming), 'Blues in Thirds' and a new master or two. The rest are minor American pieces from 1941, not helped by the vagaries of Charlie Shavers and the electric guitar of Everett Barksdale. Another retrospect is 'Ella Fitzgerald's Big Sixteen' (Verve), an anthology of Granz pieces between 1958 and 1964 which is much better than likely. Of course there is the opposition of the straight, beautifully-treated ballads such as 'Every Time We Say Goodbye' with the swingers: she joins with Louis and Oscar Peterson on 'Can't We Be Friends', and generates unaided a kinetic joyousness on 'Let's Do It' and 'Like Young'. Both are delightful: it's the soapy 'People' and misguided 'Can't Buy Me Love' that fall down.

I should not go as far as to say we have had enough of the New Orleans veterans, but much of it seems hardly more than historically interesting. 'Emile Barnes' New Orleans Band' (Storyville) is from the American Music label (1951), with Dede Pierce on one of the trumpets and the amazing Albert Glenny, who was born in 1870 and played with Buddy Bolden ('He was loud'), on bass. Barnes is a clarinettist in the Dodds tradition, intense and blue, as can be heard on 'Billie's Blues' and 'St. Louis Blues', and Dede Pierce does a fierce Creole vocal on 'Eh la Bas'; these heartening assets are balanced by Billie Pierce's interminable lyrics and some waddling trombone from Harrison Brazely. Billie and Dede turn up again on 'New Orleans Jazz' (Storyville), duetting to reasonably good advantage, but piano and trumpet are not a combination for extended listening.

A remarkable morsel on the same label is a series of 1939 transcripts from the Sherman Hotel, Chicago, of the 'Boogie Woogie Trio', Pete Johnson, Albert Ammons and Meade Lux Lewis. The vogue of this team seems incredible today, not because they lacked talent but because a little of their hard-hitting manner goes such a long way. Eight of the fifteen tracks are by Ammons, including a good 'Hersal Blues' and a spritely 'Jesse James'. From the Mayfair Hotel, London, some six years earlier, Harry Roy and his Band were dispensing ('Hotcha-Me-Cha-Cha', MFP) their curious blend of ragtime and Ted Lewis: 'Bugle Call Rag', 'Somebody Stole My Gal' and many more. Only the trombone (no sleeve information) commands respect today, but the selection is rich in reminiscence.

Delicacies abound (in contrast) on 'Blue Guitars' (Parlophone), tracks chosen from the work of that odd studio association, Eddie Lang and Lonnie Johnson – Lang mellow and feelingful, Johnson lighter and more agile. The most precious item, though, is Armstrong's 'Knockin' a Jug' (1929), included by courtesy of Eddie's presence. I did not care for 'Saturday Night Fish Fry' (one of Fontana's new stereo-mono discs), although the personnel – Eldridge, Freeman, Bryant and Jo Jones – is promising. Much more enjoyable is Howard McGhee's 'The Sharp Edge' (Fontana), on which this rather forgotten man of bop whips up some blues and ballads with George Coleman, Junior Mance and Jimmy Cobb. I should call this better than Miles.

10 May 1967

The Man from Defiance (Ohio)

'If you have not heard Wild Bill before,' says the sleeve of 'Wild Bill Davison!' (Fontana), 'it is something of a shock to your system.' But supposing you have? The record could then probably be passed over if it weren't for the fact that, of the three great white jazz eccentrics, only Wild Bill seems to have had less than his due. His affinities lie with Pee Wee Russell rather than Beiderbecke: a player of notable energy, he uses a wide range of conscious tonal distortions, heavy vibrato, and an urgent, bustling attack. At slow tempos he is melting, almost articulate. Humphrey Lyttelton has compared him with the kind of reveller who throws his arm round your neck one moment and tries to knock you down the next.

All the same, his stylistic mannerisms – the deep hoarse blurrings, the athletic in-front-of-the-beat timing, the flaring shakes – are highly conscious (the 'Wild' is more a personal than a musical sobriquet), and, imposed as they are on a conventional Armstrong basis, make Davison one of the most exciting of white small-band trumpeters. His sessions with Sidney Bechet for Blue Note are collisions of two furious jazz talents which at the same time were oddly sympathetic, and prove his ability to play in any kind of milieu; his numerous sides in the Condon tradition show him uniting with Russell in the same way. But solo after solo demonstrates that he is not a 'wild' player: each note is as perfectly shaped and pitched as if the cornet were his speaking voice, in the style of his favourites Armstrong and Hackett, and with an emotional immediacy always hard to parallel.

Today Davison is over 60, and though, as his recent tours have shown, his vitality is undiminished, he has not devised any new tricks and is now a heavily mannered performer. This record, made with members of the Alex Welsh Band, presents him with ten tunes, many of them ('If I Had You', 'How Come You Do Me') old favourites, and is loaded with theatrical codas, flamboyant statements and pushing ensembles. The first eight bars of 'Blue Again' are the best thing on the record, but a final sickening modulation upwards spoils it as a track; the blues 'Duet' and 'Keeping Out of Mischief' are much better overall. For Davison fans this is a lively collection, well worth buying: others should look for his work of twenty-five years ago.

Readers of Charles Keil's *Urban Blues* will be interested in 'Blues Is King' (HMV), performances by the celebrated B. B. King recorded live in Chicago. Keil's point was that modern blues have a kind of singer-audience solidarity that links them with religious meetings, and the plummy authoritative King certainly evokes response, yelling his maxims as if determined not to be misunderstood. Duke Jethro's organ and Bobby Forte's tenor make nice contrasts. The church comparison will be more easily understood after a playing of 'Witness For The Lord' (Ace of Hearts), especially the dynamic six tracks by the Reverend Kelsey and his congregation recorded in 1951 in Washington. Every collector should have at least one example of Negro religious community expression, and there could hardly be a better one than this.

'Fractious Fingering' (RCA Victor) is another exploration into the 1936 Waller archives, sixteen tracks all from that year except three 1929 piano solos. The titles are less familiar than usual, and include

'The Curse Of An Aching Heart', 'La-De-De La-De-Da' and 'Who's Afraid Of Love?' Even to the Waller fan Fats's successes are something of a mystery: they seem to be due to his formula, but so do his failures – what one moment is fresh as dew and genuinely funny becomes, a moment after, a stale and facetious cliché. The balance here is about normal.

Mississippi John Hurt, now about 75, made some records in the twenties but was rediscovered only recently by Tom Hoskins, since when he has enjoyed something of a vogue. Despite his name, he is no back-country bottle-neck mumbler, rather a spry guitar-for-dancing performer with a limited original repertoire (three of these tracks he made first back in 1928) and a trick of producing individual versions of familiar standards such as 'Pallet On The Floor' and 'Hot Time In Old Town'. His harmonies are rich, his singing and general manner entirely good-tempered, suggesting his training as entertainer rather than social-protest man. Another notable blues disc is Muddy Waters' 'Down On Stovall's Plantation' (Bounty), a reissue of Muddy's 1941–2 Library of Congress recordings when he was in his mid-twenties and still very much a country singer influenced by Robert Johnson.

It is hard to believe Henry 'Red' Allen is dead. Like Davison, he bent the Armstrong, or New Orleans, style to his own use, making it nervy, off-balance, harmonically unexpected; his recording career was a long one, and it is exciting to see 'The Luis Russell Story' announced by Parlophone, but in the meantime Red can be heard in a more elegiac context, with Jelly Roll Morton in 'Morton Sixes and Sevens' (Fontana). These are Morton's last three sessions, in 1940, rather hesitant, rather sad, an old master in search of a new style. Red plays as if he didn't want to hurt his feelings.

7 June 1967

The Great Russell Band

If the President of Yeshiva University in New York had sent a car for you some five years ago it would probably have been driven by Luis Russell, who at 60 did the job on twenty-four-hour call. This saddening anecdote is not to be found on the sleeve of 'The Luis Russell Story, 1929–30' (Parlophone), but then Russell was not a famous chauffeur. A jazzman from the age of 16, he graduated from

Oliver's Dixie Syncopaters to a band which he eventually took over, making its first records in January, 1929. These, and thirteen other tracks, all made within sixteen months, are to be found on this splendid reissue.

The band had a triple existence: during the same period, it was fronted by Armstrong for some of his best records of the period ('Dallas Blues', 'Bessie Couldn't Help It'); its star trumpeter, Henry Allen, made about sixteen sides with it under his own name ('Patrol Wagon Blues'); but it is in its own right that Luis Russell's orchestra will be remembered, for its fiery excursions such as 'Jersey Lightning', 'Panama' and 'Feeling the Spirit'. Like most Negro orchestras of the age, it was rather cumbrous in ensemble work, but the rhythm section had Pops Foster and Paul Barbarin on bass and drums, and it was a feature of Russell's arrangements that he never went for long without calling on one of his superlative soloists, either extendedly, or just for a break – Henry Allen, altoist Charlie Holmes, and trombonist J. C. Higginbotham. These three men were not only admirable in themselves, they formed a piquantly contrasting stylistic triangle. Allen, who makes a thrilling entry into the band's history on 'New Call Of The Freaks', brought to the Armstrong manner an idiosyncratic nerviness that made him a forerunner of modern phrasing and intervals, Charlie Holmes had an elegiac tone that makes his plaintive, downward-falling interjections all the more poignant, while the iron-lipped Higginbotham (his speciality, which even he could not keep up for long, was shattering trombone trills as on 'On Revival Day') created a blustering extrovert atmosphere by his solos in direct opposition to the other two. They are all heard extendedly on 'Doctor Blues', but they are equally exciting when they are tossing the solo ball among themselves as in 'Panama', suggesting a discussion between three utterly different temperaments. But, in fact, there is little fresh to say about this collection; it contains a second take of 'Louisiana Swing', but the rest of the tracks are classics almost without exception.

It came as a shock in Barry McRae's excellent account of the last decade or so of jazz, *The Jazz Cataclysm* (Dent), to find Parker, Gillespie and Davis described as 'giants of an earlier era'. Presumably, the younger generation think of Monk as a contemporary of Kid Ory, and indeed there is something craggy and elemental about him, as 'Straight, No Chaser' (CBS) demonstrates. Here two characteristic Monk explorations of ballads ('I Didn't Know About

You' and 'Devil And The Deep') are teamed with Quartet standards such as the title tune, 'Locomotive', and an endless piece called 'Japanese Folk Tune', which to me has a Russian tinge. This is mostly Monk's record: Charlie Rouse is subdued, and there isn't as much bass and drums as usual. Dizzy Gillespie on 'The Melody Lingers On' (Limelight), turns in some trite Latin-Americanisms with James Moody and the usual popping percussion. 'Freeman & Co.' (Fontana) is another British date with the dean of white tenors using Alex Welsh's band and the Dick Katz Trio alternately. Most of the pieces are well-worn ('Let's Do It', 'California', 'Three Little Words'), but Freeman coasts easily, snatching good solos on 'Somebody Stole My Gal' and 'Paper Moon'. The trio tracks are spoilt by heavy concessions to bass and drums. 'Mercy, Mercy, Mercy!' (Capitol) catches the Cannonball Adderley Quintet at the Club De Lisa in Chicago: the sleeve-writer avers that not to have had a recording unit there would have been like having 'no Sistine Chapel when Michelangelo got itchy to paint a ceiling'. In fact it is a good hearty evening with the Adderley brothers and Joe Zawinul (notable on electric piano on 'Mercy'), but Cannonball still sounds derivative to me, though Coltrane now instead of Parker. 'Easy' (Fontana) reissues eight mid-fifties tracks by the Clifford Brown-Max Roach Quintet, with Land or Rollins on tenor. 'Jordu' and 'George's Dilemma' spotlight Clifford's ripe trumpet, but apart from this the star is Richie Powell, brother of Bud, who was killed in the same car with Brown in 1956. His solos, particularly on 'Joy Spring' and 'Many Splendored Things', are sparklingly delightful.

'New Orleans Memories' (Ace of Hearts) offers four Bunk Johnson sides from 1945, four Kid Ory (1945) and three George Lewis (1952), all stirring good value for a guinea. Of 'Sergeant Pepper's Lonely Hearts Club Band' (Parlophone) I can say only that The Beatles, having made their name in the narrow emotional and harmonic world of teenage pop, are now floating away on their own cloud. I doubt whether their own fancies and imagination are strong enough to command an audience instead of collaborating with it.

10 July 1967

Looking Back at Coltrane

The obituaries produced by the sudden death of John Coltrane sent me back to some of his records, picked out more or less at random:

'Black Pearls', 'Live at Birdland', 'A Love Supreme', 'Africa/Brass'. For though I do not remembering ever suggesting that his music was anything but a pain between the ears, here was *The Times* and *Melody Maker* (great friends since the Jagger case) agreeing that Coltrane stood beside Hawkins, Young and Rollins in the roll of tenor players supreme. Was I wrong?

Well, I still can't imagine how anyone can listen to a Coltrane record for pleasure. That reedy, catarrhal tone, sawing backwards and forwards for ten minutes between a couple of chords and producing 'violent barrages of notes not mathematically related to the underlying rhythmic pulse, and not swinging in the traditional sense of the term' (*Encyclopaedia of Jazz in the Sixties*); that insolent egotism, leading to forty-five-minute versions of 'My Favourite Things' until, at any rate in Britain, the audience walked out, no doubt wondering why they had ever walked in; that latter-day religiosity, exemplified in turgid suites such as 'A Love Supreme' and 'Ascension' that set up pretension as a way of life; that wilful and hideous distortion of tone that offered squeals, squeaks, Bronx cheers and throttled slate-pencil noises for serious consideration – all this, and more, ensure that, for me at any rate, when Coltrane's records go back on the shelf they will stay there.

Of course, a great deal of this falls into place if one reflects that Coltrane was a 'modern' jazzman. The adjective 'modern', when applied to any branch of art, means 'designed to evoke incomprehension, anger, boredom or laughter', and Coltrane was simply part of the melancholy tendency since 1945 to remove jazz from our pleasures and place it, with all the other 'modern' arts, among our duties. Much of this was doubtless due to the fact that Coltrane was an American Negro. He did not want to entertain his audience: he wanted to lecture them, even to annoy them. His ten-minute solos, in which he lashes himself up to dervish-like heights of hysteria, are the musical equivalent of Mr Stokely Carmichael. It is this side of his work that appeals to the Black-Power boys such as LeRoi Jones and Archie Shepp; towards the end of his life, he had become associated with younger players of even wilder and more excruciating exhibitionism than himself, such as Pharaoh Sanders. It is not surprising that pianist McCoy Tyner and drummer Elvin Jones, for long his associates and admirers, quietly dropped off the wagon.

Virtually the only compliment one can pay Coltrane is one of stature. If he was boring, he was enormously boring. If he was ugly, he was massively ugly. To squeak and gibber for sixteen bars is nothing; Coltrane could do it for sixteen minutes, stunning the listener into a kind of hypnotic state in which he read and re-read the sleeve-note and believed, not of course that he was enjoying himself, but that he was hearing something significant. Perhaps he was. Time will tell. I regret Coltrane's death, as I regret the death of any man, but I can't conceal the fact that it leaves in jazz a vast, a blessed silence.

Coltrane is dead: long live Coleman! For if Coltrane 'progressed from' (i.e. was more horrible than) Parker, who but Ornette Coleman has progressed from Coltrane? Where Coltrane had two chords, Coleman has none at all, no pitch, no rhythm, no nothing. His latest two-disc record, 'Chappaqua Suite' (CBS), has a rib-tickling sleeve-note by some Frenchman which explains that an American film director, Conrad Rooks, commissioned Coleman to 'compose' some music for his film 'Chappaqua'. Thereupon Coleman and his two sidemen, bassist Charles Izenzon and drummer Charles Moffett, accompanied by Pharaoh Sanders and 'eleven other very fine studio musicians', entered into Ornette Coleman's world and 'served his music with love'.

Unfortunately, when Rooks heard the result, he was stricken with doubts: 'Should he use a music in itself so beautiful? Should not [sic] its strength do harm to the picture instead of serving it?' In a word, he junked it, commissioned another score and presumably cut his losses by selling the tapes to a record company. One can see what he means. Despite the comparatively large personnel (not given on the sleeve), the seeming hours of music resolve into duets or trios between a horn, Coleman or Sanders, the drums, and the rest of the band, the latter sustaining long chords behind a foreground of wailing and twittering and battering and uneven thumps. This is free form. Its drawback is that it all sounds alike. I noticed some sort of spook gutbucket at the beginning of side two, and some presumably satiric swing-era clichés at the end of side one, but in the main the effect is like watching twenty monkeys trying to type the plays of Shakespeare.

Coleman's playing is utterly free from hostility: he is gentle, light-hearted, almost zany, and his alto tone is really rather pleasant. No doubt this could have been film music, and it could well have been a nicer film that Mr Rooks actually made. Something about pond life, with plenty of tadpoles.

August 1967 (unpublished)

My First Name is James

Singer Jimmy Rushing is one of the unchangeables of jazz. Four-square and five-by-five, he resembles a rock round which the tides of fashion roll. The couplets he sings on Benny Moten's 'That Too, Do' in 1930 are the same as he sings with the Basie band eight or nine years later, and they are sung in the same assured way. Rushing went on singing them through the forties and fifties, and if they don't in fact feature on 'Every Day I Have the Blues' (HMV) this is a mere accident of repertoire. Change, Rushing implies – in this rather like Sidney Bechet – is for others. His voice bears out this philosophy. High, full and clear, it is oddly dispassionate, making concessions neither to comedy nor emotionalism. The blues lines – for Rushing is primarily a blues singer – are enunciated with only the smallest variations from verse to verse and decade to decade. Yet the result is the opposite of monotony. Powerful, joyous, relaxed, Rushing's voice pours down like sunshine, swinging the listener along with him, seemingly independent of mood or accompaniment. Readers of Ralph Ellison's *Shadow and Act* will recall how as a young man in Kansas City he used to hear Rushing singing four blocks away in Slaughter's Hall, his voice rising above the noise of freight from the Rock Island roundhouse. 'He expressed a value,' wrote Ellison, 'an attitude about the world for which our lives afforded no other definition.'

In 'Every Day I Have the Blues' Rushing repeats many of his standards in front of an orchestra headed by Oliver Nelson and featuring trombonist Dickie Wells. The set-up is promising: most of the tunes are blues, and Wells, besides being a jazz master in his own right, is a colleague from earlier Basie days. Yet it doesn't quite jell. The band, and in particular the drummer, has a stiff uncompromising beat that Rushing can do little to soften. On nearly every track, like Browning's wise thrush, he sings each set of words twice, a custom acceptable with ballads but not, for some reason, with blues: it gives the impression that he is short of material. Wells rambles sardonically in the background, occasionally employing sudden yelps and growls, but rarely, as on 'I Left My Baby', achieving a serious emotional statement. There is a nice trumpet on 'Every Day' (Clark Terry?), and Rushing is in good voice throughout, though from time to time the timbre of his intonation seems strained. All the same, this is genuine irrepressible Rushing, and not to be neglected.

The fifteen sides King Oliver made for Okeh in 1923 are again reissued on 'King Oliver's Jazz Band' (Parlophone), constituting one of the great series of jazz records. Although I am something of a heretic about Oliver, Johnny Dodds's clarinet and the building quality of the ensembles (as in relatively unknown pieces such as 'Ain't Gonna Tell Nobody') still justify these tracks for me, as does the presence of the youthful Armstrong. It is a long step from that first stop-chord chorus on 'Tears' to 'Louis Armstrong's Greatest Hits' (CBS), a bunch of recordings of standards with the All-Stars made in the middle 1950s. Splendid as Armstrong's Indian summer has been (remember he is as old as the century), it's not easy to find a record of this period that isn't rather ragged, and these are no exception. A swinging and flamboyant 'All of Me' (Milan, 1955) and the stock 'Sleepytime Down South' (Amsterdam, same year) make the pleasantest listening. Yet another trumpet reissue is 'Milestones' (CBS), dating from 1958 when Davis reassembled his Quintet with Cannonball Adderley on alto to make six. Although the blues pieces 'Straight No Chaser' and 'Sid's Ahead' are by this time celebrated, the presence of Cannonball is reputed to spoil the Davis-Coltrane rapport that made the Quintet so renowned. Personally, although I am not indifferent to Davis's resonant and dignified trumpet, such music as this seems to me alien to jazz in every particular. It seems to me ironic to find Cannonball lamenting recently in the *Melody Maker* that while we have a generation of kids who are raised on a constant diet of music, they don't listen to jazz and jazz is dying in consequence. 'Milestones' is the perfect explanation of this.

The Music For Pleasure label has lately launched a remarkable twenties and thirties programme which is largely outside jazz (Evelyn Laye, Jack Buchanan) but which merits investigation by any antiquarian of popular music. An unpromisingly-titled disc 'My Baby Loves to Charleston' reveals two British studio groups, Bert Firman and his orchestra and The Rhythmic Eight, playing a number of 1926–8 pieces, not all in Rust. Sylvester Ahola and Danny Polo are reputedly featured. Another MFP offering is 'Venuti-Rollini-Lang', twelve 1933 sides including the whole of Lang's last session. Rollini chops away on 'Vibraphonia' and there are two Goodman-Freeman Blue Six sides of much charm. The Venuti-Lang team remains undimmed. Freeman turns up on a local collection 'Bud Freeman & Co' (Fontana), and anyone nostalgic for big bands should try Charlie Barnet's 'Big Band 1967' (Vocalion). Yes, this is Barnet again, after retirement and eleven wives on the stand once more, a long way behind Basie but, with Willie Smith on alto, still in the race.

27 September 1967

Old Man Mainstream

I sometimes play 'Benny Goodman's 1938 Carnegie Hall Concert' (now reissued in a two-disc pack by CBS) as a kind of Scrapbook for 1913, the golden summer before the crippling barrage descended, after which things were not the same. The Goodman band was at its zenith in 1938 (Krupa and James left soon after) and however much we disparaged it at the time ('machinegun precision') it sounds pretty good now, with pianist Stacy cantering alongside the crisp, tight-reined ensembles that set a new standard in orchestral teamwork, and forgotten men like Vernon Brown making us look them up on the sleeve. The conscious spots of 'history' (pastiches of Bix and Louis), and the inclusion of the Ellington sidemen, were infinitely less significant than the appearance of Lester Young in the 'jam session' (period phrase!). Did we look into the seeds of time, and see which grains would grow?

But jazz was to suffer its own kind of nuclear fission, and when the smoke cleared everyone was found to have scuttled either to Minton's with the boppers, or to San Jacinto Hall with the old men with new teeth. All, that is, but a somewhat puzzled crowd of players, who had been young and now were not too old, who saw no reason to change the way they had always played, and whom in a year or so we began to call 'mainstream'. Webster's Third International Dictionary defines this as 'the prevailing current or direction of activity', which clearly won't do; Berendt says the term was coined in England, but I have not so far been able to put my finger on precisely when or by whom.* The mainstream musician was clearly not Muggsy Spanier (Dixieland) or Howard McGhee (bop); he was not too good for labels (Pee Wee Russell, Johnny Hodges); he was, in the best sense of the term, an upper-second musician of no over-riding character who had relied a good deal on a tradition to support him and now found it gone. He might flirt occasionally with a flatted fifth, but he was clearly never going to rework his harmonic nature.

* See 'The Panassié Sides', page 195.

'Vic Dickenson Showcase' (Fontana), made in 1953, is an excellent example of what they could do: five numbers ('Jeepers Creepers', 'Keeping Out of Mischief', etc.) treated extendedly over the two sides in a way that gave the soloists (Dickenson, Ruby Braff, Ed Hall, Sir Charles Thompson) time to get really relaxed. The rhythm section has ex-Goodmanite Steve Jordan and Walter Page, and clucks along in agreeable unobtrusiveness while the horns build. Dickenson keeps his dry humour out of the way for once, Hall exhibits that civilized sizzling clarinet that seems at once Noone and Goodman, Braff is superb as usual, and Sir Charles, while venturing a few more notes than Basie, is clearly from the same stable. Everything is done with a crispness and energy that is going to outlast a lot of today's free-for-alls.

A classic blues disc made three years later, Joe Turner's 'Boss of the Blues' (now reissued on Atlantic), presents this knotty-voiced shouter in front of a nicely balanced group of sidemen, sometimes improvising and sometimes playing Ernie Wilkins's arrangements, 'Cherry Red', 'Wee Baby', 'How Long', 'Piney Brown' – all these standards are treated with simple and increasing emotion, and the disc should be in everyone's collection. It may have been inspired by some Rushing sessions in the same vein a year or so previously, of which 'Listen To the Blues', (Fontana) is one – 'See See Rider', 'Good Morning Blues', 'Evenin'' and others, all backed by Emmett Berry, Rudy Powell, Buddy Tate, Lawrence Brown, and with Pete Johnson rather less successful on piano than with his old colleague Turner. Here Rushing's splendid blues are mixed with ballads – 'Don't Cry, Baby' is a masterly piece of enunciation – and there are many good solos snatched.

Ruby Braff is in England as I write, and the fact that he has not recorded for five years seems all the more incredible in consequence. It is tempting to over-praise his sensitive peach-fed cornet work, that mingles tradition and originality so seductively, and there is no doubt that a record like 'Two By Two' (Fontana), where he and Ellis Larkins deal with unhackneyed numbers such as 'Where or When' and 'I Could Write a Book' (all by Rodgers and Hart, incidentally), is ravishing listening of a kind we have almost lost. At the same time, honesty demands I note that Braff *toys* with a tune rather often, instead of either playing it or departing from it, and there is some out of tempo work that is not especially invigorating. However, I forgive such lapses for his reported strictures (in the *Melody Maker*) on the pop scene today: 'It's not for people . . . whose tastes are cultivated to lower themselves to the tastes of foolish children.' Yeah, yeah, yeah, as they say.

The show that recently toured Britain and the Continent, 'Jazz From a Swinging Era', showed mainstream ten years or more on, and reminded the listener of one of those ill-assorted groups of animals reputed to huddle together in a flood or forest fire – Hines, Bud Freeman, Eldridge, Earl Warren. It was an extremely disappointing presentation, which the two-disc set (Fontana) to some extent conceals; there are plenty of good solos from Clayton, Warren and Bud Johnson, but it is only Hines who amazes, as it was in the flesh. Baroque he may be, but baroque and roll.

18 October 1967

The Panassié Sides

When the French jazz critic Hugues Panassié was 22, he wrote a book called *Le Jazz Hot* (1934). It was somewhat solemn and over-categorized in the Continental manner, and gave much attention to the white players, Nichols and Bix and their associates. But when he went to America in 1938 he was on a New Orleans kick. He sought out Mezz Mezzrow, and between them they made the sides commemorated on 'The Panassié Sessions' (RCA Victor).

This anecdote rings strangely on today's ears. 'New Orleans' means now the whinnying, nanny-goat music of a bunch of pensioners, and if in 1938 Mezz had any recording associations it was with the Chicagoans. He was also, despite his defiant registrations, a white man. But it is doubtful if then the term meant much more than 'Negro' and Panassié sought out Mezzrow because they had both, by independent routes, arrived at the same conclusion: that real jazz was Negro jazz, and that the American Negroes were the most wonderful people in the world. Jazz to Mezzrow – and possibly Panassié too – wasn't a pastime, or a profession: it was a philosophy, a way to the truth and the Negroes held the key. This was not only an unpopular doctrine in the days of the King of Swing, it was a downright unprofitable one.

These sixteen sides made on the four sessions have a variety of significances. They brought Bechet and Ladnier back to the recording studios. They took the first stumbling step toward recreating that warm, relaxed mood that was entirely realized in the wonderful King Jazz sides in 1945. They were, perhaps, part of the turning of the tide towards the roots of jazz that produced *Jazzmen* in 1939 and the whole New Orleans revival. One the other hand, as music they were extremely patchy. Ladnier, who died the following year, had already lost most of his fire and invention. However Mezzrow strove to sound like Johnny Dodds, his stiff, kinky clarinet remained an eclectic taste. The last session, conceived more in the small swing-band ethos, was in a smaller league altogether. And yet, as Panassié himself points out on the sleeve, they have become 'the Ladnier-Mezzrow sides'; they have become history. Bechet, that 'Roi Soleil' of jazz, dominates 'Weary Blues', 'Really The Blues', and 'When You And I Were Young, Maggie', Teddy Bunn, guitarist from the Spirits of Rhythm, sparked the rhythm sections with Zutty Singleton and Manzie Johnson, besides contributing a unique vocal on 'If You See Me Comin''. The steady, building ensembles of 'Revolutionary Blues' and 'Comin' On', based on memories of Oliver, foreshadowed the New Orleans bands of Bunk Johnson and George Lewis. 'I wish I could have played better,' says Mezzrow in his autobiography, *Really The Blues*. 'Still and all, what we did together stands up.' It does.

Some of the best issues these days are on the Transatlantic label, and 'Miles Davis and the Modern Jazz Giants' presents tracks from the famous 'Bags' Groove' session, Christmas Eve 1954, without that particular number, but with a ravishing 'Bemsha', two takes of 'The Man I Love' (with the Miles–Monk argument cut out) and the loping 'Swing Spring'. I have never heard Miles play better than this.

Another remarkable record of a bop veteran is 'Hot House: Bud Powell' (Fontana), which presents Bud and tenorist Johnny Griffin jamming on holiday at Edenville in summer 1964. The recording is from Francis Paudras' Ferrograph, and Bud's rather eerie groans and grunts are heavily featured, but Griffin's bustling and unabashed tenor carries the record through. Bud is perfectly acceptable if only one didn't know.

There are times when I think the only jazz that never lets you down is the chugging, unadventurous, bread-and-butter blues, such as one finds on 'Eddie Boyd and his Blues Band' (Decca). One of the Chess team from back in the Fifties (and Victor before that), Boyd came to Europe with the Blues Festival package in 1965, and made a bunch of old ones ('Five Long Years', 'Unfair Lovers') with John

Mayall and his band. To the regular plaint and beat Eddie adds stinging piano on 'Pinetop's Boogie Woogie', and Peter Green's guitar is well in keeping. In fact the whole production is solid of its kind.

RCA Victor continue their meritorious Ellington programme with 'Johnny Come Lately', a group of sides spanning the Petrillo ban, 1942–4. Here we have the title number, 'Hayfoot, Strawfoot' and 'Sherman Shuffle' from the further side with Rex Stewart and Ben Webster ('C Jam Blues' is good for the latter), and a less rubicund lot from 1944–5 with vocals by Al Hibbler and Kay Davis, the best being 'It Don't Mean a Thing' with strong Taft Jordan and Al Sears. Sonny Greer belts manfully away on 'Caravan'. It might be said that the Ellington of this period was, commercially, a little under a cloud, with the war and bop and everything, but one wants it all nonetheless.

Few players are pinned more precisely to a particular set of tracks than the late Francis 'Muggsy' Spanier, who never outdistanced his Ragtime Band recordings just before the war. 'Muggsy Spanier' (Ace of Hearts) can honestly be recommended even so: eight Crosby-type big band sides from 1942, and six small-group numbers including an extended 'Careless Love'. Talking of mainstream, as I was last month, a correspondent assures me that the term was indeed coined in Britain, by critic Stanley Dance. Now we know.

8 November 1967

Delving into the Past

I am fascinated by the number of reissues there are these days. From one point of view, perhaps, the critic should ignore them: they are past history, and his duty is to the present. Yet from another they are surely worthy of notice: if works of literature were obtainable only in short bursts of eighteen months at a time, would not the literary critic sometimes give preference to Herrick, Smollett and Webster over Mr A and Miss B? Their very appearance argues that they pay their way, which again suggests that they should not be overlooked.

Enough of scruples. First there are three Ace of Hearts selections of three famous Negro orchestras, Jimmy Lunceford (1935), Andy Kirk (1936–42) and Earl Hines (1934–5). 'Jimmy Lunceford and his

Orchestra' represents the early days of this band, smooth, sinuous and remarkably arranged by Sy Oliver, but without the human touch of Trummy Young. 'Rose Room', 'Stomp Off' and 'Since My Best Gal Turned Me Down' show the Lunceford technique at its best.

'Twelve Clouds of Joy' presents the best period of Kirk's Kansas City-based band, with the sparkling Mary Lou Williams on piano and Dick Wilson on tenor: 'Little Joe From Chicago', with its Bob Crosby-like clarinet choir and boogie rhythm, and the electric guitar of Floyd Smith on 'Big Jim Blues' arouse pleasant memories. The Hines group, 'Swinging In Chicago', is the Grand Terrace orchestra, harsh, heavy and – except for Hines – somewhat archaic, like a gangster's sedan, despite the presence of Walter Fuller, Omer Simeon, Darnell Howard and Trummy Young. Hines's piano touch is like the kick of a mule. As a jazz performer he is astonishing, possessing right from his early twenties a completely original style (like Bechet and Armstrong), yet (to my mind at least) always producing music that is a little inhuman, a little comfortless, a Merlin of the keyboard one can admire but not cherish.

'The Chocolate Dandies' (Parlophone) was a studio name given to a number of groups from 1928 to 1933 – a mixed assemblage playing 'Cherry' with the Dorsey Brothers, Teschmacher, Teagarden, and engaging vocalist George Thomas; four sides by McKinney's Cotton Pickers; the Henderson groups from 1929–30 which were the most famous bearers of the name, and the Benny Carter bunch with Kaminsky, Mezzrow and Teddy Wilson organized by John Hammond in 1933. They are all here, with the Stark-Carter-Harrison-Hawkins team of 'Dee Blues', 'Cloudy Skies' and 'Got Another Sweetie Now' winning the honours. Another anthology disc is 'Harlem On a Saturday Night' (Ace of Hearts), notable for containing the five Dodds-Shavers sides from 1938. Perhaps because I grew up with them, the contrast between Dodds's tattered majesty and the unsophisticated simplicity of the youthful Shavers never bothered me: '29th and Dearborn' shows them both at their best, while the two other blues, 'Blues Galore' and 'Stackalee', have O'Neill Spencer vocals. This session also helped to introduce us to Teddy Bunn, whose guitar was heard a lot around that time.

'Out Came The Blues Vol. 2' (Ace of Hearts) presents another assortment of pre-1940 blues singers notably Rosetta Howard with Herb Morand's straining trumpet, Georgia White, Victoria Spivey, the mysterious Jesse James and others, a strange and bitter crop. It is astonishing to learn from 'Nat Gonella and his Trumpet' (Ace of Clubs) that Nat is in fact only three years younger than Louis, the idol on whom he based his style. These are Nat's first dozen or so sides under his own name with Decca, 1932–4, and it is interesting to compare Gonella's pastiche of the stageshow Armstrong with Lyttelton's of the Hot Five. On the whole Nat comes off well, having a deep sonorous tone to handle ballads such as 'Moon Country', though his Cockney-coon vocals and the fairly dreadful accompaniments weigh on the debit side.

To get around to the present at last, Duke Ellington has been playing his 'Far East Suite' (RCA Victor) for a year or two now, and here is the record. I am not fond of exotics (botanical term meaning introduced from abroad), but in fact this is in a pretty straight line from 'Caravan' and the like: eastern-sounding pieces performed by the usual orchestra. To my ears it is Duke's piano that comes through strongest, on 'Depk', on 'Mount Harissa' and most of all on a long undirected 'Ad Lib On Nippon' at the end, which has much noodling around by Jimmy Hamilton and bassist John Lamb. When Duke wasn't enjoying himself at the keyboard he was in front conducting some richly ferocious ensembles, but to be honest the record hasn't much else.

In closing, let me mention 'Nina Simone Sings The Blues' (RCA Victor), eleven pieces bordering on the blues with guitar and organ backing. Miss Simone has a passionately agile voice that deals with all kinds of material, and her no-holds-barred 'My Man's Gone Now' has got her into my collection single-handed.

6 December 1967

1968

'I'm Coming! Beware of Me!'

My favourite New Year's resolution is Cyril Connolly's for 1929: '*Resolve:* to be altogether more advanced and intelligent.' And clearly, according to Leonard Feather in the *Melody Maker*, I'm going to need to be. Of course jazz is not dying, he says, unless by jazz you mean swinging jazz, Dixieland jazz, or anything in a straight two or four. Of course that's on the way out, and still more American jazz clubs will collapse. But anything in Latin or Cuban or 5/4 rhythm, any freedom music 'in which the beat is often suspended, distended or ignored at certain points', anything with electric or electronic sounds, anything ethnic or with sitars – why, man, the scene is made. By a subtle stroke of page make-up, this cheer-leader is printed shoulder-to-shoulder with an article recalling the deaths in 1967 of Edmond Hall, Muggsy Spanier, Willie Smith, Buster Bailey, Herman Chittison, Pete Johnson, Red Allen, Billy Strayhorn, Rex Stewart, Sidney de Paris, Stuff Smith, Jimmy Archey and one or two more.

Readers of this column may rest assured that as long as there is any swinging or Dixieland jazz in straight two or four on recent records they will hear about it. The rest will be judged by the degree to which it approximates to the excitement produced by the aforesaid swinging or Dixieland jazz.

Curiously enough, the name of Feather crops up in connection with 'Esquire's All-American Hot Jazz' (RCA Victor), fifteen tracks recalling *Esquire*'s jazz polls in the years 1944–7. Poll-winner groups are a sure recipe for dud sessions, and few of these Feather-supervised blowings really jelled, but there are the well-known 1946 Armstrong pieces ('Snafu', and so on) and the Clayton-Shavers 'Buckin' the Blues'. Side two presents sides from sessions 'using *Esquire* winners as leaders' – Lucky Thompson and his Lucky Seven, Coleman Hawkins' 52nd Street All Stars, and Louis's 'Blues For Yesterday', the best piece of the album. A not-very-effective memorial to a rather marshy period. John Hammond has a better record as a session-master, and his 'Buck Clayton Jam Session' (CBS) is available again – 'The Hucklebuck' and 'Robbin's Nest'. This goes back to 1953, two side-long numbers with Clayton and Joe Newman, Urbie Green and Henderson Chambers, Charlie Fowlkes and Sir Charles Thompson sharing the honours with the Greene-Page-Jones rhythm section. The jam session, in retrospect, was a doubtful art form; like most substances, if stretched too far it sagged in the middle. The trumpets do well here, likewise the trombones, and the Fowlkes baritone is enormously satisfying, but the other reeds are tedious and I have never thought much of Sir Charles. The supporting chords to each solo, and Jo Jones's bombs, make a great contribution.

Another classic in the shops once more is the Duke's 'Such Sweet Thunder' (CBS) – twelve pieces, in case anyone doesn't know, based on Shakespearian themes. This is very rich, very pretty, sometimes very funny music, which you can link with its ostensible themes if it amuses you: Britt Woodman's 'Sonnet To Hank Cinq' and Clark Terry's 'Up And Down' are the best pieces, and Hodges has some sweet nothings to recount apropos of Juliet and Cleopatra.

If pressed, I should nominate Monk's 'Work' (Transatlantic) as the record of the month. For narrowness of repertoire and sameness of treatment, Monk beats Kid Ory by several miles, but these five tracks dating from 1953–4 are full of snap, crackle and even pop, with a prelapsarian Sonny Rollins tearing into 'The Way You Look Tonight' and 'I Want To Be Happy' in a manner that explains why everyone once thought he was good. His playing is gay, fruitful and energetic, backed manfully by Monk and Tommy Potter; 'Work' and 'Nutty' are trio pieces – Monk, Percy Heath and Blakey – and Monk and Blakey blend beautifully. 'Friday 13th' has Julius Watkins producing a curious racket on french horn, but again Monk, Blakey and Rollins shine. This is odd, idiosyncratic, quirky music, far from the killer-diller tradition, but so original that it compels attention. Another remarkable record is 'Back To Back' (Fontana), the film music by Miles Davis for 'Lift To The Scaffold' and by Art Blakey for 'Girls Vanish'. There is a strong theatrical streak in Miles that I am surprised has not been more exploited, and the listener gets a strong impression of the cafés and wet streets and suspenseful moments and rushes down the *routes nationales* that make up every French film (I never saw this one). The Blakey tracks are remarkable for Benny Golson on tenor, particularly on 'Blues Pour Vava', the high spot of the record.

'Angry Tenors' (CBS) is a title not likely to attract everybody, but in fact it presents three sessions from the mid-forties by Ike Quebec, Illinois Jacquet and Ben Webster that are serious and enjoyable.

Quebec is the roughest of the three, but authoritative on 'I.Q. Blues'; Jacquet is far from the circus performer of JATP, turning in fluent articulate solos in the Evans vein, while Webster is silky and delightful, and about as angry as a chocolate soufflé.

10 February 1968

The Hottest Record Ever Made

Louis Armstrong's 1929 'St. Louis Blues' is the hottest record ever made. Starting *in medias res*, with eight bars of the lolloping tangana release, it soon resolves into a genial up-tempo polyphony, with Higginbotham, Allen and Charlie Holmes observable behind the trumpet lead*. Armstrong shouts a couple of blues choruses not to be found in the original Handy song sheet, then after twelve bars of Higgie's trombone Louis leads the ensemble in four blistering choruses of solid riffing. By the third chorus the whole building seems to be moving. Anyone inclined to dismiss this as 'mere rhythmic excitement' might listen to the Cab Calloway band trying to reproduce it on a record six months later. The Armstrong version is unique.

Collected with this masterpiece on the first side of 'Satchmo Style' (Parlophone) are seven other 1929–30 recordings by Armstrong with the Luis Russell Orchestra: 'I Can't Give You Anything But Love', 'Bessie Couldn't Help It', the immortal 'Dallas Blues', and so on. This is one of the best periods of Armstrong's career, midway between the primitive twenties and showman thirties, and shouldn't be missed by anyone. The reverse side offers eight sides by the elusive Jack Purvis dating from the same time. Purvis was a white trumpeter of the period who made some tracks with Negro musicians of the calibre of Higginbotham and Hawkins: the first, 'Copyin' Louis', shows his affiliations. I can't quite share the sleeve's enthusiasm for Purvis's virtuosity, but it is nice to have 'Poor Richard' again.

Coleman Hawkins, of the bald pate and patriarchal, piratical beard, is now one of the grand old men of jazz. All the same, his career has been one of adaptation rather than domination. Perhaps

*In fact Allen leads up to the vocal, and plays behind it: I always thought this, but didn't dare say so.

the principal instance of this was his joining the bop revolution, during which he led bands containing Howard McGhee and Thelonious Monk – 'like a milestone', as Benny Green felicitously phrased it, 'getting up and walking along the road'. But before that his style had undergone a major change, when he switched from his fierce, bellowing manner of the twenties (remember the fourfold reiteration of that note to announce himself in 'Hello, Lola'?) to a crooning, buttery intonation in the thirties. This is exemplified very well in 'The Hawk In Holland' (Ace of Clubs), fourteen sides made with The Ramblers in 1935–7. Here is the Hawkins of 'Donegal Cradle Song', and of course, 'Body And Soul': hunched, suave and lighter-toned than today, but of considerable silky power when necessary. 'Night Hawk' (Xtra) is a 1961 album from the Prestige catalogue, in which Hawkins is coupled with Lockjaw Davis and a Flanagan-led rhythm. It's a fine collection, showing how at the dictates of fashion Hawkins came back to a harsher, more direct manner without abandoning any of his middle-period complexities. 'No Greater Love' has three superb choruses: 'Mellow Tone' dispels the legend that Hawkins does not relish swapping solos or even fours. Before we criticize the milestone for walking we should compare it with the milestones that stand still.

Johnny Hodges, an excellent example of the latter class, turns up with a name-studded band on 'Don't Sleep In The Subway' (Verve), arranged and generally directed by Jimmy Jones. The title-piece is a disappointment, having been minced up into a Latin-American hash, but there are some good Hodges originals, such as 'Heel Kickin'', together with feelingful standards like 'You've Changed'. There is one small piece of perfection, untypically called 'Blues Serenade', which Stanley Dance doesn't even mention on the sleeve; it isn't a blues, just a simple little thirty-two-bar tune played twice and worthy to stand with 'Daydream'. Ernie Royal, Jimmy Hamilton and Hank Jones are heard in support elsewhere.

John Coltrane's 'Dakar' (Transatlantic) is an odd kettle of 1957 fish, presenting the Master with two baritone saxes, Cecil Payne and Pepper Adams, and Mal Waldron on piano. On the whole it's a success, Payne being the smoother and Pepper the guttier. On 'Catwalk' in particular Coltrane is light and appealing. Yet another major reed is heard in 'Big Ben Time' (Fontana) on which Ben Webster blows ten standards in front of a British quartet. This is a pleasant and modest set, flecked with Ellingtonia, Ben's notes wilting at the edges in their accustomed way. Dick Katz on piano disproves Monk's contention that 'those simple chords ain't so easy to find nowadays'.

9 March 1968

Home Fires Burning

Britain does not often lead the world in popular entertainment, and our present pre-eminence in pop music comes as a surprise to jazz fans, accustomed as we are to achieving no more than intelligent parody. Recently, however, there have been a number of British records of marked originality that suggest we may make a name in this field also. Most people by now will have heard Mike Westbrook's 'Celebration' (Deram), a sort of suite for a twelve-piece band which has been called one of the finest in Europe, and which seems to marry the Ellington orchestral tradition to the freer harmonic and formal lines which have been explored lately. Now the Don Rendell-Ian Carr Quintet has come out with its third record, 'Phase III' (Columbia), which offers a nice blend of composition, arrangement and improvisation. This collection suggests that their eclecticism is literary as well as musical, extending as it does to 'Crazy Jane' (Yeats) and 'Neiges d'Antan' (Villon) for titles, and Coltrane and the chevaliers of free form as stylistic influences. These five players – the same that made 'Dusk Fire' a couple of years ago – are accomplished and confident musicians; Rendell's solo on 'On!' (starting with a garbled memory of 'Lester Leaps In') and Carr's astonishingly adroit choruses on 'Crazy Jane' have a bustling yet poised quality that compel attention. Michael Garrick has some nice piano on 'Neiges', and drummer Trevor Tomkin provides massive punctuation.

The Joe Harriott-John Mayer Double Quintet's 'Indo-Jazz Fusions II' (Columbia) is also a third record, and a much narrower kettle of fish, so to speak: Indian ragas and other forms given a jazzy twist, like Loussier's versions of Bach. The result isn't at all unpleasant; 'Raga Piloo' has a wild and windy quality, and the bagpipe drone over incessant plucking and tapping is hypnotic if not soporific on 'Purvi Variations' and 'Mishra Blues'. The latter lives up to its name: good bursts of flugelhorn and piano made at least one listener remember where his allegiances lay. 'At Home with Alex Welsh and his Band' (Columbia) will reassure some that Britain still to some extent stands where she did, nine tracks of arranged neo-Dixieland with good solos from Johnny Barnes ('It Don't Mean a Thing'), Welsh himself ('Please'), and that admirable trombonist Roy Williams ('You've Changed'); Lennie Hastings does his 'Oo-ya' break for good measure at the end of a free-wheeling blues 'Wood Green'.

Two more first-class mainstream releases are 'Vic Dickenson Showcase' and Buck Clayton's 'Buck 'n' the Blues' (both Fontana). Dickenson's 1953 set has a lovely long 'Old Fashioned Love' with Ruby Braff on cornet, a soft 'When You and I Were Young, Maggie', and a break-neck 'Runnin' Wild': the Fats Waller of the trombone is not my favourite soloist, but he applies himself with sobriety on this occasion. Jo Jones has a day out on drums. Clayton's 1957 session is mostly blues with Dickenson, Earl Warren and Hank Jones, though one of the best tracks – 'Ballin' the Jack' – is of course sixteen-bar. Clayton, who is an excellent player but rather clean-limbed for my taste, takes a low-down couple of choruses on 'Good Morning Blues'. Jo Jones sticks closely to cymbals, perhaps to demonstrate that he started all this modern drumming, notably on 'Cool Too', a fast blues with bop connections.

A mixed bag of Jelly Roll awaits purchasers of 'Mr. Jelly Lord' (RCA Victor – when are we going to get some really *original* reissues? Bob Howard, say? Prima with Russell? Billy Banks and the Rhythmakers?): there are the trios with the Dodds brothers, pieces by varying big bands of varying talents, and the immortal 'Deep Creek'. This last title is one of the completely original jazz records, slow, serene, its smooth surface ruffled towards the end by Procope's foreboding clarinet. One wonders what Morton thought of it, whether he felt he had realized a masterpiece or whether it was to him one more take. Personally I found 'Keep Your Business To Yourself' a heartening number, despite Wilton Crawley's clarinet, because of its swinging rhythm section. Morton had many talents, but I agree with Whitney Balliett that swinging was not one of them, or at least not much of the time.

One can compare him with his peers on 'Classic Jazz Piano Styles' (RCA Victor), pitting 'Freakish' and 'Fat Frances' against some thirties transcriptions by Waller, 1939–41 Earl Hines, Jimmy Yancey's 'Yancey Stomp' and 'State Street Special', and a couple of Ammons-Johnson duets. A similar bag is opened on 'Tenor of Jazz'

(Fontana), where the Webster-Freeman-Miller-Lockjaw quartet that had a brief season a year ago unbelt some original pieces. Personally I found the younger Lockjaw Davis a shot in the arm for Miller and Freeman, once two of my favourite tenor men but here dozy as old pears.

13 April 1968

The Dixieland Band

Every art has its mythologies, and the idea that the Original Dixieland Jazz Band invented jazz dies hard. 'In 1917 the ODJB cut the first JASS record,' says the sleeve of 'The Original Dixieland Jazz Band' (RCA Victor), and there they are, sad-faced Ragas (soon to be carried off by drink and the influenza epidemic of 1918–19) at the concert grand piano, clarinettist Shields, crew-cut Edwards, and the leader, La Rocca, apparently sprouting from the piano-top, and Tony Sbarbaro with his twenty-eight-inch street drum, woodblock and cowbells. Did they know what they were starting?

Were they, in fact, starting it? Even their most partisan supporter won't contend that jazz was born on 27 January 1917, in the '400' Club Room of the Reisenweber Building, New York. The band had played before that in Chicago and had come from New Orleans, where there were numerous other musicians in their tradition. And, since they were white, what about the Negroes? What about the blues? What about Buddy Bolden? What about Freddie Keppard's That Creole Band, which got a lot of encores at the Columbia Theatre in December 1915? These are, perhaps, deep waters. All we can say is that the ODJB was a flashpoint, a flashpoint in New York in 1917 and a flashpoint in London in 1919. After that, everybody was doing it.

This selection has six pieces from the halcyon 1917–18 period, four from the much sweeter post-England time, 1920–1, and the last of their Victor sessions in 1936. It would be perverse to deny that the first of these is the best. There is something vivacious, almost galvanic, about the ODJB that makes, for instance, King Oliver six years later sound Wordsworthianly meditative. The giddy breaks, each terminated by a Sbarbaro cymbal-crash, are the only variation on the driving ensembles, the holy trinity of the classic front line, cornet, clarinet and trombone, each voice imbued with the special character of its producer. It is said that by the time they reached record the ODJB were exaggerating their efforts for the purpose of comedy. If so, they must have been even more staggering in 1916.

Twenty years later, with the benefit of modern recording, much of this wild excitement has vanished; in fact, the team sounds rather like a Condon group on an offday. There are still not many solos, though Shields exhibits on 'Dixieland One-Step' the hard cutting edge that is behind Teschmacher and all the white twenties clarinettists and leader La Rocca is low-down and plangent here and in 'Skeleton Jangle'. Every artist has a time that does not come again and the ODJB was no exception.

I have been looking at the month's records and wondering what La Rocca would think of them. There is something close-knit and urgent that might appeal to him about 'People Get Ready' by The Freedom Sounds (Atlantic), a bunch led by Wayne Henderson, late of the Jazz Crusaders. Henderson's blunt-pencil trombone is backed by Al Abreu on tenor and a welter of popping and clucking percussion: at times ('Cucumonga') they brew up a storm reminiscent of middle-period Coltrane or Mingus; at others ('Respect' or 'Fa-Fa') the harmonies recall Lennon and McCartney. From the audience-participation viewpoint, the ODJB would rejoice with The Cannonball Adderley Quintet in '74 Miles Away' (Capitol). There seems to be a tendency to look down on Cannonball these days; since I never looked up to him, I can praise this as jolly, rather noisy stuff such as a Negro crowd wants on its nights out – and if you think that is anything like Archie Shepp, think, or rather listen, again. It is more Nat Adderley's record than Cannonball's ('Do Do Do' and '74 Miles'), but both contribute to two blues ('Bird' and 'Oh Babe') that are, in their different ways, both stirring.

I fancy La Rocca would go out for a drink during 'Miles Davis and John Coltrane play Richard Rodgers' (Transatlantic) which, by the number of times it has been reissued, is fast becoming a modern classic. Here is Miles's ice-bucket trumpet and Red Garland's effete quotations from 'Country Gardens' (spare us the clichés of bop!), and on the credit side Coltrane and Philly Joe Jones. It also has that curious track, 'Blue Room', where Miles, on his own admission, was not himself, and sounds like bad Pat Halcox. Since this is twice as good as he usually sounds, however, the sleeve claims rightly 'this track is the most beautiful of all'. La Rocca would think it just showed you.

11 May 1968

Whose Flaming Youth?

Listening to the new Miles Davis 'Nefertiti' (CBS), my thoughts strayed to the subject of reissues. Who chooses them? There formed in my mind a composite figure of someone aged 55 to 60, bent on recapturing his youth by judicious remastering. Take 'Clarence Williams Rarities' (Parlophone), for instance. Now we have had three Clarence Williams LPs already in the past five years or so, forty-eight examples of early twenties *naïveté:* do we want another sixteen? Somebody up there clearly does. Isn't it about time they started recapturing *my* youth, the golden hours of the thirties? I hesitate to mention the Billy Banks sides again, although they are to some the most exciting sides ever made, but what about Artie Shaw? What about the Bob Crosby Bobcats? What about the rest of the Commodore catalogue, and the early Blue Notes? And think of all those 78s that formed us, the Wilson-James 'Blue Mood', Johnny Hodges on Hampton's 'Sunny Side of the Street', even Hawkins' 'Body and Soul' – where are they? Get with the Munich scene, dad.

Not that 'Clarence Williams Rarities' is without interest. Covering 1923 to 1930, it features Armstrong, Ladnier, Bechet, Hawkins, Buster Bailey, Ed Allen and many more at various stages of maturity: Ed Allen is the most successful, his broad resonant cornet confident on the curiously charming 'Where That Old Man River Flows', 'Mississippi Blues' and several more. Four sides have vocals by Williams's wife, Eva Taylor, and Ed Cuffee contributes some mellow trombone. As rare, to me anyway, is 'The Aces of Rhythm' (Ace of Hearts), quartets and quintets led by that elusive trumpeter Jabbo Smith. The story is that Mayo Williams of Brunswick chose Jabbo to cut some twenty sides in 1929 in an effort to get in on the Armstrong Okeh boom, and this is supported by the Louis-like quality not only of the scat singing but of the trumpet lines as well. Jabbo is more than just a copyist, however: on 'Decatur Street Tutti' (splendid title) and 'Sweet and Low Blues' his notes, tight, hot and shaking, are hurled out over Ikey Robinson's banjo with a frenzy all his own. His playing here is so unlike his work with Duke Ellington (in 1927) that for a time it was supposed that there were two trumpeters of the same name. All in all, a fascinating revival.

Mention of Ellington recalls that 'Cotton Club Days, Vol. 3' (Ace of Hearts) brings the reissue of Ellington Brunswicks and Vocalion up to 1931. The highspot here is Johnny Hodges' first appearance on wax – 'Yellow Dog Blues', on 5 June 1928, where Rabbit leaps in with immense poignance, instantly proclaiming himself a master. Bubber Miley's deep and individual maturity on the 1926 sides, too, sets him forever apart from his successors in the Ellington growl chair. This should be bought, if not already possessed.

I am sometimes a bit sceptical of these marvellous Negro bands cutting each other at the Savoy Ballroom, for they so often failed to make it on record. 'Stompin' At The Savoy' (CBS) presents the Chick Webb Orchestra as it was in 1934–5, and I listened in vain for the 'powerhouse drumming' promised on the sleeve. Once I heard a noise like a couple of heavy suitcases being put down, but that was all. Mixed up with the rest are four sides by Taft Jordan and the Mob with Teddy Wilson, of notable grace and crispness. Much better is 'Don Redman' (CBS), smooth yet high-spirited arrangements from 1932 to 1937: Horace Henderson canters alongside the ensembles like Jess Stacy with Goodman, and there are some good solos snatched, markedly by Edward Inge's clarinet.

Coming nearer our own day, 'Charlie Mingus' (Polydor) presents six tracks from 1957, made by that interesting group including Clarence Shaw and Bill Evans that made 'Tijuana Moods'. I enjoy Mingus's hellbroth ensembles, such as appear on 'East Coasting' and 'Conversation', and regret his present withdrawal from the scene; it is nice to have more Shaw, too, whose Harmon-muted trumpet is heard on 'Memories of You'. Another classic session is Brubeck's 'Jazz at Oberlin' (Ace of Hearts), at which, as the sleeve underlines with relish, all members of the quartet were sacked or ill or quarrelling, but none the less did a splendid job. Although my strongest impression is of the asininity of the audience (applauding quotations and bass solos and gimmicky bits of technique), there are some fine spells, Desmond's milky alto getting into a tight spin on 'These Foolish Things', Brubeck pounding the daylights out of the piano on 'How High' and the like.

And so to the present, with the Chris McGregor Group's 'Very Urgent' (Polydor) – the leader pianist, at least, coming from South Africa. This is free form: yelping trumpet, percussive piano, jungle-at-moonrise ensembles, and a curious Elgarian finale that seems to incorporate the Last Post. I don't know how such pieces are evaluated. And finally, of course, as I was saying, 'Nefertiti' – six new tracks by Miles and his usual buddies (Shorter-Hancock-Carter-Williams), called by titles such as 'Riot' and 'Madness', and sounding about as jolly. Miles is one of the principal figures of present-day jazz, and I'm sure a lot of people like him, but to me he is the Charles Addams of the trumpet – without the humour, of course.

8 June 1968

Aretha's Gospel

New gal in town: Aretha Franklin. To judge from the fact that the first of her records to reach me did so about the same time as her face reached the cover of *Time*, and her act the Finsbury Park Astoria, her arrival has been a rapid one. Whether you like her singing, as exemplified in 'Take a Look at Aretha Franklin' (CBS), will depend on whether you like that brand of secularized gospel known as 'soul'. Pure gospel has always been a strange acre in the jazz territory: while employing the same techniques of mass excitement to attain the same ends, it has never progressed from its narrow and impersonal sincerity into a varied popular entertainment. Perhaps it is right that it should not: gospel, after all, is about salvation. 'Soul', on the other hand, seems to me to apply the fervent approach of gospel to the familiar properties of the popular song: the shouting, the sobbing, the compulsive repetition of phrases are the same, but the object is no more than 'my baby' and the same old generalized sexual satisfaction. Nor has it quite the simple purity of the evangelical tent: it leans heavily on that aspect of urban Negro taste which, with its saccharine organs, maudlin choirs, and lachrymose hysteria of tone, reminds one of the more embarrassing essays of Miss Gracie Fields. My verdict, therefore, is gospel yes, soul no.

Where does this leave Aretha Franklin? Still, I think, fairly well on the credit side. Those who have seen her will know that she sings with grace and dignity, and the present record demonstrates that her technique is preponderantly that of her one-time mentor, the great gospel singer Mahalia Jackson. Tracks such as 'Won't Be Long' and 'Soulville' have much of the traditional gospel fire, and in general she possesses an urgency and agility of voice that dominates her accompaniment and usually her audience. 'My Guy' is a little commercial and 'Try a Little Tenderness' near sentimentality, but not grossly so. All in all, I think this modernized Mahalia is lucky to have got a *Time* cover, but she may yet come to deserve it.

The rest of the month's issues are all interesting in their different ways. David Evans has been prowling through Louisiana and Mississippi with a tape-recorder, and in 'Up the Country' (Decca) offers some genuine examples of the vanishing country blues by Roosevelt Holt, Arzo Youngblood, Mager Johnson and others. And in utter contrast both to this, and to Miss Franklin, CBS has reissued 'Lady in Satin', Billie Holiday's last LP, put out in 1958 just a year before her death. The sleeve claims that this reissue is in response to popular demand, but if so then popular taste is morbid, for this is in most respects a painful record. Billie's voice is like burnt paper, and does not sound fully under control: the lyrics of 'For All We Know' are made by hindsight unbearably poignant.

Two trumpet veterans, Bunk and Louis, offer an interesting contrast: in 1945, when most of 'Bunk Johnson's Brass and Dance Band' (Storyville) was made, Bunk would be about 66, two years younger than Louis is now, and without Louis's unbroken playing career. All in all, he sounds splendid: supple, subtle, sad, elusive. These are all American Music recordings, a mixture of band pieces and 'brass band' tracks, with three trio pieces and Don Ewell thrown in. 'Louis' (Mercury) is twelve tracks from various All Stars groups in recent years: Louis's horn is shorter-winded than Bunk's, but stronger, and the numbers here show him in his golden sunset. 'Bye 'n' Bye' and 'Short But Sweet' seemed to me to have most swing and charm respectively, and the sleeve carries Armstrong's well-known dictum 'What you're there for is to please the people'. *O si sic omnes*!

'Expression' (Impulse) by the late John Coltrane, got five stars in *Down Beat*, although even this magazine admitted that it had its boring moments. Even assuming that Coltrane's solos seem other than the scribblings of a subnormal child, one is bound to admit that Mrs Coltrane and Rashied Ali are inferior on piano and drums to McCoy Tyner and Elvin Jones. 'Lunceford Special' (CBS) is another good wedge of Lunceford tracks from 1939–40, with two previously unissued 1933 takes thrown in. The celebrated 'Uptown Blues' justifies its reputation.

13 July 1968

The Inimitable Jimmy Yancey

Jimmy Yancey's piano style was slow, hesitant and poised, quite unlike the steady thunder of his pupil, Meade Lux Lewis. When

Lewis was rediscovered washing cars in 1935, he recorded something he called 'Yancey Special', which in turn drew attention to the earlier and still more shadowy figure of Jimmy Yancey, who since World War I had been groundsman with the Chicago White Sox. In the last dozen years of his life Yancey made several groups of sides of which this present selection ('Low Down Dirty Blues', Atlantic) is the last, made two months before his death in 1951.

Yancey displayed a wistful, measured, play-it-all-night talent, whose Spanish-tinged figures were instantly recognizable and almost impossible to imitate. He had a magnificent sense of timing (he was a vaudeville dancer in his youth), but never tried to stomp his listeners into submission, preferring to lassoo them idly with his slow-falling, inevitable phrases. Side one is all Yancey, accompanied (unnecessarily) by the late Israel Crosby on bass; side two brings in Jimmy's wife, Mama Estella Yancey, whose blues singing he often accompanied. The entertainment they provide is simple, graceful and moving. It's hard to think of anyone not enjoying it.

Several other blues discs claim attention. 'Blues On Top of Blues' (Stateside) is a studio job by the compelling B. B. King (plus orchestra), all rather samey but with plenty of good rock and soul, and 'Presenting the Country Blues' (CBS Blue Horizon) introduces Roosevelt Holts, a Mississippi singer now rising 60. Holts is an unstrained, unaffected performer, strumming along on guitar with most of the traditional vocal tricks of the country singer, but his lyrics are nonsequential and his rhythms and phrasing sometimes subtler than at first appears.

Those who treasure Jimmy Witherspoon's session at The Renaissance will enjoy 'Live' (Stateside), which offers Spoon in a live setting (sleeve doesn't say where) with Ben Webster and his Quartet (sleeve doesn't say who). The numbers are highly familiar – 'Outskirts', 'Nobody's Bizness', 'C.C. Rider' and so on – but the atmosphere is relaxed and Webster murmurs to great effect. This is a much more attractive Witherspoon record than some we have had recently. Finally, Atlantic has reissued 'Roots of the Blues', that extremely striking anthology of field recordings made by Alan Lomax and originally part of the set called 'The Sounds of the South'. Personally I find these primitive pieces to the accompaniment of cane fife, guitar, comb or slugging hammers, both affecting and exciting, and Fred McDowell and Forest City Joe give the collection some professional polish.

A new Benny Goodman record reminds me of a contemporary's

recent claim that he is currently the most underrated figure in jazz: 'Benny Goodman . . . And Paris!' (Command) doesn't really enlist me behind this opinion, though it's nice to hear it expressed. One trouble is that Goodman doesn't really fit into a Joe Newman – Urbie Green traditional front line: he sounds embarrassing, like a dowager doing the can-can. Another is that on the slow numbers ('Autumn Leaves') his tone is really too classical for words. But there is plenty of interest in Joe Newman's solos, and Goodman himself exhibits some faint excitement on 'Mimi'.

Two pre-war reissues of note are 'Clarinet King' and 'J.T.' (both Ace of Hearts), referring to Johnny Dodds and Jack Teagarden respectively. There is some silly whinnying and horse-laugh stuff on the first, but Dodds's fruity low-register and piercing upper-register vivify the little Chicago bands of 1927–9 here preserved. The rarer master of the Dodds-Armstrong 'Wild Man' is included: it isn't quite as good. The Teagarden tracks from 1929–31 are mostly Red Nichols groups, and very mixed in quality; the thrilling Louisiana R.K. 'Basin Street' is here, but why not 'Last Cent' from the same session, instead of the excruciating Scrappy Lambert 'Sally, Won't You Come Back?' Seek it out, though. Moving to the vibes, The Gary Burton Quartet's 'Lofty Fake Anagram' (RCA Victor) offers an original sound – fresh, West Coast, relaxed, intimate, Balinese: really, it defeats me, but it's unexpectedly enjoyable. Coleman Hawkins' 'Get Happy' (Atlantic) recalls a 1958 session with Milt Jackson, Flanagan and Burrell, with Bags pretty well in the ascendancy, rolling his mallets voluptuously over tunes such as 'Don't Take Your Love From Me': there are some blues, too.

I continue to listen gamely to Archie Shepp (who is wearing a beard now) in the hope that it will one day all cease to sound like 'Flight of the Bumble Bee' scored for bagpipes and concrete-mixer, but 'Mama Too Tight' (Impulse) hasn't managed this. Three pieces commemorate Robert Thompson, Ernie Henry and Basheer, 'Black artists who passed away at painfully abortive ages', as Shepp says on the sleeve. The band includes Tommy Turrentine, Roswell Rudd, Grachan Moncur III and Howard Johnson who plays tuba to good effect on the version of 'King Cotton' which closes the first track (yes, all right). Shepp says he is trying to make order out of chaos, but it sounds more to me as if he thinks that if you look at chaos long enough, order will eventually emerge. Or so you think.

10 August 1968

Twilight of Two Old Gods

Every jazz-lover at some time of his life has dreamed of assembling a band of his own favourite musicians to play for him. For some, it is more than a dream. Whitney Balliett, jazz critic for the *New Yorker*, gave a lecture at a Massachusetts Institute of Technology some time ago and brought a group with him that embodied a longing we have apparently shared without knowing it, to have Henry Allen and Pee Wee Russell play together again.

Balliett, a writer who brings jazz journalism to the verge of poetry, has made no secret of his admiration for these two players. In his last book, *Such Sweet Thunder* (Macdonald), he gives accounts of visits he paid to each of them, and there is nothing better in the whole 366 pages. Russell and his late wife Mary ('Pee Wee's playing embarrasses me') in their shabby apartment, make an odd contrast with Allen – the late Allen, one now has to say – and his wife Pearlie-Mae with their silver tea service and two little grand-daughters. Yet they have their similarities. Both families have obstreperous dogs, Winkie and White Fang, and, as Balliett says, 'Both appear to be inimitable and both have long been lumped with the wrong musical schools – Russell with the Chicagoans and Allen with New Orleans jazz. But both are, in reality, advanced musicians who play best in fast, original company.' 'The College Concert of Pee Wee Russell and Henry Red Allen' (Impulse) records them together for the first time since the 1932–3 sessions of Billy Banks and the Rhythmakers, a bunch of sides in themselves crying out for reissue in microgroove, and I approached it with trepidation. Would it exhume even for a few seconds the hard-driving telepathic teamwork of 'Oh Peter' or 'Who's Sorry Now?' Would the years of illness or wrong company slip away and show these two forever young?

Well, of course, it was a disappointment. The session had come at least fifteen years too late. Allen was 58, and within six months of his death, Russell, 60, and sounding it. They are backed by a young rhythm section, pianist Steve Kuhn, Charlie Haden and Marty Morell, who aren't really sympathetic. Four of the six tunes are blues, which narrows the range of feeling. There are bass solos. In 'Body and Soul' the tempo doubles for a chorus suddenly. The horns strike few sparks. Allen has worn best. He plays with a deep gutty tone, sonorous declamation alternating with muttered telegraphese as is his wont, doing nicely on 'Body and Soul', and really going in his first two or three choruses on 'Graduation Blues'. On both these tunes, too, he delivers one of his strangled vocals, which sound like no one else on earth. Russell is his latter-day self. What chiefly characterizes his playing nowadays is a much more classical tone – gone is not only the dirt, but also much of the intensity – and a fragmented twittery line that makes each solo sound like a Chinese saucer shattered into hundreds of pieces. In 'Pee Wee's Blues', taken more softly than usual, his delicacy turns to uncertainty and finally chaos.

Yet one would sooner have the record than not. After all, this is Allen, of whom we shall have little more, and it is touching at the end of his vocal on the blues to hear him call 'Carry on, carry on', and to hear Russell try to respond. It isn't a great performance, but it's a performance by great players.

I have recently been poring over a large illustrated publication by the Louisiana State University Press entitled *New Orleans Jazz Family Album*, obtainable through the Transatlantic Book Service, 28 Norfolk Street, WC2. This is an assemblage of as many photographs of New Orleans jazz men as could be brought together, and a fascinating lot they are. Most of the portraits in *Who's Who in New Orleans Jazz* are fairly recent, and much enjoyment can be had from picking out their subjects in the sections that follow, jazz and brass bands. These are marvellous: John Robichaux's Orchestra in 1896, looking like Wakefield Town Council; Stalebread's Spasm Band in 1899; Buddy Bolden's Band in 1894; and the numerous groups of forgotten Negroes in the sunshine of the 1900s standing in front of circus tents or sitting at the edge of fields with bowler hats, holding their violins, euphoniums, banjos, side drums and cornets in readiness to entertain the Lodge picnic or big top audience to the best of their ability. After this come New Orleans landmarks, the dance halls and bordellos, and Louis Armstrong's birthplace, and the riverboats, and even the graves. My only criticism is that for a university press book it's rather off-hand, and should certainly have had some street maps.

14 September 1968

When They Still Made Nice Noises

Cool jazz might be described as silver-age bop; take away the explosiveness, and add greater technical knowledge, and you have such music as was produced by Lennie Tristano, Miles Davis, and certain Claud Thornhill alumni around 1950. Three recent records can be linked together to give an incomplete conspectus of this mode: the first, 'Subconscious-Lee', by Lee Konitz with Lennie Tristano (Xtra), mixes some of the best sessions made under both their names in 1949 with Billy Bauer, Shelly Manne and Warne Marsh. On some tracks Tristano is replaced by Sam Mosca, who doesn't sound too inferior. 'Abstractions', by Lee Konitz (Atlantic), shows the altoist in 1955, after a spell with Kenton had hardened his somewhat milky tone. Tristano is absent, but Marsh, Bauer and Mosca are largely featured, notably on 'Donna Lee' and 'I Can't Get Started'. Both these records are characterized by a light, agreeable tone-quality, and a tendency for all instruments to sound alike as far as possible. Marsh's tenor might be an alto; Bauer's guitar has that even-running hunting style which might at a distance be mistaken for a wind instrument. Perhaps what tips the scale to credit for a hardened swing-era buff is that on the whole the musicians seem to be trying to make nice noises rather than nasty ones, and to be improvising. That goes some way these days. The third record is 'The New Tristano' (Atlantic) – not very new, in fact: 1962, when Tristano broke a seven-year recording silence. The result was called 'a milestone in jazz piano history', presumably on account of the dexterity with which Tristano mixes tempos without, as the sleeve takes care to guarantee, any tape-splicing or multi- tracking. The most noticeable characteristic is the walking bass line that replaces a conventional rhythm section (always one of Tristano's dislikes): personally I found this sombre, oppressive and ultimately damaging, the effect being of a man playing with one hand – brilliantly, of course, but still with only one hand. A kind of suite called 'Scene and Variations' has a kind of austere fugue-like severity, and on the whole one feels that Tristano had retreated into the shadows. In view of his loss of sight in boyhood this is perhaps not surprising.

Anyone without the three-disc Herman album should buy 'The Best of Woody Herman' (CBS), twelve pieces from 1945–7 including 'Apple Honey', 'Caldonia', 'Wild Root', 'Summer Sequence', 'Four Brothers' – virtually the lot. 'Bands of the Forties' (Ember) is rather a curiosity, presenting ten tracks by the orchestras of Lucky Millinder, Erskine Hawkins, Charlie Spivak and – oddly – Elliott Lawrence. The big Negro dance bands of the two first-named predominate, each having a robust, easy-moving ensemble style, well-knit and without hysterics; really, an LP of each would not be out of place. Among the side-men were Tyree Glen, John Hardee, Hilton Jefferson and Sonny Payne.

Music For Pleasure keeps up its British antiquarianism with 'The Best of Ambrose and his Orchestra' (MFP), twelve pieces dating from 1928–32 and leaning on the current popular standard such as 'Happy-Go-Lucky You', 'Love Letters in the Sand' and 'A Bench in the Park'. Sam Browne sings, Danny Polo and Sylvester Ahola play, and even the Gold Standard has a silver lining.

To look at a pillar of established art and to wonder with infuriated bewilderment how anyone ever for a single second thought he was good is a common experience in all media, and I have often had it about John Coltrane: 'Soultrane' (Transatlantic), however, gives if nothing else a demonstration of the steely quality his tone had in 1958. 'I Want to Talk About You' and 'You Say You Care' exhibit an almost arrogant impersonality that has its fascination, though the multi-note stuff obtrudes in 'Russian Lullaby' and there are regular bass solos, as if some Bullfiddlers' Union insisted that their members had a solo quota on every record made. 'A Portrait of Monk' by Bud Powell (CBS) purports to be a live recording in a nightclub, but rumour has it that this is Powell's 'Portrait of Thelonious', a studio job of Paris, 1961, with applause dubbed in. 'Off Minor' and 'Ruby My Dear' are played with strength and sensitivity, though Powell and Monk are poles apart as pianists: Kenny Clarke brushes beautifully in the background.

'Fletcher Henderson and the Dixie Stompers' (Parlophone) contains all the sides made under this name after Ladnier replaced Rex Stewart in 1927, fifteen numbers to boot. Despite the reputation of these tracks, and the star-studded Henderson line-ups, I found myself a little disappointed at the diminished jigging sameness of it all. Anyone who reckons to know Ladnier from Joe Smith will have a good time here: other familiar voices such as Hawkins, Jimmy Harrison, Benny Morton and Buster Bailey keep breaking through. Perhaps they needed better tunes: Waller's 'St. Louis Shuffle' stands out just by the old Fats melodiousness.

12 October 1968

How Long This Has Been Going On!

Should I be surprised, after listening to a month's extremely varied releases, to find a Louis Armstrong record push its way effortlessly to first place? 'The Singing Style of Louis Armstrong' (Verve), one of Verve's new two-disc packs (for the price of one), isn't new material: it's not even what one thinks of as primary jazz, being a selection of vocal tracks Louis made with the Russell Garcia Orchestra and the Oscar Peterson Trio in 1957. And yet to lay it on the turntable after several nights' elucidation of more complex performances is to put down one's pad and pencil in acknowledgement of a mastery one thought held no more surprises.

There is, to be sure, nothing particularly remarkable about what goes on: Louis sings, plays the trumpet, then sings some more. Behind him, the large shimmering Garcia band or the dapper Peterson Trio provides appropriate accompaniment. What astonishes is the ease with which this man, pushing 60, creates twenty-two valid jazz experiences simply by singing that number of well-known commercial songs without recourse to excessive mugging or bravura, just a slur here, an emphasis there, and the use of the varying textures of his amazing voice. There is not a moment's hesitation: although many of the songs (particularly in the Peterson set) are of a sophisticated smartness at the opposite pole to his own jazz reputation ('How Long Has This Been Going On', 'What's New'), he deals with them with complete conviction. I listened to all twenty-two tracks at one sitting (including three not mentioned by Jepsen), and didn't dismiss a single one as a dud.

Hard in Louis's wake comes Sidney Bechet, 'Sidney Bechet Sessions' (Storyville) presents the elusive Wax Shop session of 1947, with Mezz, Vernon Brown, James P. Johnson and others: two 1946 New York Town Hall numbers and three tracks with Joe Sullivan and George Wettling. This, too, is a gripping disc; to hear Bechet's soprano pealing out in open domination on 'Old Fashioned Love' is to experience a wave of emotion only the great players can evoke. As a whole, the collection is patchy: some first-rate Vernon Brown, better-than-hoped-for Mezz, and noble ('Slow Blues') Bechet is balanced by muddy recording, jumbled solos, James P. and the egregious Baby Dodds (the last two players I find greatly overrated).

Another Storyville disc, 'Muggsy Spanier' presents a marathon day in the Manhattan label studios in 1945 when Spanier, Pee Wee Russell, Miff Mole, Lou McGarity and others made twelve sides, with two more from the day before. This is a good sample of the merits and demerits of this school: Russell delivering some fine untrammelled solos ('My Honey's Lovin' Arms', 'You're Lucky To Me'), McGarity cutting Mole all ends up, and some energetic grunting from Carceres on baritone against Muggsy's squad of clichés, and one of the stiffest rhythm sections to date.

In more recent style 'Brubeck/Mulligan/Compadres' (CBS) shows Dave, having parted from Paul Desmond (who is reputedly writing a book on the Quartet), swapping solos with Gerry Mulligan in Mexico: the audience's applause seemed a little excessive, 'Bizarre' (CBS) was Charles Lloyd's first LP in 1963, made up of Coltrane-type outings ('Forest Flower') and ballady flute numbers ('Little Peace'). Don Friedman's piano is consistently agreeable, but as for Lloyd I found myself in harmony with the 'British jazz musician' reported on the sleeve.* British Ronnie Ross's 'Cleopatra's Needle' (Fontana) is made by a little band featuring Les Condon, Art Elefsen and Bill le Sage as well as Ronnie, and their admirers may well enjoy it.

'Blues For Bouffément' (Fontana) is another French Bud Powell offering, including 'Little Willie Leaps' and 'My Old Flame' as well as some originals. Bud is quite coherent here, but a little dull: I doubt if it would occur to the listener that this was once a great pianist; the title number has elements of emotion. Another pianist, Michael Garrick, dominates 'Black Marigold's' (Argo) which is a stew of half-baked poetry-and-jazz and harpsichord pieces plus one or two reasonable jazz vehicles for Ian Carr, Joe Harriott, Don Rendell and Tony Coe. Oscar Peterson turns up again on another Verve double, 'Jazz At The Opera House' (Verve), a showcase for Granz's stablemates Stan Getz and J. J. Johnson, not to mention the MJQ. Stan and J.J. provide the most satisfying pabulum. Gary Burton's recent appearance may add interest to 'Three-Four The Blues' (CBS), another 'first' date whereon this precocious 17-year-old vibist teamed with guitarist Hank Garland to smooth and colourful effect. 'Skip James Today!' (Vanguard) is yet another example of the in-grown, mysterious, almost-random blues strumming and whimpering that conjures an ancient melancholy for forgotten women and railroads: James has a curiously high and delicate voice, trailing, dead and dry, and repeats six of the pieces he recorded for Paramount in 1931 along with six more. It couldn't be less like Louis, but it's almost as fascinating.

9 November 1968

* As far as I remember, his view was pungently adverse.

Rabbit Jumps the Blues

It is curious that Ellington, who has never been short of orchestral velvet on which to display the individual jewels of his soloists, should have been slow to put forward the inscrutable altoist Johnny Hodges in this manner. In the late thirties, when the notion first occurred to him, Barney Bigard and Cootie Williams each had their 'concertos' and their 'units' long before Hodges, and when records did begin to appear under his name, they were inclined to be commercial and have female vocals. Very likely it was not until the late Billy Strayhorn joined the band that Hodges got his 'image' with numbers such as 'Day Dream' and 'Passion Flower', which he recorded in 1940.

But there was another Hodges, the young man to whom Sidney Bechet gave a soprano sax, and he is admirably showcased on 'Hodge Podge' (CBS), which picks out sixteen titles from 1938–9, starting with 'Jeep's Blues' and going through 'Dooji Wooji' and 'Wanderlust' to 'Skunk Hollow Blues'. Here the blues is dominant, and one can see that Bechet knew his man. It took Hodges the best part of twenty years to emerge from the Strayhorn boudoir role, and when he did so he had lost something of his urgency with the blues, as 'Duke Ellington and Johnny Hodges: Back to Back and Side by Side' (Verve) demonstrates. All the sidemen, in fact, are more inclined to ponder over such themes as 'Weary Blues' and 'Loveless Love' than belt them out, though in doing so they reveal many new facets. The second of the two-disc pack has Roy Eldridge, Ben Webster and Jo Jones presented to advantage; Lawrence Brown's crumbly trombone and Edison's one-note adventures are minor distractions.

It is generally said of Bix Beiderbecke that he was a musical genius lumbered with deadheads. Possibly, but listening to 'Bix and Tram' (Parlophone) makes me think that Rank, Signorelli and company were a more sympathetic setting for his cornet than, say, Teschmacher, Freeman, Mezzrow and Sullivan would have been. And Lang and Jimmy Dorsey, not to mention Trumbauer himself, can hardly be dismissed as nonentities. It is just their lack of the tension that the Chicagoans excelled in that provides Bix with a musically-relaxed background that suited him. Here lesser-known tracks such as 'Humpty Dumpty', 'Cryin' All The Day' and 'A Good Man Is Hard to Find' are added to the well-known 'Singing The Blues', 'I'm Coming Virginia' and others.

To my surprise, I found myself liking at least two tracks of 'Miles in the Sky' (CBS), not of course as jazz, but as a kind of soundtrack to some bleak pastoral such as a film of the Paston Letters. 'Paraphernalia' and 'Country Boy', the pieces in question, show Miles unwinding long isolated scarf-like phrases against the hoppity background of Hancock, Carter and Williams, and the record is undoubtedly beautiful in a melancholy and fenlike way.

Of 'Ornette Coleman On Tenor' (Atlantic) and Archie Shepp's 'The Magic of Ju-Ju' (Impulse) I can say only that here are two *avant garde* kings having an outing, and that you may go with them if it pleases you. Shepp's five percussionists, with their rhythm logs and talking drums, seem to be supporting a new kind of Pharaoh-Sanders-of-the-River Uncle-Tommery.

Way Down Yonder: Wooden Joe Nicholas, massive near-contemporary of Buddy Bolden, plays splendidly on 'Wooden Joe's New Orleans Band 1945–1949' (Storyville), not only with power but (like Bunk) with beauty, too. The record proves Albert Burbank to be a better clarinettist than George Lewis, if anyone needed convincing, and indeed almost as good as Dodds. 'New Orleans Joys', by the Young Tuxedo Brass Band (Atlantic), is a presentation of genuine music rather neatly divided into (side one): 'Going to the Cemetery' and (side two) 'Coming Back'. John Casimir leads on piercing E-flat clarinet, and Jim Robinson and sousaphonist Wilbert Tillman swing the band on the return. This set has been much issued since 1958, but if you don't know it you might find it affecting.

A reissue I enjoyed too much to annotate is Jimmy Witherspoon's 'Callin' the Blues' (Atlantic), the 1956 session with the Wilbur de Paris band. The numbers are all the same, but it's a pleasure to hear some real hot music behind them rather than Gerry Mulligan or strings. Art Tatum fans will no doubt already have much of 'Piano Starts Here' (CBS), Art's first four pieces from 1933 (dubbed) and a familiar session from a 1949 'Just Jazz' concert; the music is as amazing as ever.

When I began this column nearly eight years ago I opened with a mention of *Jazz on Record*. A new edition has just been published (Hanover Books), and everyone who collects jazz records ought to have it; its 416 pages are full of information and judgment. It's a good book to quarrel with: why omit 'Pee Wee Russell: a Legend' (Fontana)? To conceal how good Pee Wee was in his Condon days? But such cavils are swept away in gratitude.

14 December 1968

1969

Just a Little While

Whatever one thought of the clarinet playing of George Lewis, it is impossible to avoid sadness at his death. This small, gentle, 98lb man, who did not so much achieve greatness as have it thrust upon him, became the idol of the post-war revivalist generation in Britain. It is not too much to say that he replaced Louis Armstrong in the hearts of jazz enthusiasts as their emblem of genuine grass-roots jazz.

His life was appropriate to this legend. Born in the same year and city as Louis (1900, New Orleans), he taught himself to play the clarinet (though never to read music) and lived that odd semi-professional life common to so many New Orleans musicians till well after his fortieth birthday. He played at weddings, picnics and funerals, not to mention dances, and when no work was to be had he worked as a stevedore.

In 1929 he played his first gigs with Bunk Johnson, and when Johnson ('This ain't bunk – Bunk taught Louis' as *Down Beat* headlined it) was discovered in 1942, he asked that Lewis should be found for the clarinet chair. The band went straight to the top. It was not a happy association, but when Bunk died in 1949 the way back to genuine New Orleans had been well and truly beaten, and Lewis was free to carry on with his unsophisticated contemporaries and their simple, heartfelt repertoire.

So they played. In San Francisco, New York, London, Berlin, Copenhagen, it was always the same: unschooled, even somewhat incompetent ensembles, perhaps a little repetitive, perhaps a trifle off pitch, but singing out over a bouncing rhythm in a way that gladdened the heart, the George Lewis band became the emblem of uncommercial jazz purity.

Chris Barber, Ken Colyer, Monty Sunshine, Acker Bilk, Keith Smith – two decades of men who wanted to play jazz as it originally sounded took Lewis as their model. What did they find in his music? Many answers might be given, but mine would be excitement without tension.

So much jazz of the thirties had been based on the crescendo of feeling, the killer-diller, jam-session pseudo-orgasmic pattern of the ten-inch record; in George Lewis's music there was a different method, that of genial co-operation in recounting the tunes that had become deeply ingrained in the New Orleans Negro's way of life: 'Just a Little While To Stay Here', 'Bye and Bye', 'Old Rugged Cross', and the love songs of the beginning of the century such as 'When You Wore a Tulip', sounded even better in the twentieth chorus than in the first.

And that was really the beginning and the end of George Lewis's music. There were no tremendous finishes, astounding solos, murderous build-ups; just this happy, jogging polyphony, a gay-painted musical merry-go-round made up of numerous simple yet sensitive voices, a group of men playing with the complete conviction of performers at the heart of an unquestioned tradition.

It is just the nature of this tradition that makes it hard to assess Lewis finally as 'a clarinettist'. A George Lewis solo is really no more than the other horns resting while George goes on playing what he would have played in an ensemble – a careful, zig-zagging embellishment of the theme, in no way designed to draw attention to himself. But this was New Orleans.

'In the old days, it was always *our* band,' Whitney Balliett reports the New Orleans jazz musicologist Bill Russell saying rebukingly, 'Now one or another of the trumpet players is always resting, and sometimes the drums stop altogether. And there are strings of solos, like an Eddie Condon jam session.' Clearly the cult of personality was as unwelcome here as elsewhere.

But George Lewis did have a solo, a slow blues, usually called 'Burgundy Street Blues', that earned him from Bunk Johnson the mocking appellation of 'the composer'. It was slow, tremulous, formal, rather over-sweet, like a Victorian valentine, and seems to show something of the heart of the man, which, according to *Call Him George*, Jay Allison Stuart's readable though somewhat sentimentalized biography (Peter Davies), had few of the 'mean' qualities of the indigenous New Orleans musician.

Like many successful men, Lewis had a remarkable mother, Mrs Alice Zeno, who lived to be 96 and instilled into him a religious attitude to his life and playing. 'Remember that, son,' she would say. 'George Lewis does nothing. It is God does it.' Again, this is not new in the New Orleans context: we remember Joe Oliver, ill and poor and bandless, writing to his sister: 'I've got a lot to thank God for, because I eat and sleep . . .' And even Jelly Roll Morton, on that long, last mortal drive west in 1940, telling his wife: 'The blessed mother really taken care of me.' All the same, it explains a lot in George Lewis's playing: the resilience, the modesty, the happiness, the decency.

He made a lot of records in the past twenty-five years, and I don't know which are currently available. *Jazz On Record*, that invaluable book I mentioned before, names 'George Lewis and his New Orleans Stompers' (Vocalion) as one of the best, and I would add 'Concert!' (Blue Note). But all the early ones are good. Like Lewis himself, you can't really go wrong.

11 January 1969

Coverage

Recently I added up the number of jazz records that had been reviewed in the previous four numbers of the *Gramophone*, and found that out of a possible fifty-three I had actually heard twenty-two. Interested, I repeated the experiment in terms of *Jazz Journal*. Here I had heard forty-eight out of a possible 183.

I recount this anecdote partly to exemplify the difficulties a reviewer works under and partly to dispel the notion that my choice of the month's best records is absolute and unchallengeable. A great many records today are issued on cheap and comparatively fugitive labels, or are in fact imported from abroad on a strictly commercial basis, so that free distribution of review copies (unless a review is guaranteed) is out of the question. 'I seem to hear fewer and fewer LPs,' one pundit grumbled, when asked to select the best records of 1968.

But another factor is the excessive volatility of the jazz record world. A frequent phenomenon is the arrival of a chatty letter from (say) Mike Stickleback, announcing that he is now Jazz Press Release Officer for Hi-Note, Mahogany, Windy City, Extreme, Second Line and Old Man Blues labels and that my slightest wish with regard to any items they cover, past, present and future, will be instantly gratified if only I will ring Marble Arch something or other.

In a few weeks I send Mike a courteous note asking for perhaps three new releases; no response. I ring up; Mr Stickleback is no longer with us and in any case Hi-Note, Windy City and Second

Line are now part of Megasaurus Enterprises, Mahogany and Extreme are distributed by Oafmark and Old Man Blues has packed up; and usually they aren't as polite as that, treating my request for Mr Stickleback as a subtle form of commercial leg-pulling, or equivalent to a proposal to raise the spirit of William Ewart Gladstone.

Well, it's a difficult business, suggesting that jazz lovers should scan more than one source of information. For my part I shall go on pursuing the elusive Mr Stickleback.

The record I found most interesting this month was 'Jammin' at Sunset – Volume 1' (Fontana), Jazzart tracks from 1945. This Los Angeles company picked up several instrumentalists when big bands such as James or Kenton were in town, and cut a dozen skilled and musical tracks featuring Howard McGhee, Willie Smith, Lucky Thompson and the 16-year-old André Previn, Charlie Ventura's Hawkinsisms haven't worn as well. A parallel item, also from the Jazzart 1961 list, is 'Modern Mainstream' by the Dave Bailey Sextet (Fontana), featuring Kinny Dorham, Curtis Fuller, tenorist Frank Haynes and Tommy Flanagan in addition to drummer Bailey. This is all very airy and efficient, with good long solos for all on 'Osmosis' and 'An Oscar for Oscar', but the temperature doesn't rise quite high enough.

I wish I was fonder of the sort of studio orchestra one gets these days: 'Le Déjeuner sur L'Herbe' by the New Jazz Orchestra (Verve) is a musicianly and original occasion, studded with notabilities (Ian Carr, Jon Hiseman), full of compositional niceties and unexpected voicings, but I can't pretend it is jazz as I understand the word. 'John Surman' (Deram) is a little better, presenting this amiable young baritone man on some West Indian tracks with a quintet, then with a fuller orchestra for Coltrane-like crescendoes called 'Incantation', 'Episode' and 'Dance'; Kenny Wheeler is present to good effect. Don Ellis's 'Shock Treatment' (CBS) takes some sorting out (follow the label, not the sleeve), but if you can endure eccentric tempos ('Beat Me, Daddy, Seven To The Bar') there is much shimmering and spirited writing here, some of it electronically assisted.

A two-disc Verve Krupa pack, 'Drummer Man', mustn't be confused with the CBS 'Drummin' Man' of some years back: this is a pair of Granz sessions from 1956 and 1958 respectively by studio groups. The first is openly retrospective, exhuming vulgarities with the help of Eldridge and Anita O'Day, but the second – a dozen 1946

Mulligan arrangements – is much looser and more beguiling, with Krupa hardly audible at all. Funnily enough, no one noticed the personnel, though sleeveman Alun Morgan chances his arm. Another revival is 'Retrospect Through 21 Years of BBC Jazz Club' (Philips) – not contemporary airshots, as one would wish, but Billy Munn, Johnny Dankworth, Humphrey Lyttelton and others re-assembled with numerous star sidesmen.

Was I too generous recently to some Armstrong vocals? Verve's 'Ella and Louis' from 1956 and 1957 makes me think not. The pattern of these sides is for the two veterans to sing the lyrics of standards alternately, and it's noticeable how much tighter a grip Louis gets than Ella, not to mention his background trumpet.

8 February 1969

How Long Blues?

I am getting rather tired of the blues boom. Having for thirty years known the blues as a kind of jazz that calls forth a particular sincerity from the player ('Yeah, he's all right, but can he play the *blues*?'), or as a muttering, plangent lingua franca of the southern American Negro, it gives me no pleasure to hear it banged out in unvarying fortissimo by an indistinguishable series of groups and individuals of both races and nations. Moreover, we may be killing the goose that lays the golden eggs. The blues is tough, resilient, basic, ubiquitous. But it is not indestructible, and if we go on like this the day will come when the whole genre will be as tedious as, say, the Harry Lime theme.

However, the records keep rolling in: 'Sonny Boy Williamson Vol. 2' (Blues Classics) presents fourteen sides from 1937–45 by the original bearer of this name, accompanied by various sidekicks including Broonzy, Big Maceo, Tampa Red, Eddie Boyd and so on. This is light, agreeable music, the querulous harmonica blending nicely with the lacework of piano and guitar. 'Hand Me Down My Old Walking Stick' by Big Joe Williams (Liberty) is a much richer job, recorded last year, on which Big Joe's tremendous orchestra of a guitar (nine strings) pounds out music for dancing as well as accompanying his strong voice. Liberty is also issuing some anthologies: 'Rural Blues, 1 & 2' gives a conspectus of the post-war country styles. Lil' Son Jackson, Lightnin' Hopkins and others, moving into the era of amplification (Slim Harpo, J. D. Edwards) and – to my mind – coarsening. 'Urban Blues I' is a parallel group offering early Fats Domino, T-Bone Walker, Joe Turner and others.

Turning to jazz in general, 'Kansas City Jump' (Fontana) is a most interesting assortment, dating mostly from 1947, by groups led by Buddy Tate, Pete Peterson, Jay McShann and Earl Jackson. Tate and Peterson are tenorists, and there is some remarkable Emmett Berry: the unknown (to me and the sleeve) Jackson group, however, with two takes of 'Kansas City Jump', justify their eponymity with flowing alto, squalling half-muted trumpet, good tenor and building ensembles in the blues. Riverside label is happily back on the market again, offering a raft of middlebrow music: 'Swing Masters' gives Hawkins, Sulieman, J. J. Johnson and a Hank Jones rhythm section, dealing with the blues in various shades, 'Laura' and 'Sanctity'. 'Mulligan Meets Monk' eternalizes an enigmatic encounter in which *Jazz On Record* found Monk taking the micky out of Mulligan, and 'Bill Evans At Shelly's Manne Hole' puts the pianist in a more forthright, less Pierrot-and-Columbine mood than usual, though his first chorus of 'Round Midnight' converts Monk's sombre line into a romantic yearning.

RCA Victor have done a good resurrection job on Charlie Barnet, putting out sixteen tracks from 1939–42 that show this forceful but somewhat anonymous band at its best. Barnet was a rich boy who led a band because he liked it, and in fact was the first white leader to play the Apollo Theatre in Harlem (in 1933); his best-known pieces, 'The Duke's Idea', 'Pompton Turnpike', 'Cherokee' and 'Wanderin' Blues' (with Mary Ann McCall) are all here. Leonard Feather's sleeve-note rather absurdly calls the band one of the four that 'have passed the test of time *magna cum laude*' (the others are Duke, Count and Lunceford): 'The Right Idea', a bright thirty-two-bar riffer in the early Basie style, shows it at its most effective. 'Basie Straight Ahead' (Dot) cross-sections this band last year, giving out on nine Sam Nestico originals (a trombone player, not saxist Sal Nistico) in the accustomed manner, which is by now on the edge of a cliché – the wobbling brass flares, the blistering drumming, the cat-walking Basie piano. 'Magic Flea' is perhaps the most exciting track, featuring a frenzied Lockjaw Davis.

Such obituaries of Pee Wee Russell as have come my way have not seemed to do justice to this extraordinary white clarinet player who died last month at the age of 62. I have referred before to the trio of great white eccentrics, Beiderbecke, Russell and Wild Bill Davison – three players who achieved completely individual styles – and it seems to me that the unique quality of each was the product of conscious and consummate artistry. I don't accept the suggestion that Russell didn't know what he was doing. Listen to his solo on Bud Freeman's 'Muskrat Ramble', for instance, where he deliberately repeats that typical squeak at the beginning of two successive phrases; hear him on the Mound City Blue Blowers' 'One Hour', or the Louisiana Rhythm Kings' 'Basin Street Blues', or the Rhythmakers 'Spider Crawl' – all beautifully-shaped statements; try Condon's 'It's Right Here For You', where Russell shatters the record with half a chorus of murderous musical agnosticism, or the last eight bars of Spanier's 'Sweet Lorraine' where he homes in like a talked-down jet. Such a prolific recorder was bound to have his dull days; admittedly he clowned for the drunks at Nicks; but on his day between, say, 1930 and 1945, when his talent was really blossoming and dancing, he had no peers.

8 March 1969

The Rummagers

If I were to frame Larkin's Law of Reissues, it would say that anything you haven't got already probably isn't worth bothering about. In other words, if someone tries to persuade you to buy a limited edition of the 1924–5 sessions by Paraffin Joe and his Nitelites, keep your pockets buttoned up; if they were any good, you'd have heard of them at school, as you did King Oliver, and have laid out your earliest pocket money on them.

Everything worthwhile gets reissued about every five years.

True, the conscientious rummaging several companies are at present engaged in puts this generalization to the test. Polydor, for instance, have produced in 'Classics of the Swing Years' a remarkable bunch of little-known tracks by famous groups ranging from Webb, Lunceford and Henderson to the John Kirby Band and Jay McShann with Charlie Parker. One suspects that a good deal of them come from airshots or tapings (the reproduction is far from invariably good), and there is a general atmosphere of live non-studio action, which makes for vitality at the expense of finesse. Try at any rate to see the list of contents.

'The Delicate Swing of Teddy Wilson' (Polydor) was apparently recorded in 1945 as a kind of Muzak, but the leader, in conjunction with Shavers, Norvo and a rhythm section, deals ably with a bunch of standards. Then there is 'Earl Hines and his Band' (Riverside), a 1961 session from the Birdhouse in Chicago, on which Jimmy Archey hogs the mike, although Eddie Smith (sounding a bit like Hackett) and Darnell Howard, not to mention Hines himself, can be heard in the background.

'Bunk Johnson 1944 – Vol. 2' (Storyville) is the kind of music that will never be left out of print for long. These American Music tracks display Johnson as a leader and soloist of unrivalled relaxation and persuasiveness and make it clear that, now the unattractiveness of his personality has faded from the scene, he was a trumpeter of unique gifts. True, he couldn't do the cadenzas of 'West End Blues', but could even Louis push a group along with such lilting grace as Bunk does on 'Ballin' the Jack' and 'Precious Lord'?

It is interesting to compare him with 'Dejan's Olympia Brass Band in Europe' (77 Records), an example of a genuine-spirited New Orleans marching band of great good humour but little art: this is what you would hear if you went to New Orleans, not Bunk. It may be significant that I liked the slow-scored stuff best: the free-for-all ensembles turn into riffing, rather than organized polyphony.

Although I believe jazz was the music of America from 1890 to 1950, and deplore all alien infiltrations from other countries and centuries, I'm bound to say that I'm something of a sucker for these Indo-jazz fusions.

'Indo Jazz Etudes' (Sonet) is a delightful example of the mode: fluid, watery in the best sense, European in a strange way – dig, for instance, John Mayer's captivating pastiche-Vivaldi on 'Serenade': is it satire or what? Perhaps it's the lack of strain and Lat-Am jerkiness that appeals, or the unabashed lizard-on-the-crumbling-wall romanticism of 'Saraband', performed against tappings and cluckings and poppings, and a vague drone as if someone had put his hat down on a harmonium. Hear it.

Artie Shaw's 'Free For All' (CBS) is a bunch of sides from 1937, including 'I'm Yours', 'Nightmare', 'Free For All', 'Free Wheeling' and those magnificent tracks 'The Blues Parts I and II'. It's entertaining to note how drummer Cliff Leeman bought a cymbal halfway through the year that sounded like a metallic sneeze, and couldn't leave it alone.

From 1944–5 comes 'The Ellingtonians' (Mercury), sessions by Rex Stewart's Big Eight, Billy Taylor's Big Eight and the Barney Bigard quintet. I doubt if Ellington's sidemen ever sound quite as effective outside the band as in, but Stewart plunges and snorts to good effect on 'Zaza', and the ubiquitous Johnny Guarnieri substitutes for Duke on all sides.

On 'The 1968 Memphis Country Blues Festival' (Blue Horizon) I was greatly taken by the opening tracks by one Nathan Beauregard, 73, local, blind and yelling with a desperate serenity the old interchangeable lyrics. Furry Lewis, Bukka White and others chip in lower down the bill.

'Plain Old Blues' (Mercury) offers Art Hodes rolling the blues along with bassist Tiny Parham: those who remember Hodes's methods in the forties, trilling and rumbling and somehow playing as well, as if he had three hands, will be interested to hear how his style has crispened. Indeed, his greater sophistication may have led to a decline in taste: he takes 'How Long' too fast, and grows frivolous at the end of 'Pinetop's Blues'. Still, it's marvellous background music, if you can find the foreground.

'Mingus – Ah – Um' (CBS) has turned up again: funny how every Mingus band sounds a great rabble of players, like some trick of Shakespearian production: this is notable for 'Goodbye Pork Pie Hat' (tribute to Lester Young) and 'Fables of Faubus'. 'Pussy Cat Dues' highlights Knepper on trombone and Handy on clarinet, while Mingus pounds away behind.

13 April 1969

Record-Making History

In the dark Hitler-ridden days just before the war there were two American companies, Commodore and Blue Note, which did astounding things: they assembled living Jazz players to make twelve-inch jazz records.

Survivors from that period will recall that the jazz record is a comparatively post-war invention: up to the late thirties the output of all the founding fathers was classified as 'Popular and Dance' or even 'Novelty'.*

*Unfortunately I have lost a reader's letter contradicting this sentence with a wealth of evidence. Commodore and Blue Note, however, were the first exclusively jazz-oriented labels to issue new performances.

The disinfecting phrase 'With vocal refrain' was enough to conceal that Bix was in the ensemble, or that the said refrain was by Louis Armstrong. To make jazz records *as such*, and to issue them on the traditionally classical size of disc, was to send a shudder through the industry from which it never recovered.

The two innovators (who had nothing at all to do with each other) were Milt Gabler and Alfred Lion. Gabler ran the Commodore Music Shop, had a red-and-gold label and began by recording the Condon gang in 1938. Lion was a German expatriate who began by recording Negro artists such as Bechet, Ammons and Pete Johnson with a blue-and-white label in 1939.

To the distant fan in Britain, Commodore was the tough, white, nightclub kind of music, while Blue Note was sombre, towering, shadowy, statuesque Negro stuff. Both were successful, and after a good run sold out to the big boys. The Commodore catalogue reappeared here on Stateside; now Blue Note (the property of the Transamerica Corporation) has put out some discs anthologizing its earlier choices (present-day Blue Note records are entirely post-Parker).

Of the first five Blue Note reissues to appear, I should guess that 'The Funky Piano of Art Hodes' is the best, containing as it does eleven tracks dating from 1944–5, all by groups directed by Russian emigré Hodes. These range from seven-piecers to trios, usually led by trumpeter Max Kaminsky and with heavy drummers such as Fred Moore or Danny Alvin.

The jazz is serious and traditional, characterized by Kaminsky's curiously-impersonal honesty and the fine clarinets of Rod Cless, Ed Hall and Omer Simeon: after listening carefully to Kaminsky's horn, I conclude that its quality is of a man blowing a trumpet, rather than making it speak for him as in the case of Spanier or Wild Bill; it's probably something to do with lipwork. Nevertheless this record contains some of the best jazz issued this year. The naked sincerity of 'M K Blues' and 'Slow 'Em Down Blues' nicely matches the up-tempo 'Doctor Jazz' and 'Chicago Gal', with, of course, plenty of the rolling Hodes piano. Other issues feature Sidney de Paris and Ed Hall groups from the same era, and merit checking.

The core of 'That Toddlin' Town' (Parlophone) is four classic McKenzie-Condon sides from 1927 ('Nobody's Sweetheart', 'Liza' and the others), supported by the two numbers made by the odd Condon Quartet in the following year. Dominating figure is solemn spectacled Dutch-born Frank Teschmacher, who was killed in 1932: his clarinet solos are driving and original, a halfway-house between Dodds and Pee Wee Russell, and his alto (on 'Indiana') sounds nearly as exciting. McPartland, Sullivan and Freeman contribute to the general impression at least two of the sides give that the whole of jazz has got to be expressed in three minutes flat: well, that's youth (they were all about the age of our Stretchford gate-demolishers), and who's to say they've ever done better? It's a pity that the selection couldn't have included 'I Found a New Baby' with Spanier, the most enduring monument to this terse and dynamic school.

Does jazz gain or suffer from the Impresario Fallacy, the Let's-Call-Up-Buddy-Bolden-And-Have-Him-Record-With-Brubeck attitude? Good jazz records in the past were made by groups brought together temporarily or permanently by personal sympathy: 'Gerry Mulligan Meets Paul Desmond & Johnny Hodges' (Verve) is perhaps not a fair example of the genre, but it had me wondering rather testily why alto and baritone sax should be thought an adequate front line. Or don't things like that matter any more?

Mulligan-Desmond, however, (recorded at 2 a.m.), takes the honours with some splendid striving on 'Blues in Time' and 'Body and Soul'. Mulligan-Hodges is more phlegmatic, as if Rabbit was not going to bestir himself for the likes of Gerry, but of course they are pleasant enough.

'Bebop' (Mercury) resuscitates some Keynote 78s from 1946–7 made by Red Rodney, Al Haig and other alumni; Rodney always seemed to me one of the easier-to-take of the bop trumpeters, with a riper tone that contrasts agreeably with the asceticism of Allen Eager, and the ensemble is nicely varied with Serge Chaloff on baritone (his number, 'The Goof and I' is here). On the whole, however, the sides have lasted less well than six Tristano tracks from the same period: these including the previously-unissued 'Ghost' (it turns out to be a pretty astounding 'Night in Tunisia') show what Tristano himself called his 'scandalous efficiency' to admirable effect.

You will hardly believe it, but I have now got, after years of waiting, 'The Rhythmakers 1932' on Collector's Classics 14. Yes, all the Billy Banks sides, as marvellous as ever. Provenance is obscure: jazz shops might help.

10 May 1969

A Revival That Came Too Late

Many early jazz players had sad lives, but there was particular irony added to the misfortunes of the New Orleans men who, coming north after the Great War, suffered through the Depression and died before the New Orleans revival could set them on their feet again. The last session of clarinettist Johnny Dodds, for instance, was for Decca's tentative 'New Orleans Jazz Album' in 1940: he did it after a stroke and with all his teeth taken out. Shortly afterwards he died, aged 48, a good five years younger than Dizzy Gillespie is today.

'Johnny Dodds' (RCA Victor) contains much of what is commonly agreed to be his best work, titles made under his own name in the late twenties with fellow-townsmen Natty Dominique and Honoré Dutrey and brother Baby on drums. Such well-known pieces as 'Bucktown Stomp', 'Weary City' and 'Bull Fiddle Blues' give his full, piercing clarinet tone a prominence it could not have on earlier dates with Oliver and Armstrong, and insist that his claim to be one of the first three or four great jazz clarinettists be acknowledged.

Nonetheless, there is a kind of stiff sadness sometimes in his playing: it may be the archaism of a different tradition, but it's not to be found in the work of contemporaries such as Bechet or Jimmy Noone. This collection includes three sides by the Dixie Jug Blowers, an outfit which on 11 December 1926, was graced to advantage with Dodds's presence.

Some months the number and diversity of releases defy coherent exposition, and this is one of them. 'Gary Burton in Concert' (RCA Victor) presents America's new favourite vibist in the Carnegie Recital Hall, playing a lot of the time what sounds like a Dance of the Hoar-Frost Fairy for a Balinese Listen-With-Mother, but his cohorts (Larry Coryell, guitar, and drummer Bob Moses) get things under way from time to time. The two tenorists Harold Ashby and Paul Gonsalves appear on 'Two From Duke' (Columbia), a selection from earlier sessions of 1960–1, playing a sort of Trust House jazz which is respectable without being exciting. Remarkable for a guitar solo by Gonsalves, 'Hines + Eldridge Vol. 1' is live Village Vanguard music from 1965 and features the late Coleman Hawkins on a swinging 'Rosetta'. Hines does a Waller medley: he is a strange player, commanding, florid, resourceful, surprising, yet a little too fond of doing it different ways instead of building a mood.

'Saxophones' (Mercury) is a refreshing anthology of Keynote

pressings from 1943–6, featuring Lester Young ('Sometimes I'm Happy'), Hawkins, Willie Smith, Bud Johnson (very Lesterish), Pete Brown and others. Add some fine trumpetings from Joe Thomas, Clayton, and, I suppose, Shavers, and you have a highly enjoyable set.

The news that the late John Coltrane has left a mass of self-taped material will arouse mixed feelings: 'Cosmic Music' (Impulse) is the first instalment, dating from 1966 and 1968. The two earlier tracks ('Manifestation' and 'Reverend King') are the usual tumults of noise, the latter featuring The Master on bass clarinet. Disciple Archie Shepp takes up the torch on 'The Way Ahead' (Impulse), four tracks with a reticent Jimmy Owen on trumpet and Grachan Moncur III. Shepp sounds a shade less villainous to me on some tracks, notably 'Fiesta' and 'Sophisticated Lady'.

The Blues are always with us, and it is good news that the Arhoolie label is available in this country: 'Chicago Blues' by Johnny Young and Big Walter offers representative tracks by pioneers of the present scene which, as the sleeve says, is rapidly passing. Sunnyland Slim's 'Midnight Jump' (Blue Horizon) has something of the same quality but with the personal material ('Stepmother') of an older tradition. 'The Natch'l Blues' by one Taj Mahal (Direction) has a hippy sleeve, but the music is conservative and good.

'Oscar Peterson With the Jazz Giants' (Verve) is notable for eight tracks with Sonny Stitt who purveys passionate pseudo-Parkerisms in a way that overshadows Webster and Hawkins on other pieces. 'Mike Westbrook's Concert Band' is getting golden opinions these days, and 'Release' (Deram) offers a seamless medley with soloists George Khan, John Surman, Dave Holdsworth and others. To me it's a bit like Debroy Summers tarted up, but probably more worthwhile than 'Artie Shaw Re-Creates His Great '38 Band' (Capitol), which I'm afraid lacks the tight excitement of the original. The Shaw parts are played by Walt Levinsky.

I don't really approve of anthologies such as 'Jazz In Britain – the '20s' (Parlophone) when the Bob Cats are still unreissued, but it has a splendid ODJB 'My Baby's Arms'. My news that the Billy Banks sides are alive and well and available on Collector's Classics 14 has brought letters from an American professor on sabbatical, a wing-commander in Cyprus, and Britain's leading under-fifty novelist. Blest be the tie that binds.

14 June 1969

Armstrong Out On His Own

One of the more remarkable anecdotes about Louis Armstrong concerns a set of records in which he blows against a tape made by an orchestra – Gordon Jenkins', probably – on the other side of the continent. 'Man, they sure left some great gaps,' chuckled this master of jazz, a music noted, you will recall, for its reliance on collective improvisation.

If one puts this story at the end of his career, and his two-cornet duets with King Oliver at the beginning, the result suggests a continuous progression away from group performance to the lonely insulation of individuality, and 'Louis and the Big Bands 1928–1930' (Parlophone) stands approximately in the middle. Gone were the Hot Five, the Hot Seven, the tempestuous occasions with the Luis Russell band: instead we had a cut-out figure gesticulating in front of an anonymous musical background, hitting 250 high Cs followed by a high F.

One explanation as to why he did it argues that with Armstrong the jazz solo developed to a pitch where no one could follow, and this kind of set-up was the only course left to him. Another explanation is that he did it for the money.

Most of the sixteen tracks here offered are familiar from the old Parlophone Rhythm Style series – 'When You're Smiling', 'After You've Gone', 'My Sweet' and so on – and are characterized by that flaccid Lombardo-flavoured sax section Louis so loved, high register statements of the melody, and exuberant vocals. Indeed, some of the more trance-like renderings ('My Sweet' and 'Exactly Like You', for instance) have an eerie originality remote from the well-known mannerisms of 'You Rascal, You' or 'Rockin' Chair': one wonders if Louis had any idea of the words.

There are alternative takes of 'Some of These Days' and 'When You're Smiling', and that famous pair of sides made in 1928 with Carroll Dickerson and his Orchestra, 'Symphonic Raps' and 'Savoyager's Stomp', appear for the first time in this country (they have never been issued in America). The record concludes with the much-abused 'Tiger Rag', to my ears not a bad version of Louis's call-and-response build-up routine, of which 'Chinatown My Chinatown' is the supreme example.

Though perhaps not Louis's best, it is still good enough to out-top the rest of the month's issues in remotely the same genre: 'Ornette at

12' (Impulse) escapes this classification, being four 'live' pieces by trumpeter-fiddler-altoist Ornette in the company of tenorist Dewey Redman, Charlie Haden and Ornette Denardo on drums, whom I take to be Ornette's 12-year-old son.

Dewey is a new name to me, and proves himself to be of the terrier-shaking-a-rat school of Archie Shepp (a white rat, of course) rather than the totally unmalicious style of Coleman himself. 'New York' presents a romantic, almost sentimental, view of that ambiguous city. Young Ornette patters away efficiently enough: having seen the 7-year-old Victor Feldman in action in 1941, I don't mark him up unduly for prodigiousness.

Another disc with a drummer-leader is 'Richcraft' (Mercury), nine tracks by the Rich orchestra of 1959 on which a nine-piece brass section dominates the five-piece reeds like the rippling of silk. Buddy's jackboot drumming punches things forward, aided by notable soloists such as Earl Warren, Phil Woods, Harry Edison, Al Cohn and Benny Golson: I found it a stimulating session.

Not so 'Jambo Caribe' (Mercury), a Dizzy Gillespie record based on Caribbean themes and rhythms for 1964. The finale 'Trinidad Goodbye' has some sterling stuff by Dizzy and James Moody, but on the whole this is just another Gillespie exotic.

I reckon myself a blues lover, but it does seem a shame that a genuine Mississippi singer such as John Lee Hooker has to surround himself with organ, Fender bass and amplifiers in order to make a session like 'Simply the Truth' (Stateside). It's not so much that I dislike the heavy, anonymous thudding common to this mode (though of course I do) as that it tends to reduce a remarkable singer such as John Lee to his lowest common denominator. Once or twice ('Mean Mean Woman', 'I'm Just a Drifter') he strays down those back-country tracks again.

12 July 1969

Squalor Behind the Blues

Behind the blues spreads the half-glimpsed, depressing vista of the life of the American Negro. At almost any level the houses are shoddy; at worst, they are hardly more than lean-to sheds standing on dirt among weeds. The landscapes are the flat plains that border the national highways and are traversed by the south-running railroads, the Louisville-Nashville, the Texas and Pacific. In the scattered townships the only recreation is to be found in the 'Coloured Café', with its beer and Coca-Cola advertisements and juke-box, or, in the grim chimney-packed towns, in the blues cellars, where there is hardly headroom for the performers to stand upright.

All this and more is depicted, almost accidentally, in Paul Oliver's *The Story of the Blues*, a handsome illustrated book based on the remarkable exhibition of the same name held in the American Embassy in 1964. Put together primarily to show the personalities of the blues, and the properties of their music, it is continually supplying details that the keenest historical imagination would miss.

The bread lines, the Red Cross relief camps after the floods, compete with charms, hair-straightener, and perfumes that are clearly seen as more than half sorcery ('If you want wonderful things to happen to you, use Ma-jeek perfume . . . Might turn boyfriends into husbands'). A grim advertisement for Ramblin' Thomas's 'No Job Blues' is next to an *Insect Life* drawing of the boll weevil, the creature that devastated the post-plantation cotton crops in the early years of the century. Anyone curious about the blues, their players and the conditions that produced them, will find this book endlessly fascinating.

Something of the same sense of panorama emerges from 'The Roots of America's Music' (Arhoolie), a two-disc pack cutting four broad swathes through its multi-faceted subject. The blues, naturally enough (the name 'Arhoolie' is an old field holler), account for two of these: 'Country', with Fred McDowell, Mance Lipscomb, Black Ace and more, and 'City', with Texas pianist Mercy Dee, the fierce and athletic yelling of Big Mama Thornton, and the curious accordionist Clifton Chenier.

'Gospel and Jazz' is patchier: the Reverend Overstreet is caught at St Luke Powerhouse Church in Phoenix, Arizona, and there are remarkable guitar and piano solos from Jesse Fuller and Robert Shaw respectively; the jazz is Kid Thomas, Pete Johnson and Joe Turner, and a pseudo-Mingus offering from Berkeley.

The last section, 'Country Cajun and Folk', is most refreshing because least familiar: the sprightly mountain fiddle music, possessing a vitality of Scotch-Irish flavour, the mysterious Cajun version of it, the conventional folk songs and the incredible Nashville Street Band that rounds it off, polyphony as gay as it is confused. All in all it's a splendid gallimaufry.

Two small-group discs I enjoyed are Nat Adderley's 'The Scavenger' (Milestone) and 'The Herdsmen' (Mercury): the first features tenorist Joe Henderson and Joe Zawinul on some eclectic numbers diversified by strings and Varitone trumpet, and the second is a string of Keynote recordings made between 1944 and 1947 by groups having strong affiliations with the Herman band of the time. My pet aversion, Slam Stewart, is balanced by the handsome trumpetings of the underrated Joe Thomas.

Then there is the native product: 'Jazz Explosion' (Columbia) offers at 16s. an anthology from what the sleeve calls the Lansdowne Jazz Explosion, starting with Stan Tracey in 1965 and going up to an as-yet-unissued Harriott/D'Silva. 'Alex Welsh and his Band '69' (Columbia) emphasizes what a hit this fiery little band made at Newport in 1968, and these numbers go some way towards explaining this. Their style is a trifle slithy for comfort, though.

Anyone whose idea of a good jazz record is to sit meditating on our mortal end had better hurry on down and buy 'A Genuine Tong Funeral' by the Gary Burton Quartet with Orchestra (RCA). This bit of nonsense is subtitled 'A Dark Opera Without Words by Carla Bley' and 'based on emotions towards death', the sections entitled 'The Opening (Inside the Grave)' and 'Interlude: Shovels' and similar jollity. I like Burton, but here he is lumbered with a bass trombone and tuba and a musical concept that is, to say the least, pretty deadly.

Further extracts from the Keynote catalogue are grouped on 'Hawkins & Hines' (Mercury), small 1944 bands starring one or other or both of these notabilities plus Shavers, Wilson, Tab Smith and Trummy Young to taste. This is a kind of afterglow of the thirties that has much to recommend it. And, talking of afterglows, 'The Best of Glenn Miller' (RCA International) has such a beautiful 'Nightingale Sang in Berkeley Square' that one can almost hear the bombs falling.

9 August 1969

Change and Decay

Slowly it is creeping out that bop was no good – or, if you like, increasingly bop is being seen in its historical perspective. The latest penny on the plate is from Henry Pleasants who, you may remember, was lamenting the death of classical music back in 1961 (*Death Of A Music?*) by saying that all the musical vitality of the mid-century had gone into jazz. Now, in *Serious Music And All That Jazz* (Gollancz), he is fighting against the realization that jazz has intellectualized itself out of the market and that all the musical vitality, and so on, has gone into pop.

The parallel is strict. Classical music had its death-throes with chromaticism, and is now dead and twitching with people who slap trombones ('a slapped trombone is a glorious sound'). Jazz had its death-throes with Gillespie and Parker, and is now dead and screeching with the political diatribes ('America's done me a lot of wrong') of Archie Shepp.

Mr Pleasants is commendably honest: 'Much of the bop era seems, in retrospect, an orgy of sanctimonious self-indulgence and self-congratulation . . . What had begun as a device to exclude the square musician at Minton's and other gathering places of the new élite was sustained in more public performances to exclude the square lay listener, too.' In other words it was a private music unsupported by popular approval, and died the death.

My own reservation about this highly stimulating book is that in 1969, as in 1961, Mr Pleasants may be behind the times. Surely by now pop is showing every signs of going into a chromatic phase? How can one possibly rank 'A Day In The Life' with 'I Want To Hold Your Hand'? No doubt there is, or soon will be, free form pop. Only it won't be all that pop.

This argument was much in my mind when listening to 'Fats Navarro Memorial' (CBS Realm), for Fats Navarro, dead at 27 in 1950 of chronic tuberculosis, is being praised these days as if he were a sort of bop Bix. Having listened to these four sides, commemorating between them six sessions from 1946–7, I concluded that Navarro was a good, a very good, bop trumpeter, better if you like than the young Miles Davis, and even pushing Clifford Brown. But what does that mean? Only that he was able to play fast, high, screwy trumpet better than they could. The emotional content is limited to several Tad Dameron numbers ('Bop Carroll' among them) and some hilarious commercials to the voice of Kay Penton.

Without going outside that same series, the reissue of 'Louis Armstrong Plays W. C. Handy' (CBS Realm) should put Navarro in his historical perspective. This session, classic though it is, is not perfection: in fact, a surprising number of the tracks ('St Louis

Blues', 'Loveless Love', 'Long Gone') are pretty lightweight, but 'Chantez-les-Bas' and 'Yellow Dog Blues', to name but two, have a ranting, jubilant power about them that is bound to keep them in the lists. The moment, in the former, when Armstrong starts to sing 'Just 'fore day', and the tracks slips from its moorings into real jazz, is unforgettable.

Sometimes I think Stephane Grappelly has been unfairly overshadowed by Django Reinhardt – Django was *good*, certainly, and better than Grappelly at least towards the end of his career, but Stephane's high, swinging Goodman-style excitement shouldn't be neglected. 'Django' (CBS Realm) offers the Quintet's earliest 1934–5 recordings at a time when Django could be downright pedestrian ('Confessin'') and the sides usually took flight when Grappelly came in swift and high ('Sweet Sue').

Some agreeable Biograph issues have come to hand lately (specialist shops only), and I was interested to hear The Red Onion Jazz Band's 'There'll Be A Hot Time In Old Town Tonight' made at New York's Town Hall with Natalie Lamb singing early this year. The style of this group is very much in the vein of Colyer and early Barber (though the sleeve claims that it is less deliberately archaic): John Bucher's cornet is soft and feelingful, and Miss Lamb renders Bessie's songs accurately enough.

Another Biograph is 'After Hours Blues', 1949 recordings by St Louis Jimmy (with an excellent unknown pianist), Sunnyland Slim (rather rhythm-&-bluesy), and a raft of Little Brother Montgomery sides with two versions of his famous 'Vicksburg Blues', 1949 and 1930, both excellent.

'The Best of Benny Goodman' (RCA Victor) and 'Benny Goodman and The Great Vocalists' (RCA International) signify the growing return of interest in the king of thirty years ago. The first disc offers mostly studio performances of the numbers played at Carnegie Hall – 'Don't Be That Way', 'One O'Clock', 'Loch Lomond' and so on – and efficient though they are, they haven't quite the punch of that memorable evening. The vocal record is rather odd: 1935–9 tracks featuring regulars such as Martha Tilton and Helen Ward, and irregulars Jimmy Rushing, Ella Fitzgerald and Johnny Mercer (groogh!). The earlier sides are well worth hearing.

13 September 1969

Great Expectations

The golden rule in any art is: once you have made your name, keep in there punching. For the public is not so much endlessly gullible as endlessly hopeful: after twenty years, after forty years even, it still half-expects your next book or film or play to reproduce that first fine careless rapture, however clearly you have demonstrated that whatever talent you once possessed has long since degenerated into repetition, platitude or frivolity.

A commonplace in the more established arts, it is true of jazz also.

It is perhaps ungenerous to write such a preamble to 'Count Basie Plays Neal Hefti and Quincy Jones' (Verve). These must have been two of the earliest Basie Verve LPs, 1962–3, and each shows the band put through its paces by a first-class arranger; personally I prefer the Jones session, as it seems to stay closer to the well-tried Basie formula 'brass, reeds and rhythm, four to the bar and no messing'.

The two blues 'Count 'Em' and 'Kansas City Wrinkles' have feeling and power; in the Hefti group, Thad Jones's work on 'The Long Night' is good, and Al Aarons, another trumpet, takes the honours on 'Ain't That Right?' and 'Together Again'.

All the same, no one really believes – do they? – that the Newmans and Fosters of the sixties equal Clayton, Edison, Young and Evans, and even the celebrated Basie beat seems to have suffered by the separation of amplified bass from over-loud drums. *The Encyclopaedia of Jazz in the Sixties* speaks of 'a sharp deterioration in the musical interest', and Whitney Balliett of 'a smooth, heavyset machine that never falters and never surprises'. If Basie has kept his reputation, it is only by remorseless application of my golden rule.

Albert Ayler's 'New Grass' (Impulse) is an extraordinary piece of work, being (not to put too fine a point on it) a rock record by the master of the gothic galosh. The first track 'Message From Albert', has the usual screeching, plus some half-baked nonsense about having lived before, but after that it is all soul, Gospel, R. & B., and even Lat-Am, giving the reader the worst of both free form and funky worlds.

Much better is Ornette Coleman's 'Town Hall 1962' (Fontana), one of the earliest appearances of the Trio, though here accompanied by a string quartet that mews like a basketful of kittens while Coleman's agreeable-toned alto rambles all over the place. On the twenty-minute 'The Ark' he is exceptionally good – just before the drum solo – and I can well believe that this is one of his best records.

Some interesting and enjoyable blues records have come to hand recently: the clear, non-hysterical voice of B. B. King and his sailing guitar cut through 'His Best – the Electric B. B. King' (Stateside) in a variety of tracks both studio and live. I like B.B.'s downright homiletic numbers, especially when Duke Jethro's phlegmatic organ moans in the background. 'Bukka White' (CBS Realm) presents fourteen sides by this strong-voiced veteran Mississippian dating from 1937 and 1940, full of tunefulness, sadness and individuality, urgent in its mournful predicaments. The sleeve picture is pointlessly disgusting.

Biograph has put out an anthology of Southern and South-Western artists from 1949 called 'Sugar Mama Blues', featuring David Wylie, Frank Edwards, Pee Wee Hughes, Curley Weaver and Denis Macmillan: a rare sample for lovers of the mode. Then there is the same label's 'Oh Ma Baby – Ma Rainey Vol. 2', tracks from 1924–8 by this ancient sibyl of the blues who commanded a sombre resonance and musicality denied her junior, Bessie Smith. The title tune, with the magnificent Hendersonians, Joe Smith, Green, Bailey, Hawkins, et al, justifies her reputation as well as any, though 'Countin' the Blues' with Louis runs it close.

Finally, no one could go wrong buying 'Joe Turner Sings the Blues' (CBS Realm), the blues-shouting bartender from Kansas City doing his thing in front of hired helps Pete Johnson, Frankie Newton, Don Byas, Teddy Bunn and others.

18 October 1969

Ancient and Modern

Most jazz buffs secretly cherish a record they believe to be jazz as it really is, a norm from which everything else is a divagation, ancient, modern, good, bad or indifferent. In my case it is some of the tracks now reissued on Ace of Hearts by Eddie Condon and his accomplices of thirty years back.

'Condon à la Carte' and 'Jam Sessions At Commodore' represent the first sprightly running of the Commodore barrel around 1938–40, the label set up by Milt Gabler of the Commodore Music Shop to preserve the magnificent music Kaminsky, Russell, Stacy, Bushkin, Freeman and Hackett were making in their mid-thirties.

'I Ain't Gonna Give Nobody None Of This Jelly Roll' on the first disc, is one of the most perfectly balanced records I know. From Kaminsky's introductory whip-up on trumpet, the whole thing bounds along cleanly and inventively: Bushkin takes thirty-two bars that sound as if you are inside the piano, Russell another thirty-two of sunny intensity. The rest of the session is here, as good, if not better, notably Russell's murderous melodrama on 'It's All Right Here For You'.

The four tracks with Waller prove that the Condonites were always at home in coloured company, as is shown on the other disc where Benny Morton and Sidney Catlett join in on 'Basin Street Blues' and 'Oh Katharina!'. But it is the 1938 blues 'Carnegie Drag' I would cite as my second favourite, the sour, tough, four-in-the-morning epitome of the disillusioned Chicago mood, with Wettling's thistly percussion punctuating the solos.

Nostalgia? I don't think so: 'Bob Crosby's Bob Cats 1937–42' (Swaggie) has turned up from the Antipodes (specialist shops only), and though I fell on it avidly I found 'Who's Sorry Now', 'Five Point Blues' and 'Fidgety Feet' less tremendous than I remembered. 'Palesteena' is nice, in a Scobey sort of way, and a Marion Mann number 'Mama's Gone Goodbye', but I could have wished for 'Mourning Blues' and 'Spain', not to mention the four Shakespeare songs of 1939.

Back to the present with a vengeance with 'Spiritual Unity' by the Albert Ayler Trio (Fontana): this dates from 1964, and has Gary Peacock (bass) and Sonny Murray in support of Ayler's grizzling tenor. The first Ayler record I heard, 'Spirits' (Transatlantic), rather amused me and had a kind of Gothic originality: this, though of the same date, seems very run-of-the-mill Shepp stuff, though real enthusiasts may see something in it.

Corrupt bourgeois that I am, I found 'The Winter Consort' (A & M) much more enjoyable: Paul Winter, you will recall, was the first jazz man to play in the White House *consule* Kennedy, and here he produces a string of chilly, highly esoteric pieces with the aid of a bunch of characters blowing alto flute, darbuke, cello and baroque lute. Most of them conjure up alternate aspects of the Middle Ages, biting misery and rude clumsy gaiety until one realizes half the tempos are Lat-Am. I shall keep it, though.

The blues: 'The Blues' by Lightnin' Hopkins (Ace of Hearts) is in fact the selection of 1948–54 titles Realm issued as 'Dirty House Blues'. It's very good. The way Lightnin' tosses garbled phrases against his vividly pessimistic guitar underlines that this was one of his best periods: the subversive muttered comments are balanced by the sincere 'Long Way From Texas', and the whole is a monument to a Mid-West master of the mode.

Big Bill Broonzy ('Big Bill's Blues' CBS Realm) is a very different singer, brisk, cynical, clear, working with such studio companions as Washboard Sam, Joshua Altheimer, Black Bob and so on. There is some reputed Punch Miller trumpet on 'Trucking Little Woman', another trumpet on 'You Do Me' and all in all the collection shows the blues as cheerful group activity rather than the bitter expression of a solitary individual. 'Home Town Blues' (Ace of Hearts) repeats a pleasant Sonny Terry-Brownie McGhee anthology.

Persons wishing to be reminded of the Clyde Valley Stompers some dozen years ago should hear 'Trad Party' (Eclipse), which mixes six studio standards with some skiffly performances from St Andrew's Grand Hall, Glasgow, led by Mary Gowan. Douggie Kerr's trumpet sparks the former set which gives the disc its main appeal.

Nothing could be more different than 'Country Roads and Other Places' (RCA). Gary Burton's latest listen-with-mother for flower children. The pieces are melodious and inoffensive ('And On The Third Day' is particularly beguiling). The co-operation of Jerry Hahn, Steve Swallow and Roy Haynes sounds so easy one forgets how difficult it must be.

The latest Fats Waller garland, 'African Ripples' (RCA), mixes early piano solos with another choice of band pieces, and wholesome listening they are. Waller's voice is an elastic band that can be snapped round any tune: for example, 'Tell Me With Your Kisses' (unissued take), an untypical tune treated with typical charm and confidence. Great stuff.

8 November 1969

Just Around the Corner

A month of good will: a month of good records too. So a truce to the snide remark (All We Like Shepp), and on to the happy work of praise.

Quite the best record of this and many another month is 'Henry "Red" Allen' (RCA), fifteen tracks showing the career of this remarkable New Orleans-born trumpeter (his father was a street parade man) from 'Biffly Blues' in 1929 to 'Love Is Just Around the Corner' with a Hawkins-Higginbotham-Bailey group in 1957.

There was always something unusual about Allen's playing: even at the start he tended to sound like Armstrong in a distorting mirror, and by the end of his life an Allen solo was a brooding, gobbling, stretched, telegraphic thing of half notes and quarter-tones, while an Allen vocal sounded like a man with a bad conscience talking in his sleep. 'Roamin' is a lovely number, and there is a different, inferior 'Feelin' Drowsy' (I can't help thinking that albums with different masters of classics should be available to special order only, the normal version – rare enough to many – being issued otherwise); 'The Crawl' suggests the marathon vulgarities of Allen's Metropole stint.

A companion album is 'Wingy Manone' (RCA). This covers 1936–41, Wingy's Bluebird period, and so doesn't include 'No Calling Card' (a pity): still, there are plenty of good solos by such as the Marsalas, Chu Berry, Brunis, Eddie Miller, and a nice pianist called Carl Lanoue. In fact I fell to wondering why it wasn't better, and came to the conclusion that Wingy's threadbare Armstrong trumpet and taxing line in Waller jive was probably the cause.

Then there is 'I Thought I Heard Buddy Bolden Say' (RCA Victor), Jelly Roll Morton's 1939 sessions backed up with some 1929 trios and a Wilton Crawley, who strikes me as a forerunner of John Coltrane. The band pieces are famous landmarks on the road back to New Orleans, I suppose, but Morton's ragtime allegiances prevent them sounding anything like the records Bunk Johnson was to make in a few years' time.

Albert Ayler's 'Ghosts' (Fontana) was made in Copenhagen in 1964, and I am told it is now looked back on like Hot Five records, so buy it now if you haven't got it (and want it, of course). Sleeveman Charles Fox says that Ayler 'reinstated the primacy of melody', which on reflection I think a very curious opinion indeed. A reissue I can recommend with more warmth is 'The Thelonious Monk Quintet' (Riverside) from 1959 with Thad Jones. Jones did so well as a Monk horn it's surprising he wasn't asked again, blowing sympathetically on 'Straight No Chaser' while Monk strikes far-out chords.

One of the mainstreamers is 'Swing Masters' (Riverside), where Edison and Lockjaw Davis turn in some solid stuff over Hugh Lawson's enjoyable piano. Edison can also be heard on Count Basie's 'Standing Ovation' (Dot), which I found one of the best Basie records for a long time, more for the heavy muscularity of the band than for any solo work: 'Li'l Darlin'' is superb. Sonny Payne is here replaced by Harold Jones, a rather quieter follower, but I still regret the separation of the Basie rhythm section into its individual components and the consequent loss of the elastic composite sound of guitar-bass-drums that was such a feature of the old days.

I have a big pile of Arhoolies and other imports to work through: 'Ball And Chain' (Arhoolie) struck me as good value, with Big Mama Thornton's rather torchy soul and a new name, Larry Williams, on one side, and an unusual but satisfying session by Lightnin' Hopkins with drummer Frenchy Joseph on the other. 'Masters of The Blues' (Historical Records) presents an anthology studded with names such as Robert Johnson ('Little Queen of Spades'), Blind Boy Fuller, Texas Alexander and others. Tracks date from 1928–40, and my overall impression was of the despairing placidity of it all; a number such as Tommy Johnson's 'Canned Heat Blues', with its appealingly flighted lyric lines and gentle semi-yodels, is many light-years from today's howling, and Mr Johnson probably had a good deal more to howl about.

'Everybody's Talkin' 'Bout Sammy' (77 Records) presents British-born Sammy Rimington with his Denmark-formed band on a selection recorded in London last September. Rimington, a Lewis-type clarinet who has paid his dues in the street-parade world in New Orleans, leads pleasantly on an original choice of tunes, but the rest of the band just aren't up to Sammy's American friends. The tracks I liked best were of singer Kay Younger (very Billie-ish) where Rimington blows melodious tenor in the background.

RCA's stream of Waller selections make me think that they must sell well, which shows all is not lost: 'Handful of Keys' (RCA) offers two of my favourites, 'How Can You Face Me' and 'Dream Man', the latter with Bill Coleman's shy, intensely hot trumpet phrasing beautifully against Waller's jive; there is also 'E Flat Blues' and the title number.

Finally, Blue Note have put out three double-disc albums, covering their three decades of existence: the first, '1939–1949', contains classics such as Ammons' 'Boogie Woogie Stomp', Meade Lux's 'Honky Tonk', Bechet's 'Summertime' and 'Blue Horizon', Lewis's 'Climax Rag', Hodes's 'Maple Leaf' – a magnificent bag. The other two I'll come to later. Happy Christmas, with all that jazz.

13 December 1969

1970

Moment of Truth

I don't read as much jazz journalism as I should, but of what I did read in 1969 it is *Down Beat's* account of the Rutgers Jazz Festival that has stayed with me most vividly.

Down Beat, as you know, is the principal magazine of the American jazz music profession; it has been going thirty-five years, and has correspondents in every land from Denmark to Japan. Its policy is a comfortable, middle-of-the-road tolerance: whatever is, generally speaking, is right. And the man they sent to Rutgers was clearly cast in the same mould: let 'em all come, Dizzy, Herbie Mann, Jethro Tull, B. B. King, the Adderley Brothers – the more the merrier. He sat patiently in his seat and tried to hear good in everything, even sermons from Stones had they been present, and on the whole he succeeded, though there is the occasional wince ('I was beginning to wish I wore a hearing aid so I could turn it down').

The flashpoint, if one can call it that, came on the Sunday evening. Our man arrived late, to find the Miles Davis group launched into what proved their final number, or, as he puts it, 'in the throes of what I most deplore, a free-form free-for-all' that 'degenerated into a musical catfight'. One must salute his honesty: here was one of the groups he was most anxious to hear, and it was terrible, and he admits it was terrible. But then – and this is the point – there followed the Newport All Stars Braff, Norvo, Tad Farlow, and good old George Wein on piano, and the reporter's relief was so enormous that his encomia became almost pathetic in their hyperbole. Braff and his friends were sparkling spring water, they were 'Macbeth' and 'David Copperfield', they were incomparable, they were as eternal as sex and sunlight: 'man, this is what it's all about.' In his enthusiasm he asked a 17-year-old girl what she thought of them. She said: 'It's music to go shopping at Klein's by.'

Now the point of this anecdote is two-fold: first, all kinds of jazz are not equally good, no matter what editorial policy may be; some of it is ravishingly exciting, and some a musical catfight scored for broken glass and bagpipes, and you have only to hear the two in succession to grab the one and reject the other. Secondly, jazz (that is, the form of Afro-American popular music that flourished between 1925 and 1945) means nothing to the young. This should strengthen us in our devotion to it. True, we must give up any notion we may have been cherishing that beneath our hoar exteriors lurk hearts of May: we may dig jazz, but the kids want something else. Our passion for this extraordinary and ecstatic musical phenomenon that lasted a mere twenty or thirty years in the first half of our century must now take its place alongside similar passions for Hilliard miniatures or plain-chant.

With this in mind, it's not surprising that I found the last two two-disc albums of Blue Note's 'Three Decades of Jazz' a record of a decline. Most of the heroes of the revolution are represented with the exception of Parker: on the first set ('1949–1959') are Bud Powell, Monk, Miles, Clifford Brown, Coltrane and Rollins; and in the second ('1959–1969') Dolphy and Coleman, with attendant lords such as Lee Morgan, Lou Donaldson and Jimmy Smith. Coltrane and Rollins sound amazingly clean-toned and upright compared with their sixties' selves, but although I quite liked the Clifford Brown contributions few of these sides seemed to me masterpieces.

I enjoyed Jimmy Smith's 'Yardbird Suite' (splendid Kenny Burrell and Art Blakey) and The Jazz Messengers' 'Moanin'' from the first set (which is easily the better); the second hasn't much to recommend it, unless you like 'The Sidewinder' or an Ornette number 'European Echoes' which turns into a drum solo. One can trace the growth, too, of certain noxious and choking weeds that hastened our music's decline: Lat-Am rhythms, for instance, or the endless jogging excursions into the riff-and-rumble of sock-and-soul.

Antiquarians will go for 'The Arcadian Serenaders' (Parlophone), which shows lead trumpets Wingy Manone and Sterling Bose combining in 1924–5 with the good hard clarinet of Cliff Holman. As Brian Rust points out on the sleeve, it's amusing how Bose's style changes after he heard Bix. 'Jazz From New York 1928–1932' (Historical Records) is a curious *olla podrida*, yielding on examination Oliver's 'Call Of The Freaks', Allen's 'Swing Out' (different take), The Ten Blackberries' 'Rent Party Blues' (O my Hodges and my Nanton long ago!), Casa Loma's 'White Jazz' and a mass of minor Goodman-Pollack-Berigan material, mostly not too good.

Pianist Cecil Taylor has a strong following, and on 'Nefertiti, The Beautiful One Has Come' (Fontana) he, alto Jimmy Lyons and drummer Sonny Murray make characteristic uproar. Weaker stomachs may prefer 'The Swing Piano' (Polydor): Hines, Tatum and Wilson; music to go shopping in the fields of heaven by.

10 January 1970

Resurrected Big Bands

A great deal of the history of any art is taken up with the simple struggle between what the artist wants to do and what the customer wants to pay for. Once upon a time the jazzman, whose one ambition was to woodshed the righteous stuff after hours with a few friends, was forced to spend his life in a big band earning a living. Today a great many jazzmen would like to play in big bands, but the public is not so keen. We don't want to dance to them, they make pretty tedious television viewing and we certainly don't want the cost of one tacked on to a night out. It follows that the existence of a big jazz band today is a precarious thing: it may not even extend beyond the recording studio.

'Faces' (Polydor) is the first Kenny Clarke-Francy Boland that has come my way: based on Cologne, its international line-up has a strong British element – Tony Coe, Jimmy Deuchar, Ronnie Scott and others. This particular disc is a vastly-inflated version of the meet-the-boys number ('Rhythm Is Our Business', for instance) popular in the thirties: a suite in four parts (each with a pretentious title such as 'Vortographs'), each made up of pieces show-casing an individual player; Benny Bailey's trumpet and Derek Humble's alto pleased most. 'The New Don Ellis Band Goes Underground' (CBS) has been called progressive rock but to me, with its Lat-Am gospel and quarter-tone trumpets and something called a ring modulator, it suggests that we live in a world of wops, all melting into one another –a quotation, I hasten to add before you ring the Race Board, from that undervalued play, *The Apple Cart*.

Lionel Hampton's band, on the other hand, never has any difficulty in getting work, which shows that there is still a public for the raving, romping, stomping flag-wavers that it purveys. The secret of the Hampton band's fascination (well exemplified on 'Hamp's Big Band', RCA) is the contrast between the flamboyant vulgarity of the ensembles and Hampton's delicate vibes – delicate perforce, because one can't really be vulgar on the vibraphone. This is a splendid record. Audio Fidelity from 1959, with Cat Anderson and Donald Byrd contributing to the plate.

Other bands abound. There is 'The Benny Goodman Story' (Coral), the soundtrack of the film, with the usual stalwarts plus Stan Getz dating from August 1955. Artie Shaw's 'September Song' (RCA) offers three Shaw teams, 1938–9, 1940 and 1945, the second with strings: the numbers include fringe stuff like 'You're A Sweet Little Headache', with Helen Forrest singing. And Woody Herman is preserved on Coral at a hitherto undocumented point in his career: 1943–4, when he had such unexpected powers under his baton as Ben Webster, not to mention Bud Johnson, Hodges, Nance and Dave Tough.

No one should miss 'The Jumping Blues' (Coral), Jay McShann's band from 1941 to 1943, with teenager Charlie Parker in the reeds. McShann plays blues piano; there is some sub-Rushing singing by Walter Brown, who fronted the group when McShann was drafted. I'm not simply being perverse when I say that the best alto comes from John Jackson and that the band steadily improves with time and size. 'Spinning The Webb' (Coral) presents thirties Webb with fine section work, Taft Jordan, Bobby Stark and Sandy Williams, and early Ella.

Another is 'Swing That Music' (Coral), Armstrong pieces from 1935 to 1944, an intensely interesting picture of Louis going through a personal depression. I don't believe the story that Armstrong, after his marvellous improvised pageantry of the late twenties, suddenly discovered that playing the tune was much better: it must have been forced on him by his manager and the record companies, as they tried to force it on to Waller and Billie Holiday.

'The Immortal King Oliver' (CBS) presents a mixture of well-known occasions such as the duets ('Tom Cat Blues') with Jelly Roll, with Sara Martin's 'Death Sting Me' and two takes of the Creole Jazz Band's 'Mabel's Dream'. I don't care for Oliver: any solo not full of that childish wa-wa stuff is suspected to be by Ward Pinkett or Dave Nelson. But the atmosphere is nice. And don't neglect 'The Alex Welsh Dixieland Party' (Columbia), a good-humoured outing with at least one ('Sleepy Time Gal') good track.

14 February 1970

Blues A-Plenty

It is not surprising, historically, that the decline and death of jazz (or its transformation into something utterly unlike itself, whichever way you like to put it) has been succeeded by a bursting-out of the blues, a form which until then had been a subordinate area of jazz, though a compelling one. It is as if the appetite of the audience, starved of its proper food of warmth and beat, had fastened on this essentially Negro music and founded a whole popular culture on it.

As a result, there is a market for almost any kind of blues nowadays, ranging through the entire spectrum from the toothless mutterings of some rehabilitated veteran of the thirties, through the spruce electronic whanging of the South Side entertainers, to the white imitators, whose efforts shade off into the different world of beat, pop or what you will. It's hard to tell whether the blues are suffering from such over-exposure. A music in which, as Paul Oliver puts it, a 'stockpile of traditional phrases' serves as 'an indispensable substitute for original thought' would seem likely to be soon exhausted. Good blues records, however, still sound attractive: I wish traditional instrumental examples of the form were somewhat easier to come by.

'The American Folk Blues 1969' (CBS) is becoming a hardy annual: last year's group was brisker than usual, mostly from the Arhoolie stable, and included the late lamented Magic Sam, Clifton Chenier (the Cajun accordionist), Earl Hooker and Whistling Alex Moore. An entertaining evening. Clifton Chenier turns up again on 'Black Snake Blues' (Arhoolie) with brother Cleveland on rub-board, and demonstrates the curious territory he inhabits, halfway between Louisiana Cajun music and the juke-boxes.

A richer medley is found on 'Mississippi Delta Blues' (two discs, Arhoolie), which shows that 'the Negroes who live in the unpainted shacks along these forgotten roads' still keep up their inherited skills. I especially liked the Como Drum Band's drum-and-fife music (oddly indigenous to this part of America), but there are many other performers, including Walter Miller, Furry Lewis and Houston Stackhouse, who does a version of Tommy Johnson's marvellous 'Canned Heat Blues'. The second disc is given over entirely to R. L. Burnside and Joe Callicott.

Furry Lewis on 'Presenting the Country Blues' (Blue Horizon) and Bukka White on 'Memphis Hot Shots' (Blue Horizon) are two renowned performers with differing styles. White is much more agreeable to my ear, giving a stirring programme of rough-and-mumble lyrics against harmonica and strumming guitars. Otis Spann ('The Biggest Thing Since Colossus', Blue Horizon) and 'John

Littlejohn's Chicago Blues Stars' (Arhoolie) are more urbanized sets, the slow numbers especially feelingful, drums thwacking deliberately as the amplified guitars sing in leisured ecstacy.

Few single talents can have had a more extensive showcasing than Oscar Peterson's in Polydor's boxed four-disc 'Exclusively for my Friends', sides made in Germany over 1963–8 under non-commercial conditions. This is a beautiful piece of recording and Peterson fans will relish it: the question is whether such sessions do not lead to over-indulgence. The different piano of Fats Waller invigorates 'Ain't Misbehavin'' (RCA International), a somewhat crowd-catching selection of Waller standards and favourites ('I'm Gonna Sit Right Down', 'Hold Tight', 'Feet's Too Big') with some pretty solos to open and close the proceedings.

The new Miles Davis 'In a Silent Way' (CBS) has had a big reception in Britain: can Miles be turning into one of those fortunate artists who can do no wrong? It is very much his studio self, with three electronic pianos shimmering and spangling in the background while Davis and Shorter do their things in an unhurried and generally out-of-tempo atmosphere. Towards the end a regular beat faintly obtrudes (*Down Beat* calls it 'a striding rock rhythm') and as a whole it's a great deal pleasanter to listen to than Miles's public kind of music. But jazz?

'Swingin' with Gene Krupa' (RCA International) proved a delightful surprise, concealing within its noteless sleeve four sides made in 1950 with Wild Bill Davison and four more from 1936 with Goodman, Eldridge, Berry and Stacy, with Helen Ward to sing two vocals. The Davison tracks have a horrible male singer, unfortunately, but the celebrated cornet can be heard expostulating to good effect behind.

Going farther back, 'The Immortal Johnny Dodds' (CBS) rounds up a miscellany of twenties numbers with Lovie Austin, Blind Blake, Natty Dominique and Ida Cox: the sleeve gives Ladnier on five sides, but Rust proposes Dominique or Schoffner. 'Jackass Blues' is a winner, whoever it is.

Dexter Gordon's 'The Dial Sessions' (Polydor) offers a set of trumpetless 1947 sessions whereon Gordon deals rather roughly with ballads such as 'Ghost of a Chance' and indulges in long cutting contests with Wardell Gray ('The Chase') and Teddy Edwards ('The Duel'). Alternative takes: tenor fans only. Wider appeal from Johnny Griffin on 'The Man I Love' (Polydor), a Copenhagen club bash with

Kenny Drew, who contributes fine piano in a generally heartening occasion.

14 March 1970

The Colour of Their Music

It would be a bold man who tried today to differentiate between jazz performances by the colour of the players, for, quite apart from the race thing, intensive communications have led to a full blending of environmental styles. Yet during my own lifetime there have been several successive received ideas on the subject: black jazz was crude and limited, white jazz sophisticated and clever (*c* 1925). White jazz was commercial and derivative, black jazz sincere and for kicks (*c* 1935). Black jazz was really something else, white jazz was a bunch of kids trying to play like old men (*c* 1945). And, of course, white jazz was thin, stiff, intellectual, whereas black jazz was vital, swinging, instinctive: they not only did it with a better grace, they did it more natural (*passim*).

Without wanting to reawaken old controversies, I still think it's possible to instance this or that as good white or black jazz, with the implication that the other race could not have done it as well and no offence meant. An example to hand is the two Art Hodes' Chicagoans sessions from 1944 on 'Sittin' In – Vol. 1' (Blue Note). Here Kaminsky, Cless, Coniff, Hodes and the rhythm present a nicely-balanced programme of four blues and four standards such as 'Maple Leaf' and 'She's Cryin''; the texture is strong and stirring, based on Hodes' rolling blues piano but lit with Kaminsky's shouting open horn. The first three choruses of 'Yellow Dog Blues' are as relaxed and stimulating blues ensemble music as any I have heard. 'Doctor Jazz' and 'Changes Made' are up-tempo and hectoring. 'Slow 'Em Down Blues' and 'Shoe Shiner's Drag' slow and packed with feeling. Five stars from anyone's planetarium.

Compared with, say, Red Nichols or Brubeck, this is Negro-tradition jazz. Why do I call it white? Well, first, the rhythm has a kind of Gothic heaviness, which communicates itself at least to Coniff, whose trombone is markedly unathletic. Secondly, there is a certain brutal volume about the ensembles which, while exciting, is untypical of Negro playing, which tends to be tactful and glancing. But, above all, there is a harsh consistent agreement of style, almost an agreed melodrama, as of men who have decided what jazz is and how to play it. This might be termed convention, but it makes its effect: suppose the front line had been Eldridge, Bigard and Dickenson! What quotations, what 'dry humour', what tonal adventures! Well, let's not push it too hard: it is a grand record, overlapping to some extent with 'The Funky Piano of Art Hodes' but to be bought none the less.

A sequence not to be ignored is the Polydor Jazz Masters series, now well into the teens: some of those I have seen are distinguished by delightfully-pointless Grandville drawings on the sleeves. The George Lewis ('Doctor Jazz') is Hollywood 1953, and with Monette Moore talking her way through 'Burgundy Street': 'Misery And The Blues' presents a Teagarden 1954 group, with McPartland and Ed Hall variously featured in a tougher-than-usual set: Mingus's 1957 'Duke's Choice' seems a kind of travelogue music with trumpeter Clarence Shaw airing his rare talent, while Stuff Smith's 'One O'Clock Jump' provides some 1967 continental examples of the work of this veteran violinist that will be news to anyone born since the General Strike. Smith's work differs from other violin players in that he doesn't try to be a Goodman-type clarinet, but saws away at the four strings more in the Venuti style. Ellington's 'Cottontail' is 1956 vintage, a moment of uncertainty in the Ducal career (or so I should guess), and so made up of standards 'featuring' particular soloists – a nice Hodges 'Daydream', Hamilton on 'Funny Valentine' and 'Deep Purple', Gonsalves in a breakneck 'Cottontail' and so on. Only the first track 'The Blues' presents anything like orchestral cohesion.

Better by far is 'Flaming Youth' (RCA), 1927–9 pieces from one of the Golden Ages: the first chorus of the title piece comes over with all its original excitement, Miley stuttering and snarling, Braud's wooden-bass right up to the mike, reeds billowing, Greer's cymbal coughing vehemently – this is the staggering twenties Ellington in all his marvellous glory. Buy it. It makes 'In A Mellow Tone' (Riverside) seem pallid in contrast, 1957 stuff led by Clark Terry and released earlier as 'Duke With A Difference': Hodges and Gonsalves dominate.

'Paul Whiteman II' (RCA) moves from 1927 to 1935 (with an oddity from 1920): Bix is on five tracks, including 'No Sweet Man' and 'Dardanella', and later on we hear the Teagardens and Berigan bringing things up to date. It rather overshadows 'Jazz in Britain' –

The Thirties' (Parlophone), though this has more variety: ODJB pianist Billy Jones and his band from 1936, a soggy Gonella, some heavy-handed Billy Cotton, but lightsome Sylvester Ahola with The Night Club Kings and Coleman Hawkins giving out the pay with 1939 Jack Hylton to good effect.

Let-Me-Out Department: the *Melody Maker* now has monthly record reviews of Cage, Stockhausen, et al. A case for a change of name?

18 April 1970

Fragments of a Golden Age

'Halley Richardson's shoeshine parlour in Oklahoma City,' muses Ralph Ellison in his book *Shadow and Act*, 'Where I first heard Lester Young jamming in a shine chair, his head thrown back, his horn even then out-thrust, his feet working on the footrests . . .' Dating from 1929, the anecdote is a worthy addition to a literature full of such epiphanies, and reminds us that jazz was never confined to the triangle drawn between New Orleans, Chicago and New York.

There were the great cities of the Middle West, San Antonio, Denver, Dallas, and above all Kansas City, each with their dance halls, their bands, their favourite players, and there were orchestras (Alphonse Trent, for example, or Troy Floyd) whose concentration on the rich pickings to be made in the region has cost them the immortality the New York studios might have conferred. Not all took the same view: The Missourians (later the Cab Calloway band) walked out of the Cotton Club before Duke Ellington walked in, and names such as Andy Kirk and Count Basie testify to the magnetism The Apple could always exert on country outfits.

'Kansas City Jazz' (Coral) gathers up some fragments from one particular golden age, as compelling in its way as that of New Orleans: a time when the town was, in the parlance, jumping. 'You would hear music twenty-four hours a day in Kansas City,' said Jo Jones, and it was here that Coleman Hawkins met his Waterloo, encountering some local yobs by the name of Lester Young, Herschel Evans and Ben Webster at the Cherry Blossom.

Most of the tracks here presented were recorded in New York in 1940 by such Kaycee alumni as Basie, Kirk, Mary Lou Williams and Pete Johnson, and the most typical moments in them are also the best – the start of Johnson's '627 Stomp', the piano free and kicking; the plain first chorus of Eddie Durham's 'Little Girl', with the leader's guitar embellishments; the last chorus of Basie's 'Good Morning, Blues', when the whole band sweeps in before Rushing has finished and sings out a perfect 'head' twelve bars, or the two contrasting tenor choruses (Evans and Young, who else?) on 'Doggin' Around', the trumpets riffing elastically behind them; Joe Turner's 'Piney Brown Blues', recalling the Sunset Café where Joe was bartender. The list is not endless. Other tracks are undistinguished: Lips Page's group sounds like one of those gutless little groups that spoiled Billie Holiday's records in the early forties. But as a whole the record is memorable.

Rooting in the early Blue Note bag continues to good effect, and 'Swing Hi – Swing Lo' presents some mid-forties groups largely dominated by Ike Quebec, whose tenor combines nicely with Tiny Grimes's Christian-like guitar and Roger Ramirez's piano, notably on 'Blue Harlem'. Jimmy Hamilton and the Duke's Men contribute a little masterpiece 'Slapstick', with Carney's baritone more agile than usual. 'Blue Note Classics Vol. 1' offers twelve assorted takes of Hodes chamber groups with, variously, Nicholas, Simeon, Kaminsky, Baby Dodds and others, who make fine jobs of 'Squeeze Me', 'Bugle Call' and 'Maple Leaf Rag'. The Port of Harlem Six are added for good measure.

Time was, when a man had snuffed it, you heard no more of him, as Macbeth or someone said, but 'Selflessness' (Impulse) has Coltrane in his habit as he lived, or rather two habits, bad and worse: the 1963 style with Tyner, Garrison and Haynes doing 'My Favourite Things' at Newport, and the title piece with Pharaoh Sanders and Donald Garrett, made two years later and showing all present up to the neck in what I can only call polycacophony. There's a long stretch of McCoy Tyner, showing him still unsmirched, but then chaos comes again with a vengeance. The 1963 sides are listenable by contrast.

'Louis In Los Angeles' (Parlophone) is an important segment of Louis's recording life from 1930, fronting two bands of which the common link was 16-year-old Lionel Hampton: 'Ding Dong Daddy', 'In The Market', 'Body And Soul', 'You're Drivin' Me' (two takes) and others, plus the duet 'Dear Old Southland', 'Mahogany Hall' and 'Ain't Misbehavin''. This, generally speaking, is Louis-and-background, but his good-humoured virtuosity is so compelling that the ear capitulates. 'The Best Of Louis Armstrong' (RCA International) is the 1959 Audio-Fidelity, Armstrong-Plays-Oliver session, which for some reason didn't quite come off, but judge for yourself.

On the big band front, 'Charlie Barnet Vol. II' (RCA) pursues this group through 1939–41, with 'Leapin' At The Lincoln' and Charlie Shavers doing 'Echoes of Harlem'. 'Harlem Express' (Coral) is the famous Jimmy Lunceford outfit, 1934–6, including such triumphs of arrangement as 'Organ Grinder's Swing'. Recent additions to Doug Dobell's valiant 77 label include guitarist Frank Evans' suite 'Mark Twain' and 'Shepherd's Delight', by the Dave Shepherd Quintet. If you think you can't enjoy Goodman-group pastiche, think again, or let your feet think for you.

9 May 1970

Those Marvellous Sides

Space is short, so let's lay it on the line: you are unlikely to encounter a better record this year than 'Billy Banks and his Rhythmakers' (CBS/Realm). Or any other year for that matter.

What's good about it? Well, I have written on this subject before, and will try not to repeat myself. These four sessions in 1932, famous as they are, are obscure of provenance: it seems that Irving Mills (Ellington's manager) wanted to record Banks, a young singer he had discovered, and asked Eddie Condon to pick up a supporting group. In fact the groups Condon produced played such exciting jazz that Banks was left off the last session, Henry 'Red' Allen and Chick Bullock doing the vocals instead.

The men who took part were Allen, Pee Wee Russell, Joe Sullivan, Fats Waller, Jimmy Lord, Tommy Dorsey, Happy Cauldwell and Zutty Singleton, and in 1932 they were mostly in the first prime of youth and strength; they picked an assortment of blues, standards and oddities ('Yes, Suh'), and simply jammed them to death in solos and ensembles that for some remain the plainest demonstration of what jazz is – a bunch of Americans, white and Negro, blowing up incandescent versions of a broad spectrum of kinds of tune.

After all, Armstrong is only Armstrong, and Ellington only Ellington, but in the Banks sides you have perhaps a dozen men, all of great individual talent, instinctively combining in a common language to generate a hard-hitting, unaffected excitement, not without humour but utterly without kidding. The last three choruses of 'Yellow Dog Blues', for instance, were reproduced by Wilder Hobson in his book *American Jazz Music* (1938) as an example of what collective improvisation should be.

It says a lot for Banks that he was not swamped. His high, light voice has something of the imperturbability of Jimmy Rushing, but concedes more to drama (the second chorus of 'Margie' for example): he was more a vaudeville artist than a jazz singer. When Henry Allen takes over, the difference is marked.

Footnotes for the class of 1940: there are alternative takes of 'Yellow Dog Blues', 'Mean Old Bed Bug Blues', 'I Would Do Anything For You', and 'O Peter' as well as the originals: also the little-known 'Take It Slow And Easy', and a new take of 'Who Stole The Lock' that made me burst out laughing. The last-named number is the only representative of the last session. Nothing is said on the sleeve about Banks's reputed claim that Krupa was on one of the sessions, and indeed it doesn't sound likely.

It's interesting to compare this with 'Chicago Jazz' (Coral), three groups of four sides each made in 1939 and 1940 by pick-up bands directed by Condon, McPartland and Wettling respectively. These all-white tracks are not so good – how could they be? – although there is plenty of good jazz on them. The Condon tracks are somewhat heavy and laboured, starring Pee Wee Russell and Dave Tough on the loud cymbals: a pity they have not used the version of 'Friar's Point Shuffle' issued in 1940, potentially the best number. McPartland plays some charming neo-Bix on 'Sunrise' and 'Sugar', but his companions are watery. The Wettling group with Charlie Teagarden, Floyd O'Brien and Jess Stacy, offer an intensely hot and elegant satire 'Sister Kate' and a mellow, bouncing 'Bugle Call', but the others are dull. However, it is spirited jazz of its kind.

'Barney Bigard/Albert Nicholas' (RCA Victor) links these two New Orleans Creole clarinettists without much effectiveness. Bigard's contribution is two complete sessions from 1940 and 1941 (the 'Charlie the Chulo' and 'Brown Suede' ones), dreamy riffy lukewarm near-Muzak whose appeal has never reached me: Carney and Nance cheer things up on 'C Jam Blues'. Nicholas is heard among 'Bernard Addison and his Rhythm' and 'The Little Ramblers', groups playing in 1935 with much more verve and push. Stridesman Joe Turner Wallerizes with the first group, but the second is better, warmer and with Ward Pinkett on trumpet. Nicholas is not so perceptible.

I listened conscientiously to 'Cecil Taylor at the Café Montmartre' (Fontana) and didn't want to send a gunboat to that establishment more than four or five times. Altoist Jimmy Lyons and Taylor plus Sonny Murray (drums) kick up one long shindy and three short ones, which don't let me stop you from hearing: they're your ears.

It reminds me, however, that since I last wrote the demise of Ellington's superb altoist Johnny Hodges has been announced. Hodges brought as much beauty into jazz as Coltrane did ugliness (a large claim, but I'll stick to it), but Coltrane got *The Times* obituary and Hodges didn't: that's the world we live in. Towards the end of his life Hodges' alto tone had become refined to the point at which it hardly seemed like an instrument: more like someone thinking. And, indeed, that's what it was.

20 June 1970

Looking Back at Lyttelton

If offered three wishes by a good fairy, I should exchange one of them for absolute mastery of what Walt Whitman called the key'd cornet: my mind has been made up on this score since the age of, say, 14. But what exactly should I play? I suppose in the end it would turn out to be very like what Humphrey Lyttelton plays on '21 Years On' (Polydor), strong, good-natured stuff deriving from the Armstrong-Oliver-Condon tradition, a repertoire of standards such as 'Fidgety Feet' mixed with nice tunes like 'I'll Close My Eyes' that are fun to do.

There would be plenty of good long ensembles, and solos for front line and piano. The bass and guitar/banjo would devote themselves to the beat, assisted by the drummer who would have no Lat-Am kitchen-wear among his traps but be able to terminate numbers with a four-and-out coda as well as any man in Illyria. Such, after all, is jazz, free alike of antiquarianism and experiment.

This two-disc set, recorded live at the Conway Hall, is intended to commemorate Humph's first recordings in 1948–9 and his original band. The trumpeter, to be sure, is rejoined by Fawkes and Keith Christie, though the rhythm is different and includes some cloven-footed characters who have played with Sonny Rollins and Tubby Hayes, but the line-up recaptures a fair measure of the 1954 'Humph At The Conway' atmosphere. 'Snake Rag', 'Cake-Walkin' Babies',

'Bucket's Got a Hole In It', 'Mezz's Tune', 'Old Grey Mare' – all these are solid stirring performances at medium-fast tempo, and the audience revels in them. Balance is faulty: Peter Staples' Wettling-type drums are too prominent. The rhythm sometimes submerges the melody for long periods. Lyttelton at slow tempos is effortful, and with all tempos unvarying in volume. The piano is tinny. All the same, there isn't so much good new jazz about that you can afford to ignore it.

Another fine album in the same tradition is 'Original Blue Note Jazz – Vol. II', reissuing 1944 titles by Sidney de Paris and James P. Johnson, each in much the same company, including each other. De Paris plays good open horn in 'Joy-Mentin' and with mute and growl in 'The Call of the Blues' and is strongly supported by Vic Dickenson and Ed Hall. Two versions of 'Everybody Loves My Baby' are equally effective, with Big Sid Catlett providing the four-wheel drive. I am as fond of Bix Beiderbecke as most people, but 'Bix and Tram 1928' (Parlophone) is a rather mawkish, cachou-scented collection of commercial tunes with vocal refrains by the age's *castrati*-type crooners such as Scrappy Lambert and Noel Taylor.

The credit side is Bix's leads and rare breaks and solos, demonstrating once more the chime-like quality of his playing, as if his notes were hit with mallets rather than blown down a (by all accounts) beat-up cornet. Anyway, there are enough mad-sweet pangs here, to quote Whitman again, to make the record worth buying, but only just.

And then the blues . . . Really, living when the blues have really come into their own, when they are the equivalent of everything from 'Love in Bloom' to Gilbert and Sullivan, one finds more records than one can shake a stick at. Riflings of the Bluebird catalogue continue with Sonny Boy Williamson's 'Bluebird Blues' (RCA), Walter Davis's 'Think You Need a Shot' (RCA), and Big Joe Williams's 'Crawlin' King Snake' (RCA).

As Samuel Charters says, the Bluebird blues was a stereotyped product in the thirties, using a set group of musicians to rattle out a standard formula, however genuine it may have been. Of these three I liked Sonny Roy best, his voice mixing with his fierce harmonica and sometimes ('Whisky Headed Blues') with a mewing mandolin. A more recent Big Joe Williams disc is 'Classic Delta Blues' (CBS), made in 1964 and highly praised in the United States: these tracks are often the specialities of other men – Robert Johnson,

Charley Patton, Tommy Johnson, Skip James – and Williams uses a six-string guitar rather than his majestic nine-stringer.

Much more enjoyable is 'I Ain't Gonna Pick No More Cotton' by John Henry Barbee (Storyville). Remembering Barbee's tragic appearance in this country in 1964 – suffering, without knowing it, from a malignant disease – I put off playing this Copenhagen-recorded set for some time, but in the end found it strong, melodious, dignified and passionate (especially 'I Heard My Baby'). Another better-than-average record is Mississippi Fred McDowell's 'I Do Not Play No Rock'n Roll' (Capitol). True, a lot of time is taken up with talk ('That's what the blues come from. A reel'), but McDowell's rich and sonorous yelling ('Everybody's Down On Me') is effective in blues (or reels) and spirituals alike.

Paul Oliver's second anthology 'The Story of the Blues' (CBS) is four sides of grouped pieces (pianos, guitars, girls, groups) and is as deeply rewarding as his first. A prize for the historically-minded.

11 July 1970

Wells or Gibbon?

'Every man', wrote Schopenhauer, 'mistakes the limits of his vision for the limits of the world', a quelling sentiment that came to my mind when I was pasting up a recent bunch of press cuttings. For, however they buttered their words with subsidiary praise, there was no doubt that this was what even the friendliest of my reviewers was saying. 'A pity he had to spoil things', one of them wrote, 'by holding back history.'

The book in question, a collection of my writings on this page through the sixties, had advanced the view that 'modern' jazz (I attached a special, non-chronological meaning to the adjective) was no more jazz than modern painting was painting or modern poetry, etc. I even hinted that in jazz we had witnessed a capsule history of all arts – the generation from tribal function, the efflorescence into public and conscious entertainment, and the degeneration into private and subsidized absurdity.

What the reviewers said was that it was not jazz that had degenerated, but Larkin: I was simply one more example of the regrettable fact that our ears grow old and sometimes shut up altogether (a sign that we should do likewise).

Well, jazz writers are either Wells or Gibbon, onwards and upwards or decline and fall: where did we differ? After much thought, I selected a contention by another reviewer as a kind of test case: 'Men like Parker and Sonny Rollins . . . inherited most of the old jazz virtues, and anyone attuned to jazz should not take long to recognize them.'

This is the party line of the Wellses. Assuming it means that 'most of the old jazz virtues' are to be found in Parker and Rollins (it doesn't actually say so), then I and the rest of the Gibbons reject it. The wonderful music that swept the world during the first half of this century, so wonderful that it sang songs about itself ('Everybody's Doing It', 'It Don't Mean a Thing If It Ain't Got That Swing'), was of limited appeal, but that appeal was new and definite: a certain area of musical and rhythmic sensibility was being played on for the first time. It could, perhaps, be defined, but its provocation was so strong and blatant that this was felt to be unnecessary (Fats Waller: 'Lady, if you has to ask', etc.). It originated from Negro folk music and is with us now, in an infinitely vulgarized form, in beat music, rock and roll, rhythm and blues.

When Parker and the rest started bopping, therefore, their aim was to sell something as unlike jazz as possible to jazz audiences. They did this partly because they wished to recapture the lead, so to speak, by playing something the white men couldn't, but mostly, I should say, because the jazz nerve had been over-stimulated. They were intelligent men, musically, and jazz bored them. What they produced, therefore, was the conscious opposite of jazz – dead tone, no collective improvisation, no 'good old good ones' (or rather different g.o.g. ones), a kind of anti-syncopated klook-mop rhythm, and of course chromatic harmonies rather than the familiar diatonic of all the lullabies, love songs, hymns and national anthems that lie at the base of every nation's musical consciousness.

Now I am a simple soul. If someone offers me salt instead of sugar, or a waltz instead of a march, or bop instead of jazz, then I can't help pointing out that there's been some mistake. This is all I was doing: why did my critics object?

Our difference may be a semantic one. I am sure we both agree that there is a discernible basic difference between, say, Muggsy Spanier and Freddie Hubbard. What I am saying is that in consequence the word used to describe what Spanier plays should not be used to describe Hubbard. What they are saying is that the word used for Spanier should be extended to include Hubbard. Which is right?

Behind this confrontation, I fancy, lies a number of opposed prejudices. The Wellses want to extend terms, to stretch points, to see things change. The Gibbons want words to keep their meanings, to be definite, to see things stay the same. Whitney Balliett, in a recent number of the *New Yorker*, reports Duke Ellington as saying that he wants to drop the term jazz in favour of something wider, 'Afro-American music' or something like that. Duke is a Wells; Louis Armstrong, on the other hand, has talked about 'that modern malice . . . you got no tune to remember and no beat to dance to'. Louis is a Gibbon.

Well, either camp has a pretty good leader. All I would say to my critics is that the jazz that conquered the world (and me) was the jazz of Armstrong, Ellington, Bix and the Chicagoans. What Parker, Monk, Miles and the Jazz Misanthropes are playing can be Afro-American music for all I care, but it isn't jazz. Jazz is dying with its practitioners, Red Allen, Pee Wee Russell, Johnny Hodges. Not to admit this is . . . well, holding back history.

15 August 1970

Listening with a Difference

Recently there has broken out the familiar argument about whether it's better to go to live jazz performances or to stay at home with your records. Some say, understandably, that five minutes among the shot and smoke of the field is worth a lifetime's armchair strategy.

Mr Derek Langridge, however, in an interesting little book, *Your Jazz Collection* (Bingley), makes the obvious point that '"live" listening to jazz has drastic limitations. In time it cuts off the past, in space it reduces to the accident of where one lives . . . The real jazz lover must be a record collector.'

Others eschew academic considerations; if the fans of 1970 won't pay money to hear the cats of 1970, then jazz is economically dead. For the past two months Albert McCarthy, one of the editors of *Jazz Monthly*, has been pointing out that the reason for the decline of jazz as a paying proposition is that people don't like it any more; bop, and even more, *avant garde*, has lost the following that the swing era had built up. People won't even go out to hear records; attendances at the Glasgow Jazz Record Appreciation Society recitals are such that this season may well be the last of a series that has lasted since 1933.*

Lockjaw Davis, in this month's *Jazz Journal*, makes the point more pungently: 'You can keep this freedom music. Who is going to pay a second time to hear a guy wearing a sheet go rootle-tootle up and down the scale?'

As one whose reaction to jazz concerts has sometimes resembled that of the exquisite officer to the 1914–18 war ('My dear, the *noise* and the *people*'), I find much of this sympathetic. There is another point, however, that I never see mentioned: that jazz men play more obviously, more vulgarly, more repetitively, in public than in the recording studio.

An example of this is Cannonball Adderley's 'Country Preacher' (Capitol), a live argy-bargy from some Chicago church where 'Operation Breadbasket' is in full swing; loud yammer-hammer soul, knockabout farce, no sustained effects, nothing really to remember.

Cannonball's first Riverside album, 'Nardis', dating from 1958, with Blue Mitchell, Bill Evans and Philly Joe Jones, is on the other hand some splendid high-flying bop, making one realize where Cannonball got his reputation. He and Mitchell score on 'Minority' and 'People Will Say'; Philly Joe comps authoritatively.

'Bill Coleman was one of the great unrecognized jazzmen of the late thirties,' says the *Encyclopaedia of Jazz*. True indeed: I was always being disappointed by Fats Waller records because they weren't as good as 'Dream Man' – Coleman, of course, lithe, precise, utterly swinging, and with that hint of raucous shouting that characterizes all great trumpeters, even Bix. 'Bill Coleman à Paris, 1936–38' (Parlophone) catches him in his prime, playing with French/American orchestras such as Willie Lewis and Eddie Brunner and such stars as Herman Chittison, Grappelly, Adelaide Hall, Frank Goodie and the Reinhardt brothers. Coleman, who combined complete mastery of his instrument in all registers with an unceasing flow of ideas, is supposed to derive from Armstrong, but he has nothing of Louis's deliberate theatre: Charles Fox finds the word to describe him on the sleeve – 'quicksilver'.

*I don't know whether it was. There is certainly a Glasgow Rhythm Club today (1984).

Avant-Gardiste John Tchicai is half Danish, and 'Cadentia Nova Danica' (Polydor) was recorded in Aarhus in 1968 (it had been played in Britain earlier in the year). A suite of many moods, ranging from the chilly andante of the beginning to the folksong 'L'lanto del Indio' and the heavy percussion of 'Orga Fleur Super Asam', it still has a good measure of goon-like frenzy. A surprising and moving blues record is 'J. B. Lenoir' (Polydor). Lenoir, who visited Europe in 1965, combines an old-style Mississippi whine-and-whimper intonation with newspaper subjects such as Vietnam.

12 September 1970

Definitive Digging

The publication of another definitive work of jazz reference, *Who's Who in Jazz* by John Chilton (Bloomsbury Bookshop), underlines once more how indebted to Europe the jazz world is for its works of scholarship.

America, naturally enough, produces numerous jazz books, most of them of a much greater authority than we could ever pretend to, but in the field of patient, computer-like assemblage of facts Europe is unsurpassed. Where would discography be without Rust and Jepsen? And now we have John Chilton setting out the biographies of over 1000 jazz musicians in a handsome 450-page work replete with photographs, many of them rare.

Inevitably it will be compared with Leonard Feather's *Encyclopaedia of Jazz* and its supplements. Chilton's scope is in some respects narrower: his sub-title is 'Storyville to Swing Street', and he doesn't define this except by saying that every musician in his pages was born before 1920 (the converse doesn't hold true). This means that his coverage of jazz, as opposed to bop, musicians is fuller than Feather's: taking the letter 'L' as a sample, I found that while Chilton had fifty entries and Feather 112, twenty-two of Chilton's (or forty-four per cent) were not in Feather. Such a statistic reinforces one's initial impression that this is one of the essential jazz books.

Chilton is more austere than Feather. He confines himself to dates and places – and, curiously enough, causes of death. Not everyone can claim an end as sensational as Al Killian's ('murdered by a psychopathic landlord'), but there is a plethora of heart attacks, strokes, cancer and even 'complications following an attack of mumps' (Clarence Brereton). On the other hand, he is generous to his subjects' weaknesses: drink and drugs are never mentioned. Only Don Murray, we learn, 'resumed drinking', but we had not heard that he had stopped – or, for that matter, started.

On the credit side, however, one can only marvel at the repeated arrays of detail Chilton has, with enormous pertinacity, unearthed from transatlantic sources. His entry for Ladnier includes the 'Southern Tailor' shop venture with Bechet (1933), which one would be sorry to lose sight of: his spellings include the now-accepted Teschemacher and Roppolo. Caution: entries are not always in strict alphabetical order – Lanigan and Lugg, for instance, in the section I looked at closely.

One sometimes forgets – with reason, these days – what a *pretty* instrument the guitar can be. There have been several reminders recently: 'Blue Guitars Vol. II', for instance, by Eddie Lang and Lonnie Johnson (Parlophone), has one side of Lang soloing with big-fisted accompanists such as Schutt and Signorelli, European on 'April Kisses' and Afro-American on 'Church Street Sobbin' Blues', where the low notes are like big bloomy plums. The other side, though more overtly Negro, with Lonnie Johnson, King Oliver and singer Texas Alexander, I found rather less interesting: more riffs here, that substitute for improvisation.

The Charlie Byrd Trio's 'Which Side Are You On?' (Riverside) presents a 1961 Byrd at the Gate, uncharacteristically pounding his way through 'Just Squeeze Me', a bossa nova and a sidelong 'Which Side Are You On?' Only on 'Why Was I Born?' does he indulge the gentle chord-sprinkling from his acoustic guitar that was his chief charm.

Kenny Burrell's, 'Asphalt Canyon Suite' (Verve) has Burrell in front of some Johnny Pate-organized orchestra to no bad purpose: the suite is blues-oriented, strongly so, but better than the Lat-Am 'Things Ain't' on the other standards side. The Wes Montgomery Trio is resurrected on 'So Do It' (Riverside), a set dating from 1969 with James Clay on tenor, containing more jazz than Wes was sometimes content to let us have.

I missed Chris Barber's 'Battersea Rain Dance' (Polydor) when it first appeared, and was expecting something more exciting than this turned out to be. There is a tendency nowadays to praise anything unlike an artist's usual run of work: because Barber is known as a traditional player, this mélange of souly samba-ish riffery was hailed as an advance. In fact it's the sort of thing that is more fun to do than to listen to: the absence of bands between tracks merely serves to underline their similarity. The admirable Pat Halcox can be heard from time to time struggling within this Cannonball bag.

I am rather late in mentioning Miles Davis's two-disc 'Bitches' Brew' (CBS), a second instalment of the kind of noise first offered on 'In a Silent Way', electronic pianos and all. I would many times sooner listen to this than the cut-yourself-a-slice-of-throat-Whitey stuff some artists produce, but all the same its Muzak-like chicka-chicka-boom-chick soon palls. Far more interesting is 'Clifton Chenier's Very Best' (MHSP), eleven tracks by the master of that strange Cajun style of dance music Chenier is known for. To listen is to take a trip up the authentic river.

10 October 1970

The Trial of Faith

This column has run into difficulties, because for the next six months I must write it from an institution (I prefer not to particularize) in which I am separated from my hi-fi and my records. Instead of sitting at a point of acoustic perfection from which radiate shelves of jazz history, I am alone with an old and unreliable player and such new issues as the companies consent to send to my new and somewhat intimidating address.*

The experience is a testing one, and I am not yet sure what it will reveal. Men shipwrecked on a desert island with a sauce bottle are reputed (in time) to find its label as entrancing as a lyric poem: will my few fortuitous review copies take on a more commanding stature in the same way? Or is my faith being put on trial: do I like jazz under adverse conditions, or only when buttered with high-quality reproduction and salted with selections from my own racks?

Perhaps I was lucky to have Lightnin' Slim's 'Rooster Blues' (Blue Horizon) to strengthen my resolve. Slim is one of the first generation citified-rural singers: born in Louisiana in 1913, he began recording in the middle fifties and this collection is of tracks made for Excello in 1959–60. He has a strong, rough delivery, tremendous beat, and the querulous harmonica accompaniment of Lazy Lester adds genuine

*In fact All Souls College.

earthy counterpoint. 'Rooster Blues' and 'Long Leanie Mama' are unmistakable ancestors of rock setting the feet tapping, while 'Bed Bug Blues' exhibits a passionate remonstrance that reinforced my belief that anyone who can listen to the blues unmoved had better let them alone.

Not that it is so easy to let them alone these days, for blues lie at the heart of rock, and rock (to quote Mick Farren in the *Melody Maker*) 'today . . . is so powerful a force that it will draw a quarter of a million people to sleep in the open for days on end. It can spread tolerance or invoke violence. It cannot be ignored.' Strong words, but even if one can accept the more philosophical claims that are currently being made for the music ('a source of energy and a means of generating solidarity') it's still only certain elements in the blues isolated, coarsened and amplified. It may affect audiences more strongly, but this is only to say that home-distilled hooch is more affecting than château-bottled claret, or a punch on the nose than a reasoned refutation under nineteen headings.

On the other hand, it inevitably makes run-of-the-mill blues seem a little casual and conversational, as indeed it's their nature to be: for every 'Smoke Stack Lightning' there are a thousand anonymous mumbles about babies going away and not getting loving no more and the like. 'I Have to Paint My Face' (Arhoolie) is a group of field recordings by Chris Strachwitz featuring Sam Chatman (a nice 'I Stand and Wonder'), Big Joe Williams, Bukka White (interminable), and local worthies such as R. C. Smith.

'Lonesome Lonely Blues' (Blue Horizon) by Lonesome Sundown (real name Cornelius Green) is slightly disappointing, insofar as he came up as a sideman of Clifton Chenier, and one might therefore expect Cajun-tinged variations which don't in fact materialize, but there's some pleasant tenor by Lionel Prevo on the title number, and 'I Woke Up Cryin'' has a dignified sadness.

'Fletcher Henderson and the Dixie Stompers' (Parlophone) is a mammoth (eighteen tracks) collection which, with the earlier disc on PMC 7056, makes up the whole recorded output under this name. The present set covers 1925–6 from 'Spanish Shawl' to 'Alabama Stomp', and is notable for the prominence of Joe Smith and for Coleman Hawkins' forays on bass sax. There are plenty of good moments on both sides, but I could wish that the whole proceedings had been slowed down to half speed and both tunes and soloists been given more chance to expand. There is a Keystone-cop jerkiness about almost every track that may have been exciting at the time but which today seems forced and arid.

The Count Basie Orchestra resembles a Roman legion setting its four-square example in the teeth of universal degeneracy and the approach of free-form heathen, and repeating the discipline of its routines with grim independence. 'Basic Basie' (Polydor) has a mess of standards such as 'Idaho' (a spirited opener) and 'Sweet Lorraine' and was made just a year ago with Lockjaw Davis and Bobby Plater doing most of the reed solos. Harold Jones drops rocks at calculated intervals.

Talking of that kind of thing, 'The Dynamic Drums of Louis Bellson' (Columbia) presents a 1968 Bellson band with some experiments with Varitone saxes and guitars instead of a regular reed section. There are not many soloists and the brass is distant. Bellson fans, however, will get plenty for their money.

21 November 1970

Founding Fathers

Perhaps it isn't surprising that both records produced to celebrate the seventieth birthdays of Duke Ellington and Louis Armstrong should land on my desk in the same week. They were, after all, born within fifteen months of each other in 1899 and 1900,* the sons, respectively, of a White House butler in Washington and of nobody in particular in New Orleans.

But it is always a matter for rejoicing when an artist reaches three-score years and ten without having given up and with his international reputation still undiminished, and in a world where fashion and money and temperament take ruthless toll of its servants it is appropriate to salute these two great Americans and the tenacity which enabled them to fulfil their destinies.

The records are in many ways characteristic and interesting. 'Duke Ellington's Seventieth Birthday Concert' (United Artists) is a two-disc pack comprising tracks from two British concerts (Bristol and Manchester) in November, 1969, and really has nothing to do with Duke being 70, an age which he had attained the previous

*James Lincoln Collier, in *Louis Armstrong* (1984), discounts 1900 as the year of his birth, suggesting 1898.

April. But in a way this is the point: Duke makes nothing of his age ('In 1939, when I was 17', as he sometimes quips), and the best memento of his seniority is that he is still working, still assuring us he loves us madly, still coaxing from that changing-yet-eternal band of half-mesmerized sidemen the authentic Ellington music.

And here is a concert: Cat, Cootie, Rabbit (for the last time), Carney, Gonsalves, Procope, all featured, all splendid, all numbers tied together by the leader's announcements: this is something to keep when the reality is beyond us, the sunset of a great composer and a great orchestral jazz tradition. Incidentally, '4.30 Blues', with Procope on clarinet, is really something.

'Louis Armstrong and His Friends' (Philips) is much more commemorative, and much less successful. This was conceived as a birthday date, and the studio was crowded with eminences such as Condon, Braff, Hackett, Miles Davis, Coleman and others: Louis doesn't blow these days, so choirs and strings were imported as background, or even foreground, for his warblings.

What is interesting here is the change of repertoire. The *pièce de résistance* (in more senses than one) is 'We Shall Overcome', and it isn't unimpressive in a Cup-Final kind of way, everyone joining in to give an impression of overwhelming solidarity; but, coupled with Lennon's 'Give Peace a Chance', doesn't this suggest that now Joe Glaser is dead, Louis is being wheedled into the radical ranks?

There are old favourites, too, such as 'Mood Indigo' and 'What a Wonderful World', and a rather horrible personal item called 'Boy From New Orleans', in which Louis repeatedly refers to himself as 'Old Satch'. Imagine Ellington saying 'Old Duke'!

Set of the month, though, is Benny Goodman's 'Swing Classics' (Philips), a bunch of tracks seemingly recorded live when Benny was leading a small group in the fifties, featuring Braff, Urbie Green, Quinichette and Teddy Wilson. Goodman's tone is increasingly Beaux-Arts, there are bass solos, the tunes are old hacks led spavined from the familiar stable and virtually all degenerate to riff endings, yet within five minutes I was stamping and whistling. How is it that Teddy Wilson can still make 'Body and Soul', 'Rose Room', 'After You've Gone' and the rest sound springy, new and live?

Don't neglect, either, 'London Date' (Philips), Goodman with his British bunch last year doing fine except for the heavy slugging drumming that seems the orchestral vogue these days.

Beiderbecke students will want 'Bix and Tram – 1929 Plus'

(Parlophone), which showcases Bix in his 1929 decline. For those who think that Bix could do no wrong this is salutary listening. The other side is mostly 1927, before the clouds gathered, but I must say that Trumbauer's C-melody sax seemed the main attraction throughout, as for instance on 'Louise' when he seems to be anticipating not only Lester Young but the cool light-toned Chicagoans such as Boyce Brown.

More Bluebird blues appear on 'Got to Reap What You Sow' by Jazz Gillum (RCA) and 'Pearl Harbour Blues' by Doctor Clayton and his Buddy (RCA): Gillum's tracks seem to me like the productions of some romantic novelist, perfectly good for their kind, but indistinguishable from each other and in the end rather boring. Clayton (on the first side only) is high-pitched and rather dull on some 1942 pieces, but is much more flexible in 1946: his 'Buddy' (Sunnyland Slim) takes it from there in 1947 and is really a much better performer. 'Travellin' this Lonesome Road' (RCA) is an anthology from 1927–38 of Cannon's Jug Stompers, Walter Davis, the fascinating Clifford Gibson and others. This is really the best buy of the three.

12 December 1970

1971

Minority Interest

Reviewing jazz records in January might be described as scraping the barrelhouse: there certainly don't seem to be many around. But is it only January? When, in search of Christmas presents (that annual conversion of one's indifference to others into active hatred), I wandered into a few 'record departments', I was shocked to see how little of the stock therein could be called jazz.

Rank on rank of shiny LP covers all depicted the same thing: a bunch of young people, mostly male, with clothes and faces appropriate to criminal vagrancy, stood scowling at me in attitudes eloquent of 'We're gonna do you, Dad'. Their names, so far from implying any national, familial or artistic kinship, were phrases or even single words chosen at random in a kind of imagist or even surreal poetry – The Light Brigade, Deuteronomy, Lace, Pale Ways, The Low Foreheads. Only in a far corner did I find a small rack labelled 'Jazz' that contained the sleeves of some dozen LPs by Ellington, Basie, Ella Fitzgerald, Jacques Loussier and Ambrose.

Now of course one knew that this sort of transformation had taken place; one had watched jazz magazines fold up or turn into rock organs; one had seen (or had it been only a nightmare?) Jimi Hendrix elected by the fans to a jazz pantheon instead of Johnny Hodges; nevertheless, to see it expressed in concrete palpable terms did rather bring home one or two disagreeable truths that may be formulated thus:

(1) No jazz today is popular;
(2) The least unpopular jazz is reissues;
(3) Hence the only jazz issues from the big companies today are reissues, few and far between;
(4) Current jazz comes on obscure, imported, highly expensive labels, and the ordinary public never sees or hears it.

Well, perhaps I am simplifying: Christmas always upsets me. But there's no doubt that a staggering change in the direction indicated has taken place over the past five years.

'Those who care can only go on caring' – and buy 'Swinging in

Chicago' (Coral), a round-up of two 1934 Chicago sessions by Earl Hines and his Orchestra, plus four sides from a New York one the next year. This was a fine band, with Walter Fuller's trumpet and Armstrong-like vocals, Darnell Howard and Omer Simeon in the reeds, and Trummy Young taking the bone bits in a way reminiscent of Jimmy Harrison, but the best thing about it was Jimmy Mundy's charts, setting a tradition that ran up to Goodman. His scores were strong, simple and punching: listen to 'That's a Plenty', how the phrasing falls naturally into singable units, and later resolves into swinging riffs for the take-out. The reed section on 'Sweet Georgia Brown' and 'Bubbling Over', the trombone trio on 'Fat Babes' are different aspects of an orchestra that was always playing a living beat. And then, of course, there is Hines's kicking piano behind the ensembles, or coming through in solo passages that still seem fresh-minted.

Dear old Miles Davis recently denied that any English musician could 'really play': maybe not, but Doug Dobell, that doyen of Charing Cross Road, has recently produced two notable sessions. 'Our Kind of Music' (77 Records) has Brian Lemon fronting, or backing, Sandy Brown, Tony Coe, Bruce Turner and Johnny Picard in a string of varied presentations which everyone clearly enjoyed. Bruce Turner is my man, on alto in 'Strike Up' and tenor on 'Virginia', but Picard is good too, and there is an oddly-effective 'When My Sugar' with only Dave Green's bass for rhythm.

Then there is Eddie Thompson's 'By Myself' (77 Records), which shows a strong two-handed talent at play rather in the Tatum tradition, but balancing Art's endless arpeggios with Waller-like stride. It's certainly good to hear a piano being treated like this; the tracks I like best, though, were the simpler treatments that allowed emotion to come through, such as 'Then I'll Be Tired', 'Memphis in June' and even 'Robbin's Nest'.

There are British players – Lennie Bush, Diz Disley, Alan Clare – on 'Stephane Grappelly and Friends' (Philips), a session of last June when veteran Grappelly showed how he could still whip up enthusiasm with his single string pseudo-Goodman style, coupled with exoticism ('Girl from Ipanema') and balladry ('Like Someone in Love'). A very listenable record, displaying a much more varied talent than in the days of 'one more, Steph'.

Books: I hope someone is going to publish Stanley Dance's *The World of Duke Ellington* over here: I've been poring over the Scribner edition, which is largely compiled on the *Hear Me Talkin' To Ya* principle, but none the less constitutes a full-length portrait of this aristocrat of jazz orchestras. Lastly, all librarians should slam in an order for Donald Kennington's *The Literature of Jazz* (Library Association), a highly erudite summary of sources to date.

25 January 1971

Miss Bessie to You

The news that CBS intends to reissue Bessie Smith's total recorded output (160 sides) on ten LP records is as magnificent as the music itself. Miss Bessie ('Nobody called her just "Bessie",' says Zutty Singleton, omitting to mention that you got a smack in the chops if you did) was a tall gangling girl from Chattanooga, Tennessee, who was left an orphan at the age of nine and as a result worked in scuffling road shows until Ma Rainey took her up and taught her to sing the blues.

Her first record appeared in 1923 and was an instant success: from then until the Depression she was a national figure among Negroes, a kind of Gracie Fields of the blues.

Her style was not greatly dissimilar from that of Ma Rainey, and personally I have always had a sneaking preference for the older woman's pieces as being less monotonous, or more tuneful, than some of her pupil's, but Bessie Smith's voice has a deep, unhappy, surging quality that marked her off at once from her contemporaries. As a person, 'she was rough,' a fellow-singer admitted, but this seemed to add itself to the plangency of her intonation.

Unfortunately this didn't last: by 1930 the Negro record-buying public was more interested in the greater sophistication of Ethel Waters, and Miss Bessie lost her public. She was incapable of 'going commercial': she simply sank lower in the entertainment scale, and drank to forget it. In a way her decline resembled Joe Oliver's – the failure of a great talent to adapt itself to changing taste – but for all her heavy drinking there is no evidence of bad health, nor of substantial loss of voice. In 1933, as is well known, John Hammond recorded her for the British market: in some ways these are the most striking sides she ever waxed. Her death in 1937 in a road accident ended the question of whether she could ever fight her way back.

'The World's Greatest Blues Singer' (CBS, two discs) presents the first sixteen numbers she ever recorded (all 1923) along with the last sixteen (from 1930 to 1933): subsequent discs will continue this opposition until the two sequences meet in the middle. Her first recordings were with piano only, the somewhat inane Clarence Williams on the first side, the pounding Smack on the second, and show her voice already able to switch from simple majesty ('Midnight Blues') to the swooping, bending, yelling phrases of 'Beale Street Papa'. From the first few bars of 'See If I Care' on the second disc it's clear that Miss Bessie's voice had grown 'meaner' with the passing of years, but the music is more varied. Her tracks with the Bessemer Singers and James P. Johnson are invigorating, while two sides with Ed Allen and four with a Louis Bacon/Charlie Green group offer a harsh tearing sadness.

The album closes with the four Hammond sides, which (in my view) blow to the winds the idea that Bessie Smith was in decline. Backed by her best accompaniment since the 'Blue Boys' (Newton, Teagarden, Chu), she belts out some non-blues numbers (by then Miss Bessie was convinced that her blues days were over), at least two of which ('Buggy Ride' and 'Down In The Dumps') are as good as anything she ever did. As an end to her recording career they are superb, but also more than a little sad: clearly there was so much more that could have come.

I had it in mind to pillory 'Bennie Moten's Kansas City Orchestra 1923–5' (Parlophone) as exactly the kind of thing we don't want when there is so much thirties music waiting to be reissued, but having played it I'm bound to admit it has its attractive side. This is mainly supplied by Lamar Wright, later a trumpeter with Cab Calloway, who dominates these different small groups with a clear and attacking tone, making collectors' pieces of 'Baby Dear' and 'Sister Honky Tonk'. Woody Walder's clarinet is something of a trial, but Thamon Hayes's trombone satisfies and Moten's semi-ragtime piano appears on 'Goofy Dust' and 'Kater Street Rag'. There are many worse buys.

'The Glenn Miller Story' (RCA) will, I suppose, be something for the addicts of this band: its twelve tracks seem to be airshots from the very early forties and include most of the Miller warhorses – 'In The Mood', 'Jug', 'Pennsylvania', 'Kalamazoo' and so on. Featured soloists are Bobby Hackett, Tex Beneke, Billy May and Clyde Hurley, and apart from discographical problems it all runs smoothly. 'Buddy and the Juniors' (Harvest) offers Buddy Guy, Junior Wells and Junior Mance rattling away at the blues with a throbbing sincerity and most of it fills the blues slot for the month more than adequately.

13 March 1971

White Tie and Tails

Most of the records that have managed to reach me since the end of the postal strike have been of British music, thereby giving rise to reflections about British jazz in general. What unexpected alcoves its history contains!

Did you know, for instance, that at the Café de Paris in 1932 a group called the New Dixieland Band did a one-night stand that proved so successful that the management kept them on for several weeks? Their original front line was Alfie Noakes (trumpet), Lew Davis (trombone) and Sid Lenton (clarinet), the first two of whom were appearing regularly with Lew Stone at the Monseigneur, but when these few weeks were over these 'hot men' had to go back to being what Condon once called 'a jigger of whisky in a pint of milk'.

An admirable conspectus of the life they led is given by Decca in their four-disc set entitled 'The Bands That Matter', selections from the thirties output of Jack Hylton, Roy Fox, Lew Stone and Ambrose. I should explain (for readers under forty) that in pre-war London well-off people 'went out for the evening' in something called 'evening dress' to dine and dance at certain hotels and restaurants. These institutions were so prosperous that they were able to engage bands of twelve or fourteen pieces to provide music, and their leaders, through the medium of 'late night dance music' on the BBC and the 78 rpm gramophone record became national figures.

Jack Hylton (Eclipse) was a Northerner who got the Legion d'Honneur (did someone mention the MBE?) and led the first British band to broadcast to America (at 3 a.m. on the Lucky Strike Hour). His band was heavy and melodious, though listeners should dig that Bix-lives! coda from Philippe Brun on 'We Just Couldn't Say Goodbye'. Roy Fox (Eclipse) was an American who had an excellent line-up including, from time to time, Nat Gonella, Harry Gold, Ivor Mairants, Lew Stone himself, Tiny Winters and many others: 'Corinne Corinna' with Nat's vocal, shows the band lumbering in the wake of jazz. Lew Stone (Eclipse) took over and kept most of the Fox band when the latter was ill, and seemed to coax from them a more forthright and swinging voice as on 'Look What I've Got' and 'Plastered in Paris'. Ambrose (Eclipse) was in some ways the aristocrat of them all.

I recommend this last set not because of its jazz interest (most of the bands perpetrated hotter performances than can be found here) but for its enormous historical, not to say nostalgic, value: remember Denny Dennis? Al Bowlly? Sam Browne? Elsie Carlisle? But it does suggest that the British jazzman, throughout the decades, has only copied the American of the moment, whether it has been Paul Whiteman, Glenn Miller, George Lewis or Chuck Berry, thereby condemning himself to the role of eternal plagiarist. A matter of dejection? Not necessarily: jazz is an international language, not a local dialect.

Harry Beckett's 'Flare Up' (Philips) is an admirably professional example of a British group employing the progressive argot of the jazz sixties with verve and conviction. Beckett, on trumpet and flugelhorn, has been around the British scene since the fifties, and here unites with such as John Surman, Mike Osborne and Alan Skidmore to produce nine ingenious and colourful pieces, adroit mixtures of scoring and ad lib. Of course I hate this *kind* of sound, but even so it seems good.

Then again there is Alex Welsh's 'The Roaring Twenties' (Marble Arch), a rather more pedestrian pastiche of the Wild Bill/Pee Wee Commodore music. 'Charleston' has plenty of bounce, and 'Shim-Me-Sha-Wabble' exhibits Archie Semple's uncanny ability to get inside Russell's tuxedo: devotees of this mode will have a bargain.

America at last: 'Blues and Things', by Earl Hines and Jimmy Rushing (World Record Club), is an agreeable 1967 session with Budd Johnson doing his soprano 'Summertime' and staunch support from Pemberton and Jackson. Rushing sounds throatier than usual, but stirs up 'St Louis' to good effect: the most charming piece is the simple sensuality of 'Save It Pretty Mama'.

16 April 1971

How Things Get Better

Nothing fascinates me more in any art than shifts of critical opinion, the way things can change from wonderful to awful, then back to wonderful again. 'It is useful to compare', writes *Down Beat* a trifle smugly of Ornette Coleman's 'The Art of the Improvisers' (Atlantic), 'the universally enthusiastic response this LP will inevitably receive . . . to the disinterest (sic), antagonism or simple misunderstanding he aroused back then.'

'Back then' was 1961, around the time this record was made, and the reviewer may have been thinking of *Down Beat*'s own fulminations of that date. 'Orgy of squawks . . . horrible joke . . . anti-swing . . . chaotic' are some of the phrases that catch my eye as I run it down a review (by the editor, no less), certainly a bit different from their language now.

These seven tracks were made in 1959–61 by Coleman and Don Cherry with either Haden, La Faro or Garrison on bass and Higgins or Blackwell on drums. I would agree that Coleman's music sounds better to us now than it did then, but this is only because we have had much worse things to put up with in the interim – Coltrane's hideousness, Shepp's hostility, Davis's Chinese-restaurant Muzak. In comparison Coleman sounds no more than a bop nightmare: one of these pieces, 'The Legend of Bebop', is a kind of blues that recalls the Parker-Miles sides, virtually Dixieland to the seventies. 'The Fifth of Beethoven' has a Coleman solo that is only a little to one side of Parker, performed under a constant pressure of ideas that recalls Young. 'Just for You' is a slow ballad that sounds as if it is trying to be beautiful. This is as near as I can get to the predicted enthusiastic response. If you like Ornette, then this is reputedly his best period, and the odds are that you will find this disc intensely exciting.

Louis 'Country 'n' Western' Armstrong (Avco Embassy) seems to me an excellent idea gone a little wrong: C-&-W songs usually have a rather detailed narrative content that Louis's gargling mannerisms don't easily adapt to, and the supporting group could have been earthier, with, say, a fiddle. On the other hand, the easy swing and mid-Victorian properties ('precious ring') of this kind of music suits Louis down to the ground, and some of the tracks ('You Can Have Her', 'Wolverton Mountain') had me hollering. An all-vocal disc, it's presumably a product of Louis's semi-retirement: a pity it wasn't made ten years ago, for then we might have had some of that golden horn to finish the tracks.

Someone should do a piece on the background mode: jazz as the overall pattern, or music for turning on to. Maybe this is an unfair description of Gary Burton's 'Good Vibes' (Atlantic): it's a rich carpet with virtually two of everything (electric organ, bass, guitars) on the job, lamming away at a country-and-rock deviation from the earlier Burton Balinese. For my part I enjoyed it: Gil Evans did 'Las Vegas Tango', and the last piece, 'I Never Loved a Man' has lovely knocking by Burton.

'Benny Goodman Today' (Decca) has had some rave reviews, which is gratifying since Benny was playing with a British mob he had taken to Stockholm. The repertoire still derives (wisely) from the thirties, with 'Let's Dance', 'Roll 'Em', 'Blue Skies' and 'One O'Clock Jump', and there is certainly plenty of punch in the ensembles: 'Stealin' Apples' (composed Waller, arranged Henderson) is a pretty good example. Having said this, I'm bound to say I didn't care for the squealing trumpet (Derrick Watkins?) that disfigures 'Willow Weep', 'Roll 'Em', 'Sing, Sing, Sing', and so on, nor Goodman's own neo-Boyd Senter approach that suggests he is completely fed up with some of these routines. Bill McGuffie works steadily away at the piano.

The frog-like face on the sleeve of 'The World of Harry Roy' (Decca) takes me back to the National Programme, Friday Night, 10.30, but in fact this collection was recorded between 1944–50, which wasn't Harry's best period. It was a curious band: even though Roy and his brother Syd joined with Lew Davis back in the twenties to ape the ODJB, Roy's band never had the authenticity of Stone's or Ambrose's, jazzwise. It was too dominated by Ivor Moreton and Dave Kaye, ragtime, and Harry's own pseudo-Cantor vocals. Here we have some rags ('Leicester Square', 'Piccadilly') and non-blues ('Mayfair', 'Park Lane'), plus 'Guilty' sung by Eve Lombard and 'There Ought to Be a Society' sung by Joy Nichols. Buy as nostalgia dictates.

'Miff Mole's Molers – 1927' (Parlophone) is heart-warming period music, mixing timeless solos (Lang, Pee Wee Russell) with the corn of Vic Berton's drumming and four Sophie Tucker vocals. Personally, I think Red Nichols at this time had a lot to offer ('Alexander's Ragtime Band', 'Imagination'), and Pee Wee ('The New Twister') showed there was a lot to come. Check titles with 'The Thesaurus of Classic Jazz' (Philips), lately reissued.

15 May 1971

Voices as Instruments

Some years ago it started to be a form of approbation of a jazz singer to say he (or she – usually she) 'used his voice like an instrument'. I was never very happy about it; to start with, it ran counter to the accepted theory that the basis of jazz instrumental intonation was using your instrument like a voice, and a Negro voice at that – wide vibrato, thick, rasping, and so on.

Secondly, it seemed an attempt to devalue the *words* of a song: if the object of a singer of the words 'I love you' was not to make you think she (or he) loved you, but rather to skitter around the notes on which these words were scored, then something had gone wrong with jazz singing. One remembered, too, Lester Young's dictum that the best way to improvise on a song was to think of its words while you were doing so.

There has always been a market, however (think of Lambert, Hendricks and Ross), for vocal imitation of instruments as such, and 'The Early Mills Brothers' (Coral) presents this remarkable Negro quartet which, on the night they forgot their kazoo, invented their own instrument-faking. It was no accident that, after they rose to fame, they recorded with Armstrong, Ellington, Cab Calloway and Ella Fitzgerald: their performance was instinct with jazz. It comprised a tight, laconic close harmony against a swinging acoustic guitar, followed by imitation of muted trumpet against a scored sax section and a bass, plus a little scatting to taste, and these early numbers ('Georgia Brown', 'Sweeter Than Sugar', 'Some Of These Days') are still pretty good listening. There are no dates on the sleeve: one gets the impression that the Brothers, like the Ink Spots, grew commercial as time went by. How about an LP of the Spirits of Rhythm?

The instrument-voice business obtrudes, too, in 'Ella & Basie' (Verve), which I should be inclined to call hoo-hah among the trumpets; Ella banishes her balladry in favour of a hard, agile blending of her lyrics with the brassy Basie 1963 outfit. Much of her scatting is the Calloway (as distinct from the Carroll) kind, but in

'Into Each Life Some Rain Must Fall' she whoops and yells freely against the unsentimental slugging ensemble to good effect.

I found the two small-group tracks 'Them There Eyes' and 'Dream a Little Dream' the most pleasing. 'Sweet and Hot' (Coral), also Ella, dates from 1952–8, and comprises some ballads and quickies with rather dated orchestral backing, with the emphasis this time on the words.

Record of the month, though, is 'Louis Armstrong' (RCA), a bunch of tracks made in 1959 by Louis with the Dukes of Dixieland, and then held up for contractual reasons. The sleeve calls it 'one of the last examples of Armstrong playing trumpet with his instrumental faculties not only intact, but functioning at close to optimum level': I think this is true.

The tunes are standard – 'Back o' Town', 'Sweethearts on Parade', 'Sugar Foot Stomp', and so on – but they are freshly treated and Louis's own bursting energy dominates the scene: he tends to ascend to his own goldenly celestial upper register as a matter of course, but 'Cornet Chop Suey' and 'Bucket Got a Hole in It' are pitched at a human level. There are six Louis vocals, plus some expendable vocal contributions from Frankie Assunto, whose trumpet is, on the other hand, more than adequate. I should mark this LP much higher than the other made by Louis and the Dukes for Audio-Fidelity.

'Louis and the Good Book' (Coral) is made up of sessions from 1958 with the All Stars and the Sy Oliver Choir and Orchestra. The tunes, mostly spirituals, are exceedingly fine: 'Nobody Knows the Trouble I've Seen', 'Swing Low', and 'Sometimes I Feel Like a Motherless Child' are some of the most affecting of melodies, and Louis puts them over well, singing and (occasionally) underlining the piece with open or muted horn. There are also stretches of conversational mugging in a religious vein that remind the listener of Louis's preacher act back in the old days: indeed, this disc includes remakes of 'Shadrack' and 'Jonah', but to my mind they haven't the vividness of the 1938 versions.

An extremely enjoyable Ben Webster record called 'Atmosphere for Lovers and Thieves' (Polydor) shows the master tenor-player in Scandinavian company, running through a group of ballads in 1965 when he was on tour there. There is a nice rendering of 'Blue Light' ('Transblucency') with a small band, but most tracks are with a Kenny Drew accompaniment, Ben breathing out the melodies with accomplished negligence.

Finally, a British disc 'Mosaics' (Philips) by the Graham Collier Music was made live in December 1970, and includes Harry Beckett and Alan Wakeman among others in an orgy of freedom. The latter's soprano sax on 'Theme 2' is specially masterful, bearing out Charles Fox's prophecy that he is 'destined to be a soloist of the highest class'.

12 June 1971

Let It All Come

This is one of those months when it is the very variousness of jazz that most impresses, and somehow seems good: purism is all very well in its way, but when the same stylus can wake from their dormant grooves both Sun Ra and the New Orleans Owls, why should ears be eclectic?

The former, at any rate, has been with us longer than the uninitiated might think: he was playing piano in Fletcher Henderson's band in 1946, which suggests he is at least in his forties now, but this curious interstellar genius who was taught music by 'Nature's God and . . . Mrs Lulu Randolph of Washington DC' has for long been a spearhead of experimentalism, first in Chicago and then in New York.

'Pictures of Infinity' (Polydor) presents him with a flock of assorted horns (most of whom double on drums) and drummers (one of whom doubles on flute), plus a tautologously-named bassist, Nimrod Hunt. Better miss the fifteen-minute 'Somewhere There', with its mock air-raid drum solo, and try 'Saturn', with its long John Gilmore solo, a tenorist said to have influenced Coltrane, and 'Song of the Sparer', a slow drifting piece I see I have labelled 'not un-nice', wild praise for me.

All lovers of traditional jazz will know discographer Brian Rust's label, Vintage Jazz Music: several issues now appear acknowledging CBS on the sleeve, though not the label. 'The Little Ramblers' (VLP) was an in-group from The Californian Ramblers, and offers Adrian Rollini on goofus and bass sax with assorted colleagues, latterly Nichols and Mole. Rust loves this kind of music, and pleads on the sleeve that 'the light-hearted, utterly relaxed jazz . . . reflects the sunny times during which it was recorded' – 1924–5, in fact.

Maybe, but I preferred 'The Charleston Chasers' (VJM) of a year or so later, Bix-like leads from Leo McConville and Nichols and assorted clarinet and saxes from Jimmy Dorsey, Pee Wee Russell and Fud Livingston. Most of these tracks were in the CBS 'Thesaurus of Classic Jazz'. Then there is Volume Two of 'The New Orleans Owls and the Halfway House Orchestra' (VJM), 1926–8 tracks from these two New Orleans groups, the second with Albert Brunies with Sidney Arodin, the first with fierce Bill Padron cornet on 'The New Twister'. VJM Records reside at 12 Slough Lane, Kingsbury, London.*

From the same era comes 'Miff Mole's Molers' (Parlophone), seventeen sides from 1928–30, five (again) from the Thesaurus. I don't go for Mole's solo work greatly: it seems too designed to show he can manage difficult intervals, but in number after number he shines. 'Moanin' Low' is a lovely track; one chorus Jimmy Dorsey, one chorus Miff, then a lazy ensemble and out. If only it had been the 'Last Cent' Louisiana Rhythm Kings! The second side has three versions apiece of 'Navy Blues' and 'Lucky Little Devil'.

The most surprising record of the month is Ray Charles's 'My Kind of Jazz' (Tangerine): instead of Charles's hysterical lachrymosities, I found ten band numbers of considerable sophistication and punch. The first half of the Charles stage show is usually plain band, I know, and in the absence of any sleeve information I presume this is what's here. The band (not a big one) is sparked off by a fender bass and plenty of souly Lat-Am percussion, and has jetting spirited trumpet and matching saxes. 'I Remember Clifford', 'Passe-o-ne Blues' and 'Side Winder' are the most satisfying of a remarkable set.

'Blue Memphis Suite' (Barclay) surrounds Memphis Slim, born Peter Chatman, with numerous British instrumentalists, the principal – and title – piece being a string of vocal blues with some autobiographical intent. Memphis as a vocalist is rather submerged by his backing, where lead guitar Peter Green is prominent, but his nice slow piano emerges on 'Feel Like Screamin' and Cryin''. The other side offers separate performances, notably 'Mason-Dixon Line': a great deal of thought has gone into the presentation, which is far from the mumbling tradition.

* And still do.

On 'The Montmartre Collection' (Polydor), expatriate Dexter Gordon joins Kenny Drew with bass and drums in Copenhagen in 1967, Dexter's neo-Lester tenor dealing with a couple of Rollins pieces 'Sonnymoon For Two' and 'Doxy' plus 'For All We Know' and a frightful modal thing called 'Devilette'. Drew's piano provides relief from what I find a dull tradition of tenor-playing, not improved by bass solos from Niels-Henning Orsted Pederson, who may be the best bass player in Europe but who still can't raise the tension. 'I Remember Django' (Polydor) has Grappelly and Barney Kessel quite failing to reproduce the original Hot Club excitement, but performing very elegantly none the less, Grappelly with a wistfulness that quite belies the tight excited squealing of his early days.

10 July 1971

Armstrong's Last Goodnight

'Whereas Louis Armstrong by his artistry has through the universal language of music brought comfort, pleasure and understanding to people throughout the world . . .'. The quotation is from a 1958 citation in the House of Representatives at the State House in Boston, and demonstrates that the recent acclamation of Armstrong in the press and on radio and television was not something it took death to evoke. Long before his end, Louis had conquered the world, even America.

For his fans, throughout whose lives Armstrong had been something inexhaustible and unchanging like the sun, this universal endorsement of him as a great artist and a good man was some small consolation. We had given him our allegiance in the teeth of our elders' contempt: 'Jungle music . . . and why doesn't he clear his throat?' Now we were shown to be right. Armstrong was an artist of world stature, an American Negro slum child who spoke to the heart of Greenlander and Japanese alike. At the same time he was a humble, hard-working man who night after night set out to do no more than 'please the people', to earn his fee, to pay back the audience for coming.

The plaudits will continue for some while yet. But the sift of time is unceasing: soon we shall be looking at Louis over a gap of five years, then ten. The books will come out (how about a selection of his letters?); the wilful tide of taste will turn. Armstrong will become as distant as Oliver. What will the twenty-first century say of him?

It is only by imagining such a perspective that one can organize one's thoughts. As an artist, Louis was first of all inclusive: he was the deep river into which flowed all the tributaries of jazz. He was never original in the sense that Parker was original: he simply did what everyone else was doing twenty times better. Nevertheless, he out-distanced them. From playing with a band he changed to playing in front of a band: it played the tune, he sang the words, then blasted the roof off with his golden obbligato. He listened to what the audience applauded, and tried to give it to them.

There is no doubt that in the thirties he went through a period of exhibitionism that was as tedious as it was astonishing. To think of all that inventiveness, all that power, going into hitting 250 high Cs on 'Shine' is heart-breaking, yet that was all America encouraged Louis to do. Why wasn't it Armstrong who brought about the New Orleans revival? He had the youth, the knowledge, the stature – but he was as much in the grip of his managers as his slave grandparents had been in the grip of theirs. When it came, and he was sent out on the road with the All Stars, his playing could not meld with them. Ten years older, Bunk Johnson could sway like a reed among reeds: Armstrong was an alp among villages. So the All Stars dropped away: Teagarden and Bigard became Young and Hucko, then Big Chief Russel Moore and Joe Darensbourg. Only Armstrong remained, like a great chef putting on the same meal every night.

Yet the greatness was slow to fade. When after a severe bout of emphysema the trumpet could no longer maintain even the 'straight lead' Louis so advocated, his singing – perfectly pitched, perfectly timed – could bring tears to the eyes. The all-inclusive talent had hardened, and narrowed, and grown isolated, but it still contained the essence of jazz. The records are there to prove it. Let us be thankful for their permanence.

In the great ironical takeover of western popular music by the American Negro (and remember the saying 'Let me write a nation's songs, and anyone you like may write its laws'), Armstrong stands with Ellington and Waller as one of the Trojan horses that brought it about. Mick Jagger at Altamont in 1969 is the logical outcome of Louis bringing the house down with 'Ain't Misbehavin'' in 1929, and the process isn't finished yet. When it is, the chances are that Armstrong will be remembered as much as an agent for replacing one culture with another as an individual artist. If so, it won't be his fault: nothing, in this line, is ever anyone's fault.

In the meantime, let us take pride in 'The Melody Maker Tribute to Louis Armstrong' (Polydor three discs): this is selections from the 1970 Queen Elizabeth Hall concert to commemorate Armstrong's seventieth birthday. Dominated by the majestic Lyttelton, it features many of Britain's best traditional players – the Welsh band, Bruce Turner, and the Fawkes-Chilton group being outstanding – and I defy anyone to listen to the final 'Sleepytime' track without being glad that this country made its feelings about Armstrong clear once more before his death. Buy it: as well as making your oblation to greatness, you'll be getting a lot of good jazz.

21 August 1971

Ducal Portraits

New Ellington records go to the top of any month, even when, as in the case of 'New Orleans Suite' (Atlantic Super), they aren't world-beaters. This was commissioned by George Wein for the 1970 New Orleans Jazz Festival, and is made up of five 'sketches' and four 'portraits', all nine composed by the Master himself.

Of the portraits, 'Louis Armstrong' is negligible; 'Sidney Bechet', which, according to the sleeve, was intended to bring the late Johnny Hodges back to the soprano sax, makes do with Gonsalves in oriental vein; 'Wellman Braud' is (nuff said) a bass solo. Only 'Mahalia Jackson' manages to be moving, with Norris Turney's flute and an extraordinary ensemble scored (again according to the sleeve) for three clarinets, tenor and flute.

Of the other five pieces, 'Second Line' is Duke at his gayest, a bouillabaisse of Procope's clarinet, thirty-two bars of Cootie and a snorting trombone duet between Booty Wood and Julian Priester. 'Blues for New Orleans' presents some of Hodges' last solo work (he died before the 'portraits' were recorded), but it isn't especially striking, and the record seemed to me to change key twice, a hateful thing. 'Aristocracy à la Jean Lafite' is in three-four time and has Fred Stone flugeling away in mod vein.

It's nice to have two good more-or-less-trad English records to recommend: my enjoyment of the two-disc 'Get Rollin'!' by Chris Barber (Polydor Select) was limited by my receiving only one disc, the second, but it shows, first, that Barber is continuing to mix trad with rock and soul, and, secondly, that he has two superb new men in altoist John Crocker and guitarist John Slaughter. Both these are heard to splendid advantage on 'Jeep's Blues', achieving a pure piercing attack on their respective instruments, quite a joy. 'Ubava ZZaebava' goes on for nearly a quarter of an hour, churning up a sort of Wardour Street Mingus at times, and has some more Slaughter. If the first disc is as worthy this would be a good buy.

Steve Lane's Famous Southern Stompers ('In Concert', 'Stomp') are an older tradition altogether, mostly Oliver and Morton, and produce an easy, rather bright-toned purist music, replete with washboard and ragtime piano of Ray Smith. This is thoroughly enjoyable music (there is a singer Michèle, who has at least one good track, 'That's You, Baby'): my only criticism would be of its slightly academic air that refuses to let a number come to the boil but gets the breaks right.

Miles Davis has a lot to answer for. 'Joe Farrell Quartet' (Philips) shows this reed-man/flautist fronting one of Miles's rhythm sections (Corea/Holland/DeJohnette/McLaughlin) in some jingling reminiscent of his later manner. Of all the various modes of modern non-jazz, this sugar-fairy kind seems to me the oddest, but no one could call it unpleasant, save perhaps for 'Motion'. Herbie Hancock's 'Mwandishi' (Warner Bros.) goes rather further with what I take to be electronic effects, suggesting that Shep Fields's Rippling Rhythm has got mixed up with a gourd band from somewhere. Eddie Henderson plays pealing trumpet and Julian Priester declamatory trombone; Hancock is not much in evidence, though he wrote two of the tunes.

A really enjoyable record is 'Wess to Memphis' (Stax): Frank Wess's flute has a wild and windy quality on 'Under Hog' that is keen and thrilling; on 'Wessward Ho' he is liquid and summery.

Antiquarians are being well served by VJM Records: this month 'Celestin's Tuxedo Orchestra' preserves thirteen New Orleans 1926–8 tracks and shows the tradition approaching the Depression. Celestin makes a feature of stop-choruses, and his muted work trembles towards the real McCoy at times, but it is a great privilege to have such recondite issues. The same goes for 'Fletcher Henderson's Orchestra' (VJM), Henderson's Columbia sessions between 1923–4 which despite occasional farmyard noises and slaptongue reeds offer good Redman and Charlie Green, with Louis coming in for the last two tracks, 'Manda' and 'Go 'Long, Mule', and soloing on each.

'Oh! Red' (VJM) offers a live backroom recital by Speckled Red made in 1960, and very exhilarating his trim rolling piano is against his blues singing, 'Milk Cow Blues' being one of the best. 'Maggie Jones Vol. II' (VJM) continues the 1925–6 output of this classic blues singer, ably helped by Joe Smith, Charlie Green, Louis Metcalf and Clarence Williams. And lastly two reminders: Armstrong's 'Hello Dolly!' (Coral) has some charming latterday performances and is available again, and Sandy Wilson's 'Valmouth' (Pye) may not be jazz but is fascinating all the same with big-voiced Cleo Laine scattering the Firbankery as Mrs Yaj.

18 September 1971

Veterans' Rally

'The World's Greatest Jazz Band' (Atlantic) is the 1970 equivalent of Bunk Johnson's Superior Jazz Band in 1942; that is, a group of veterans purposely brought together to play in an outmoded style. Yes, veterans, for while Bunk was 63, Jim Robinson was 50 and George Lewis only 42, and here we have Lawson (59) and Haggart (56), not to mention Butterfield (53) and Freeman and Dickenson (64 each).

These are the survivors of the Bob Crosby band of the thirties and the Condon tribe of the twenties to the sixties, white men (leaving aside Dickenson and drummer Gus Johnson) whose memories go back pretty far, to Bix, to Armstrong in his twenties, even to King Oliver.

Their title, therefore, is less braggadocio than a statement of fact: they are the world's greatest, etc., because there's almost no competition, and they have been brought together for that reason, because their sponsor wanted to hear the old music again. According to the sleeve, the kids come up and say 'We've never heard anything like this live before!' and apparently enjoy it. As Haggart says, 'What is there not to like?'

As to that, I should say the occasional sense of strain and over-excitement; Wilber *passim*: 'Doodle Doo Doo', the ritual bass solo ('Smile'), Dickenson, if you don't like him. But overall the music is full-blooded and happy; Freeman is splendid on 'That D Minor

Thing' and 'The Eel', Butterfield on 'What's New', nearly everyone on 'My Honey's Lovin' Arms'. It's a two-disc pack, and has riches too great to count. Watch your copy, though; mine had two sides the same.

As good if not better is 'Henry Red and the Kid' (Metro). Fourteen sides made in 1959 by Henry Allen with the Ory band. One would guess that this would be oil and water, Allen's original rather nervy trumpet against threadbare favourites of Lower Basin Street, but in fact the whole set is individual and arresting. Ory's starkly primitive trombone is an admirable foil to Allen, whether the latter is playing it straight ('Tishomingo') or with the slurs, flurries, trills and growls of 'I Got Rhythm': Bob McCracken's clarinet doodles musically enough. Another remarkable two-disc set is 'The Ebullient Mr Gillespie' (Metro), the whole of three sessions from 1959, again, most of which was issued as 'Have Trumpet, Will Excite'. For once the claim is justified: Gillespie dominates on trumpet with only Mance and Les Spann to share the solo work, and whether open or muted, does a decent job, free from bass solos, vocals (nearly) and Lat-Am flamboyance. Mance does a good build-up on 'Willow Weep', nearly turning it into a blues, and Spann is nice on flute on 'Moonglow'.

Was it Bobby Hackett who said: 'It's sure funny hearing those kids trying to play like old men'? 'One Night With the New Iberia Stompers' (77 Records) brought it to mind, but in fact this is a thoroughly agreeable record by trombonist Mike Casimir, trumpeter Tony O'Sullivan and other honorary New Orleansians. Of course this kind of thing is pastiche, but which would you rather have on your mantelshelf, reproduction Staffordshire or concrete stuck with broken glass? The music – 'Mobile Blues', 'At A Georgia Camp Meeting' – strokes and soothes, being not so much shortwinded as the style of men who know they have to play all night and are pacing themselves. The clarinet is off-mike, unfortunately, but all in all it's a delightful disc.

Back again with EMI and Chris Ellis to the white twenties for 'Tommy, Jimmy and Eddie, 1928–29' (Parlophone) – the Dorsey Brothers, in fact, and Eddie Lang. Here are many old favourites – 'Freeze an' Melt', 'Hot Heels' and 'Walkin' the Dog' – and many old masters apart from the three named, such as McConville, Signorelli, and Schutt. I have always thought Jimmy Dorsey's passionate clarinet underrated, and his 'Prayin' the Blues' offers a chance for rectification. Also on this disc is that intensely melodious 'What Kind of Man Is You?' with the youthful Mildred Bailey, Bill Rank, and either Secrest or Margulis doing the Bix. What a lovely era! The only curiosity is five sides by Boyd Senter and his Senterpedes. Senter, a barnyard clarinettist, is perfectly appalling, but some of the Tommy-Jimmy backgrounds are worthwhile.

Back in our time there are a bunch of Braff solos on 'Hear Me Talkin'!' (Polydor) made in 1967 with the Welsh group and some visiting Wein-led Americans. Ruby is highly mannered as usual, and I'm not sure Welsh doesn't carve him on 'No One Else But You'. Miles Davis does the sleeve-note for Joe Zawinul's 'Zawinul' (Polydor), which is predictable as Joe was his pianist once and this is very much one of Miles's style. Pretty, jingly, with trumpet and flute and percussion thick on the ground; one of the tunes is 'A tone poem reminiscent of his grandfather's funeral'. Don't get too excited.

11 December 1971

Records Reviewed

As far as possible records have been listed under artist responsible, e.g.

Adderley, Cannonball: 'African Waltz' (Riverside), 48

Where two artists are jointly responsible for the record, both have been listed, e.g.

Armstrong, Louis and Duke Ellington: 'The Great Reunion' (Columbia), 109

Where one artist is responsible for one side of the record and another for the other, both have been listed, e.g.

Armstrong, Louis and Jack Purvis: 'Satchmo Style' (Parlophone), 200

Where more than two artists are responsible for the record, it has been listed by title, e.g.

'American Folk Blues Festival' (Polydor), 86

For a number of years in this column, records were distinguished by their labels only, and not by their numbers. Although numbers were eventually included, it has not been thought worthwhile to exhume them for this book, as many of the records have by now been deleted. Readers seeking individual numbers none the less should look them up in a reliable indexed source such as the *Gramophone*, or in the annual *Jazz Catalogue* published by *Jazz Journal*.

There are no cross-references.